What real Business Leaders, Owners and Entrepreneurs are saying about Built to Grow . . .

'A must-read for the modern business leader. At last, practical real-world strategy you can understand and act on to get instant but sustainable results. Royston delivers a clear and much-needed blueprint for scalable business growth. No matter how good you think you are, you should read this book to stay at the top of your game.'

Sháá Wasmund MBE, Author of *Stop Talking, Start Doing* and *Do Less, Get More*

'Royston is an inspiring and practiced business leader. His book transcends other management books, by walking us through a practical, simple, yet dynamic framework that really works in unlocking the potential to grow your business. The framework provides clarity on what vision, strategies and measures really matter in achieving growth goals and Royston's commentary helps agile and progressive thinking. At a time of digital revolution this has never been more critical.'

Louise Swain, CEO, Alliance Homes

'The entertainment world is chaotic at the best of times, but add the impact of rapid technical disruption and well funded new international entrants and it creates a world where established players have to focus on rapid change and constant market evolution to survive. Royston's advice and model helped us make sense of this situation and focus on what's important to compete. So much so, that in the first twelve months of trading since execution we experienced double digit EBITDA growth in a market hemorrhaging value.'

Stuart Cain, Managing Director, The Ticket Factory and Eight Feet Tall

'*Built to Grow* is both challenging and thought provoking with a range of practical examples and lessons that are of relevance to leaders in the private, public and third sector who are serious about building a high performing organization.'

Richard Stevens, HR Director, Chief Minister's Department, States of Jersey

'*Built to Grow* is jam packed with practical and simple to implement methodologies and tools to improve salesforce effectiveness. Royston and his team have helped us understand what our business growth formula is and we have now put AMR into action to the point where much of what you will read in this book is now part of our day-to-day language and behavior'

Leigh Webb, Sales Director, Ainscough Crane Hire

'Royston is a passionate, practical and engaging business leader, who inspires the commitment of those he leads and advises. *Built to Grow* is an insightful interpretation of his results driven model, that combines proven practices to unlock the potential in your people and achieve a culture of growth.'

Phil Jones, Global Vice President, CSM Bakery Solutions

'We have been fortunate enough to work with Royston in building our teams and our business over the past 2 years and he has been instrumental in supporting the growth of our team, providing new ideas, as well as clear, easy to apply guidance. He is an inspirational coach, provides great positive challenge and has played a key role in the transformation and growth of our business through our people. He's a delight to work with and great to have all of his wisdom and guidance in one book!'

Laura Brown, Retail Director, Harrods

'Many business books talk about the importance of the customer, however with *Built to Grow* it's refreshing to see a business growth strategy where genuinely the customer is the focal point of the entire model. The Customer Strategy Chapter is packed full of practical ideas that any Business Leader could instantly implement to build a customer centric business. Achieve this goal and accelerated and sustained business growth will be inevitable.'

Maggie Wheeler, Managing Director, The Focus Group and Founder of Customer Experience World

'Royston's work helps both the individual and the organization reach their full potential by providing simple yet effective techniques that are transformational. His performance and results driven model is balanced by practical concepts that empower people to excel, leading to a dynamic and highly productive organization. Everyone wants to be on a winning team and Royston provides the blueprint for success. Read this book, study and apply his techniques, and you will be a winner!'

Raymond A. Melee, Development Director, Gatwick Airport

'The finance chapter of *Built to Grow* is jam packed with insights and thinking which every "commercially savvy" business leader needs to know in order to build a profitable business. Finance is not just the job of the finance team, but an integral part of a high performing businesses performance culture. *Built to Grow* really delivers this message in a simple, engaging and compelling way.'

Ajay Handa, Chief Financial Officer, GatenbySanderson

'As an impatient executive team, we found working with Royston to implement the business models and principles in *Built to Grow* has delivered tangible growth, a committed talent base and a flourishing AMR Strategy!'

Donna Baddely, Executive Director, Corporate Services, Curo Group

'Finally, a book that puts the marketing agenda firmly on the boardroom table. *Built to Grow* recognizes the role shift of marketing and provides insights and ideas on how to stay one step ahead. Knowing your customers, understanding their needs and building a targeted customer communication strategy is fundamental to any business growth plan. *Built to Grow*, with its practical tools and ideas, simplifies how you can achieve this and deliver tangible results fast.'

Jane Parry, Head of Marketing and Communications, Canaccord Genuity Wealth Management

'Our business journey with Royston has been enlightening, enjoyable and tough. *Built to Grow* has had a fundamental impact on how we operate, with a combined focus on costs, productivity and a pro-active sales strategy we are transforming into a high performing team. We are creating a leader culture that is stretching the organization and has provided a platform for talent to flourish. We believe that we are becoming the provider of choice, employer of choice and the investment of choice in our industry and the partner of choice for trust, fund and pension solutions. Highly recommended a must have!'

Louise Bracken-Smith, Business Owner, Entrepreneur, Fairway Group

'If I were to sum up the book I would say it's "written with the reader (and leader!) in mind". In today's business landscape I would challenge any leader not to find the content of this book a must have tool to truly stand back and consider the DNA of their approach, their business strategy and most importantly how they are unlocking the potential in their biggest asset...their people.'

Jayne Owen, Group Learning and Development Manager, Princes Limited

'Royston has supported me within my own growing business and in a corporate environment. In both situations the ideas are practical, effective and universally relevant. At times they may seem simple and mere common sense . . . the key is applying them rigorously to see the long-term growth benefits. Follow his ideas and you, your people and your business will achieve massive growth.'

Graham Nicoll, Advisory, KPMG Enterprise

Built to Grow

How to deliver accelerated, sustained and profitable business growth

Royston Guest

This edition first published 2017
© 2017 PTI Worldwide Limited

Registered office
John Wiley & Sons Ltd, The Atrium, Southern Gate, Chichester, West Sussex, PO19 8SQ, United Kingdom

For details of our global editorial offices, for customer services and for information about how to apply for permission to reuse the copyright material in this book please see our website at www.wiley.com.

Wiley publishes in a variety of print and electronic formats and by print-on-demand. Some material included with standard print versions of this book may not be included in e-books or in print-on-demand. If this book refers to media such as a CD or DVD that is not included in the version you purchased, you may download this material at http://booksupport.wiley.com. For more information about Wiley products, visit www.wiley.com.

Designations used by companies to distinguish their products are often claimed as trademarks. All brand names and product names used in this book are trade names, service marks, trademarks or registered trademarks of their respective owners. The publisher is not associated with any product or vendor mentioned in this book.

Limit of Liability/Disclaimer of Warranty: While the publisher and author have used their best efforts in preparing this book, they make no representations or warranties with the respect to the accuracy or completeness of the contents of this book and specifically disclaim any implied warranties of merchantability or fitness for a particular purpose. It is sold on the understanding that the publisher is not engaged in rendering professional services and neither the publisher nor the author shall be liable for damages arising herefrom. If professional advice or other expert assistance is required, the services of a competent professional should be sought.

Library of Congress Cataloging-in-Publication Data

Names: Guest, Royston, author.
Title: Great by design : how to deliver accelerated and sustained business growth / Royston Guest.
Description: Chichester, West Sussex, United Kingdom : John Wiley & Sons, 2017. | Includes index.
Identifiers: LCCN 2016029041 (print) | LCCN 2016042883 (ebook) | ISBN 9781119318095 (cloth) | ISBN 9781119318132 (pdf) | ISBN 9781119318156 (epub)
Subjects: LCSH: Strategic planning. | Small business--Growth.
Classification: LCC HD30.28 .G8346 2017 (print) | LCC HD30.28 (ebook) | DDC 338.6/42--dc23
LC record available at https://lccn.loc.gov/2016029041

A catalogue record for this book is available from the British Library

ISBN 978-1-119-31809-5 (hardback)   ISBN 978-1-119-31813-2 (ebk)
ISBN 978-1-119-31815-6 (ebk)

10 9 8 7 6 5 4 3 2 1

Cover design: Wiley

Set in 10/14pt ITC Avant Garde Std Book by Thomson Digital, Noida, India
Printed in Great Britain by TJ International Ltd, Padstow, Cornwall, UK

To my beautiful wife Jane and wonderful children Eloise and Ethan. You give life context, purpose, and meaning.

Contents

Acknowledgements

To reach this point has certainly not been a solitary journey. I have reached out, coached, been coached and mentored, spoken, consulted, had a meal and drunk a few glasses of wine with so many clients, colleagues, friends, and family. To name everyone here would be a book in itself, however you know who you are and from the bottom of my heart a massive thank you to you all.

Without my loyal clients and customers I wouldn't have the 20 plus years of experience packed in to *Built to Grow*. I look forward to continuing to work with you and helping you grow your business and realize your personal and professional goals.

Thank you to the many well-known companies, organizations, sportsmen and women, authors, actors, and actresses referenced. The great work you do provides a shining example of what works in the real arena of life and perhaps as importantly . . . what doesn't.

I'd like to thank my publisher, Wiley, for bringing *Built to Grow* to life, and together, creating the opportunity to contribute our part in building a more sustained, commercial world one business and organization at a time.

Heartfelt thanks to my team at Pti Worldwide; Kate, you have been with me from the start. Your loyalty, energy, and vision are valued beyond words. Pti is like your second child and you should feel proud of the business you have helped build, the positive difference you make every day, and the businesswoman and mother you have become.

Luke, I have watched you grow and develop into an inspirational leader and great consultant. Your work ethic, commitment, and drive are admired and I have no doubt at some point in the future I will be writing a foreword for your book.

Jane, your talent as a business leader and professional never fails to astonish me. Your ability to zoom out to see the big picture and zoom into the detail is a unique skill. *Built to Grow* would not be the book it is without your eye for detail, positive challenge, and break-through insights.

Laura, my Executive Assistant, you have the patience of a saint. I know I am not always easy to manage, but you do it with relentless energy, consistency, and calmness. You truly are unflappable.

And all my colleagues at Pti. I am so proud of the great work commitment, focus, and drive you demonstrate every day in helping our clients grow their businesses and unlock people potential.

Colin Brown, the hours we spent piecing together *Built to Grow* making sure every word, every sentence, every paragraph, and every page counted was a labour of love. I hope you look on our time together with fond memories. You are an inspired writer and a man of genuine integrity. Thank you.

And most importantly to my family.

My dad, Bill, for being a friend as well as a father. You created life experiences and opportunities for me to develop and grow which played a significant impact on who I am today. I hope I make you proud of the business professional and father I have become.

Jean, my stepmum for treating me as your own.

My mum, Pat, for your tireless devotion and sacrifice in bringing me up, shaping my values and beliefs about what is right and wrong and how to live a fulfilled life. Being a parent myself, I now know what unconditional love means and on reflection, wish I had appreciated it more as a child growing up.

My sister, Justine, you have always had my back. To watch you grow into the successful businesswoman, mum and wife you are makes me feel proud.

My in-laws, Mary and Eric. Mary, I told you I would include you in my book, or perhaps I was just fearful of the consequence of not including you! On a serious note, in life you can count on one hand the individuals you can call who will drop everything and be there for you in a heartbeat. You both fall into this camp and I am eternally grateful for your love and support.

And finally my wife, Jane, my soulmate and best friend and our two beautiful children, Eloise and Ethan. I am blessed beyond words and so proud to be able to say I am your husband and your daddy.

About the Author

From an early age Royston nurtured his entrepreneurial spirit spending weekends and summer holidays working in his father's construction business.

A relentless itch to join the working world saw Royston kick start his career at the age of 16, enrolling on a construction apprenticeship programme. He worked from the ground up, literally.

His thirst for learning and making things happen saw his career fast track at companies like Balfour Beatty managing high profile projects like the Liverpool Institute for Performing Arts, founded by Paul McCartney. A working stint in America gave Royston valuable insight into operating across cultural boundaries and different mindsets.

On returning to the UK, Royston was involved in the privatization of the Rail Industry and major Private Finance Initiatives (PFIs) with Jarvis before joining Hoogovens, a Dutch business, where he was involved in mergers and acquisitions.

The breadth and depth of 'hands on' business experience led to Royston starting his own consultancy and people development business in 2005, Pti Worldwide, of which he is CEO.

Driving sustainable and profitable business growth fast whilst unlocking the real potential of individuals are the two professional missions of Royston and the Pti team.

A mission spanning over two decades, 27 countries, and tens of thousands of businesses across a multitude of sectors, enterprises, and governments.

Through exposure to such a broad array of organizations, Royston has created a unique databank and set of breakthrough distinctions and insights into what it takes to build a truly high performing organization, which delivers accelerated, sustained, and profitable growth.

Whether speaking, facilitating, consulting, or coaching, Royston's passion to make a real tangible difference is at the forefront of his work, and what sets him apart from his peers.

Royston is married with two children and splits his time between Jersey and the UK.

Introduction

If you asked a cross-section of business leaders, business owners, and entrepreneurs what their biggest business challenge is, I'm confident you'd hear the same recurring thought: growing their business in a sustainable, predictable, yet profitable way, quickly.

It's a reality that most businesses never reach their full potential, always yearning for the thing that will catapult them into significance, but never really finding it. The simple reason is a mismatch between the lofty vision that guided their founders and eventual leaders, and the ability to turn that vision into anything practical.

Fixing that mismatch is one of the goals of *Built to Grow.*

The practical strategies of the Business Growth Transformation Framework®, detailed throughout this book, are precisely that: practical, tried, tested, and proven to be effective. As a result, *Built to Grow* has been a long time in development. Concepts within have been put through their paces in the real world laboratory of some of our most successful clients including large companies such as DHL, Virgin, Harrods, and Santander; mid-tier organizations, SMEs, and small/home businesses, all across a diverse range of sectors.

By reading this book, you'll learn what business leaders, business owners, and entrepreneurs have done to ensure their greatness isn't just a coincidence, but an act of purposeful design.

Why *Built to Grow*?

Building a great business rarely happens by accident. Businesses we admire most have been structured for growth by their founders and business leaders, using principles similar or identical to the ones I will share.

There are two non-conflicting concepts at play in *Built to Grow*. The first is a planned, structured framework, which, if followed closely, is assured to grow your business; the other is the element of speed. Hopefully you view your business as something that will continue to thrive for a long time, but that doesn't mean it should take a long time to grow. The Built to Grow model is partly in recognition that entrepreneurial and business vision is closely tied to impatience. You've got an idea and you want to build it now.

If that's true for you, this book is an essential action guide.

What *Built to Grow* Is Not

Business growth theories are not hard to come by. A cursory Google search will uncover thousands of ideas of varying quality, some of which may be useful to you. The challenge in all fields of theoretical thinking, however, is that so few of the ideas presented can be backed up with results founded on real-world testing. It's certainly true that you have little interest in your business being a guinea pig, and that's where the ultimate strength of *Built to Grow* lies.

This book rejects any theoretical modelling that my team and I haven't tested and applied in real life, multiple times. It is not merely a book of ideas. By its very nature, *Built to Grow* is not intended as a passive read, but as a blueprint for you to achieve accelerated, sustained and profitable business growth.

How to Use *Built to Grow*

I am a big believer in coaching, which comprises a substantial share of what I devote my time to on a daily basis. As a result, I chose a coaching framework to demonstrate the Business Growth Transformation Framework® (the model at the core of *Built to Grow*).

I recommend you dedicate quality time to reading each chapter and consider how you can apply the principles within your own business. One useful technique I adopt, which you may find useful, is to scribble your thoughts and comments in the page margins, underline passages that are most compelling, and refer regularly to the content. This makes it simple to find the most relevant information whilst embedding the behaviours as you read and re-read. It may go against all your instincts to mark a book, so as the author, I am giving you my unreserved permission right now.

The Added Benefit to You

The Business Growth Transformation Framework® comprises, at its heart, nine interlocking strategies with each strategy focusing on a particular business area. Consequently, there is a high probability that readers will have a deep affinity with one particular section, and perhaps not others. It may be your instinct as a Financial Director, Financial Manager, or Accountant, for example, to jump straight to the Finance and Governance chapter to find some brand new insights in that field. Please suppress that urge. The intention of *Built to Grow* is to give you a broad and interlocking insight into *all* key aspects of business growth; some of which you will be well versed in and others you may have limited or no knowledge of at all.

A marketing expert should be able to read the Finance and Governance chapter and walk away with some real Aha! moments. A finance expert should have Aha! moments having read Marketing Strategy, Business Development, and Sales or any of the other chapters.

Think about how beneficial it would be if your colleagues had a better understanding and appreciation of your job function. And vice versa, the benefits to them of you understanding and appreciating their function at a deeper level.

Specific expertise is invaluable in order to achieve excellence in your area of responsibility, but business owners, business leaders, and entrepreneurs who choose to build companies through purposeful design, smooth their way forward by being familiar with all interlocking strategies and how they add immense power to one another.

As a final note, I wish you every success on your journey of transformation. You're going to feel challenged at times and frustrated at others, but if you are relentless in your approach, I am confident in saying that your accelerated, sustained and profitable business growth will be inevitable.

Chapter 1

The Fundamentals of Business Growth: Your AMR Strategy

Strategically, the primary purpose of a business is to Acquire, Maximize, and Retain the right customers. Everything that contributes to this is an investment; anything which doesn't, is a cost!

Because *Built to Grow* is focused on how to deliver accelerated, sustained, and profitable growth in your business, it makes perfect sense to launch straight into the fundamentals of business growth . . . and your AMR strategy. In this chapter, we're going to peel back the layers of the onion, get to the root of business growth and, using simple, practical ideas, give you insight into how you can deliver consistent, repeatable, predictable results in your business.

The First BIG Idea

Strategically, the primary purpose of a business is to Acquire, Maximize, and Retain the right customers. Everything that contributes to this is an investment; anything which doesn't, is a cost. Which activities in your business are an investment, and which are a cost?

Without customers, businesses don't exist. That's a simple fact which no business owner can dispute. The challenge is that most business owners, business leaders, and entrepreneurs over-engineer their business growth model, making it more complex than it needs to be. They introduce layers of management that stifle and delay decision-making. They create unnecessary systems, processes, and procedures that dilute the focus of their people from doing what they do best: Acquiring, Maximizing, and Retaining customers. Then they wonder why they're not delivering market or industry leading performance and growth!

You see, regardless of your industry, sector, business type, or whether you're in a B2B or B2C environment, there is a formula for success in delivering accelerated, sustained and profitable business growth. However, most business leaders, business owners, and entrepreneurs are either not aware of the success formula and its fundamental principles, or are simply not following it. I'm going to walk you through the success formula and detail the precise steps to personalize and apply it to your business.

Remember our first BIG idea:

> *Strategically, the primary purpose of a business is to Acquire, Maximize, and Retain the right customers. Everything that contributes to this is an investment; anything which doesn't, is a cost.*

Let me break this into a couple of component parts:

1. 'Strategically, the primary purpose of a business . . .'

    Note the key word here is *strategically.* Over the years, customers and delegates have challenged me by saying 'Royston, isn't the primary purpose of a business to fulfil a customer need?' My answer to this question is always: 'Yes, you are 100% right'. However, in the context of your business growth formula, this is a given. Here we are focused on your business growth not your business essence.

    My focus is to help you build a business with the potential to deliver sustained growth, and therefore it is important to deepen your understanding of the fundamental principles of business growth and the levers you can pull in your business to achieve it.

2. '. . . Acquire, Maximize, and Retain the right customers'

   This statement contains the core principles, the hub of your business growth formula. Attract, Maximize, and Retain are three key words, which together form your AMR strategy. Lock those three letters firmly in your mind, as they are going to be a thread that runs throughout this book.

Your AMR Strategy

During good economic times, new business was probably easier to come by, and it didn't really matter if you lost a customer, because there was always another waiting in the wings. However, in a competitive market where multiple providers are chasing the same customers, and those customers are more demanding than ever, a structured, systematic, and sustainable business growth strategy is more important than ever.

Now, you may say *'but what about reducing costs, surely that will increase my profits and therefore help me grow my business?'* Again, this is true, but what I want you to focus on is unlocking the untapped potential of unlimited growth. Reducing costs is finite; you can only ever cut back so far before arriving at a base cost to serve and deliver your customer proposition. It's never a long-term strategy for sustained growth.

Buying other businesses can be another way of driving growth, but with that comes additional cost and usually a significant amount of change to manage.

What I'm focused on is accelerated, sustained and profitable organic, year-on-year growth underpinned by your AMR strategy and the answers to the Four BIG questions. All of which add breadth and depth to the business growth formula.

The Four BIG questions:

1. How do you increase the number of customers?
2. How do you increase the average order value?

3. How do you increase the average order frequency?
4. How do you increase the retention of customers?

The first question addresses the 'A' of your AMR strategy, questions two and three the 'M', and finally question four the 'R'. Which question do you think most businesses focus their time, effort and resources on? It's the first – increasing the number of customers.

While this is certainly key for business growth, the amount of time you should focus on new customer acquisitions isn't the same for all businesses. The maturity of your business and the size of your existing customer base, when aligned to your growth ambition, will determine how much focus you need to place on the 'A' part of AMR.

Having worked with tens of thousands of businesses of all different shapes and sizes, experience tells me that most businesses spend too much time on this question altogether. Only a select few businesses have a business growth strategy that integrates all four questions aligned to an overarching AMR strategy and a deep-rooted understanding of the customer lifecycle.

I always remember reading this headline in a UK business newspaper:

'A million customers come back to energy provider.'

Now, the challenge I have with this headline is: why did they lose a million customers in the first place?

Let me share a compelling story that may suggest they lost those customers because they were looking in all the wrong places. Perhaps the same is true for you.

There's a story called *Acres of Diamonds* by Russell H. Conwell which describes a Persian man named Al Hafed who lived many years ago and was very contented with his life as the owner of a large farm with orchards, grain fields, and gardens. One evening, however, his world is turned upside down when a Buddhist priest stops by to warm himself by the fire and begins to talk about how the world was made. He concludes his story with a description of diamonds, the rarest gems of all. The old priest tells Al Hafed that if he had a handful of diamonds he could purchase a whole country, and with a mine of diamonds he could place his children upon thrones through the influence of their great wealth.

That night, Al Hafed went to bed feeling poor despite all that he had, because he didn't have a diamond mine. Finally, early in the morning, he woke the priest and asked him: 'Will you tell me where I can find diamonds?'

The priest said, 'Diamonds? What do you want with diamonds?'

'I want to be immensely rich,' said Al Hafed, 'but I don't know where to go.'

'Well,' said the priest, 'if you will find a river that runs over white sand between high mountains, in those sands you will always see diamonds.'

So Al Hafed sold his farm, collected his money, asked a neighbour to look after his family, and went off in search of the river on white sands. For years, he wandered, spending every penny he had, until eventually, frail, hungry, and reduced to rags, he gave in to his despair and threw himself into the sea, never to be seen again.

But that's not the whole story. Shortly after he bought the farm from Al Hafed, the new owner led his camel out to the garden to drink one day, and as the camel put its nose down into the water, he noticed a glint of something shiny. Realizing that the object sparkling in the river that ran over white sands through the back garden of the farm was a diamond, the farmer began to dig for them and so were discovered some of the greatest diamond mines in the world, making the farmer wealthy beyond his wildest dreams.

Al Hafed had never seen them because he had never looked in his own back garden. Had he looked more closely at what was right in front of him, and not been distracted by what he thought would be better elsewhere, he wouldn't have suffered poverty and starvation, but enjoyed acres upon acres of diamonds.

There is a danger for every business owner, business leader, and entrepreneur of obsessing about finding new customers, all the while failing to notice the 'acres of diamonds' – the customers we've already invested the time, effort, and money to acquire.

Business growth is about acquiring the right customers through the front door of your business, and building a compelling value proposition that fulfils their needs and wants. It's about delivering your products and services through an exceptional customer experience and maximizing the value and worth of each customer.

And finally, because of the great value and experience you deliver, it's about keeping the back door of your business firmly shut by giving customers good reasons to stay with you for the long term, thus driving your retention strategy.

Your Business Growth Formula: How the Numbers Work

So let's look at how AMR works in practice and why AMR working in unison is how successful businesses deliver accelerated, sustained, and profitable business growth.

In Table 1.1, you can see the turnover/revenue effect of the 'A' and the two 'M's: 100 customers, each of whom spends £100 per year and buys from you twice. A quick calculation shows that you'll have £20,000 per year in revenue.

Now, let's do what most companies do and only look at acquiring new customers. A sound idea, but one that, as we've already demonstrated, is not a true growth strategy alone.

In Table 1.2 look at the second line and you'll see that a 10% increase in customers, without any change to the other two variables, leads to a 10% increase in revenue. Increase one of the variables and you get a linear, incremental revenue uplift.

Table 1.1   The turnover/revenue effect

Number of Customers (A)	Average order value (M)	Average order frequency (M)	Turnover/ Revenue
100	£100	2	£20,000

Table 1.2   The turnover/revenue effect; increasing the number of customers

Number of Customers (A)	Average order value (M)	Average order frequency (M)	Turnover/ Revenue
100	£100	2	£20,000
110	£100	2	£22,000

Table 1.3 The turnover/revenue effect; increasing the number of customers, average order value, and frequency

Number of Customers (A)	Average order value (M)	Average order frequency (M)	Turnover/ Revenue
100	£100	2	£20,000
110	£100	2	£22,000
110	£110	2.2	£26,620

Business growth really starts to become fun when you focus on all three variables of your AMR strategy at the same time. In the third line of Table 1.3, we've increased all three variables by 10%, and you can see how the uplift in growth is totally different.

If you focus on one variable, you get 10% growth. Work all three variables at the same time and you get 33.1% uplift!

Small changes make a BIG difference

You see, the fundamentals of business growth are not complicated. When you have an AMR strategy, underpinned by the Four BIG questions and you work all variables of the formula at the same time, you don't just achieve linear growth. The multiplying effect of the variables working together gives you exponential business growth – hence the 33.1% uplift through just a 10% increase in each of the three variables.

In Table 1.4 you'll see a more realistic picture of differential uplift across all three variables: 23% growth in customers, 16% in order value, and 5% in order frequency. The impact on your turnover/ revenue is nearly a 50% uplift!

Table 1.4 The turnover/revenue effect; increasing the number of customers, average order value, and frequency

Number of Customers (A)	Average order value (M)	Average order frequency (M)	Turnover/ Revenue
100	£100	2	£20,000
110	£100	2	£22,000
110	£110	2.2	£26,620
123	£116	2.1	£29,962

The Profit Impact

This business growth formula is not just a model to drive top line revenue growth. It's no good getting to the end of a financial year to discover you've made no profit. Taking two of our examples, let's work the formula to understand what impact driving the top line in the right way can have on the bottom line profit.

In Table 1.5, Example 1 illustrates £20,000 turnover/revenue, assumed fixed costs of £9,000, and variable costs of another £9,000. Profits therefore equate to £2,000.

In Example 2 in Table 1.5, the turnover/revenue line of £26,620 was created through increasing each of the three variables: number of customers (A), average order value (M), and average order frequency (M) by 10% (as demonstrated in Table 1.3). Now, it is prudent to factor in a slight increase in our variable costs in order to manufacture or deliver the increase in product or services as a result of the 10% uplift. However, as we're only talking about a relatively small increase of 10% across the variables, let's assume no impact on our fixed costs. Look at what happens to our profits. A 231% uplift! Now that is the business growth formula in action.

We still have one final BIG question to consider, the 'R' in our AMR strategy: How do you increase the retention of customers? If you keep your customers for a second year, you can earn a second year's spend (remember in our first example, Table 1.1, 100 customers spent an average of £100 twice per year for an annualized revenue of £20,000).

Table 1.5   The turnover/revenue effect; impact to bottom line profit

Factors	Example 1	Example 2
Turnover/Revenue	£20,000	£26,620
Fixed Costs	£9,000	£9,000
Variable Costs	£9,000	£11,000
Profit	£2,000	£6,620
Profit increase %		231%

Imagine if you retained all 100 customers for five years . . . that would equate to £100,000 of locked-in revenue. This is a dynamic I refer to as Lifetime Value (LTV) and it's the essence of our 'R'. Let's look at how this works in real life.

Lifetime Value (LTV)

What is the lifetime value of a customer in your business? Understanding this is fundamental in creating your sustained business growth model. Let's use a real world scenario, in order to bring this to life: your weekly grocery shop.

An average family of four living in the UK will probably visit the supermarket at least once a week for their main family shop and let's say spend on average of £100 each time. During any average year, they'll probably go on holiday for two weeks, so if we factor this into the model, we can predict they will visit their local supermarket 50 times per year. That makes the average value per year £5,000 (50 times x £100 average spend).

But that's not even close to being their lifetime value. If they are a regular shopper over five years, the LTV to that supermarket is £25,000 from all those £100 trips (50 times per year x £100 average spend x 5 years). Retaining a customer suddenly becomes a very valuable thing to do.

This information becomes a fundamental piece of a very important puzzle: how much to spend on customer acquisition. If you know how much a customer is going to be worth to you over their lifetime, their LTV, you can calculate how much you're prepared to spend to acquire them. Without this insight, you're acquiring new customers blind, adding more pressure to your business model, particularly if you're overwhelmingly 'A' focused.

It also enables us to gain some important perspective. If you lose a customer, you don't forfeit someone who could earn you £100 next week, but someone who could earn you £25,000 over the next five years! Culturally, that is a different way of thinking and certainly should propel you to focus on the importance of retaining customers.

Applying this to your business

What is a customer worth to your business? Not just during year one, but over their lifetime . . . what's their LTV? Be careful not to just calculate the turnover or revenue figure, think about what they are worth in terms of profitability. After all, as we've demonstrated, that's the real measure of success of the business growth formula in action.

Cost to acquire customers

It's amazing when you actually calculate the real lifetime value of a customer, how it changes your priorities. With this clear focus, you can calculate what you are prepared to spend on sales and marketing to acquire new customers. Let's look at some well-known companies to help crystallize our thinking:

Gillette and other leading shaver brands charge a premium for refill razor blades. However, the first purchase you make, the razor itself, is comparatively cheap. They're prepared to sacrifice the initial profits on the first purchase, knowing they will recover them with each successive purchase. Hence during a new campaign launch, a new razor will be heavily discounted by as much as 50%. Of course, all the additional 'back end' products – shaving foam, face wash, moisturizer – are the add-ons focused on maximizing the customer LTV.

Inkjet printer manufacturers adopt the same approach. You buy a printer for virtually nothing, in comparison to what it can do for you, but to keep it running you have to purchase ink refills, which have been calculated as the most expensive liquid on Earth – more than premium vintage champagne!

Websites that offer a premium product, such as LinkedIn Premium, will often allow users to enjoy a month or two for free in order to get you hooked. They make up the cost of those two free months over the next 24 months or even over an open-ended contract with no fixed termination date.

Gyms do the same thing: they'll offer you the first month for free, on the signing of a contract, because over the LTV of that contract, they have factored in the profit margins they require.

In the last two examples, there are usually cancellation clauses, which enable you to stop your contract before your first payment. Of course this is a risk providers face. However, they rely on the laws of probability, in that far more people will activate their contract after their first free month than will cancel, so the majority of projected revenue isn't at risk.

These acquisition strategies work because the business understands the LTV of its customer; they are therefore able to offset a higher cost of acquisition.

Understanding your customer cost to serve

Another consideration, once you have acquired customers, is how much does it cost to serve them?

Nowadays, many businesses use multiple channels to promote and sell their products (i.e. online, face-to-face, or through a contact centre), so perhaps a more pointed question should be: what does it cost to serve your customers *by channel*? The competitive and challenging business landscape has definitely focused the minds of business professionals to interrogate their cost base and understand the cost/profitability of customers more than ever.

This topic could be the focus of a whole book in itself. However, for now, we'll focus on two key drivers of analysing cost to serve: advancements in technology and the changing demand and sophistication of the customer.

It's no big surprise that there has been phenomenal growth in web-based businesses such as Amazon, CompareTheMarket.com, ASOS, and Play.com. This e-business model gives the consumer complete control over when and where they choose to shop. For the business, it can deliver a leading edge 'cost to serve' business model centred on automation, therefore reducing people, bricks and mortar, and infrastructure costs.

A traditional business model may need a rethink, particularly if there is an expensive face-to-face component. A high people head-count and a network of real estate might be critical components of the proposition, yet they drive up the cost to serve. Without an in-depth understanding of cost to serve and conscious decision-making in relation to LTV, AMR, and the Four BIG questions, many business growth models are fundamentally flawed.

The principles of business growth are certainly not complex, and you shouldn't over-engineer them. To help you on your journey of tailoring the business growth formula to your business here are two case studies which apply the AMR formula and are reaping the benefits through accelerated, sustained and profitable business growth.

AMR in Action

Case study 1: McDonald's

When you think of AMR in action, there's a good chance that McDonald's comes to mind because of one simple, yet powerful question: *do you want fries with that?* That simple question is symbolic of McDonald's mastery of customer maximization, but let's be honest, the company delivers in outstanding fashion across the entire spectrum of AMR.

From a modest start at the beginning of the 1950s, McDonald's today operates more than 36,500 restaurants in 118 countries, and employs 420,000 people who serve more than 68 million customers every day. At the time of writing, McDonald's had also increased shareholder dividends for 25 consecutive years, making it one of the S&P 500 Dividend Aristocrats. Let's look at how it applies AMR and the Four BIG questions to great effect.

Acquisition

How does McDonald's increase the number of customers?

McDonald's clearly understands the value of high frequency locations. You're never more than a few miles from one in any major urban area. They have outlets in airports, train stations, motorway service stations and, in many instances, they build on their convenient locations by adding a drive-thru component so customers don't even have to get out of their vehicles. Once inside a McDonald's restaurant, the look and feel is consistent so that customers know how it works and what they can order without fuss. In recent years McDonald's has also been inventive in the way it appeals to different demographic audiences, modifying its opening times so that restaurants can serve early morning audiences for breakfast and late night audiences for dinner, with many outlets operating 24 hours a day.

In recognition of the challenge from 'coffee shop' competitors such as Starbucks, McDonald's has adapted its offering to include the McCafé concept with quality coffee and coffee shop-style food, pastries, and doughnuts. It has also expanded its appeal to a day-time business audience by offering free Wi-Fi and through the design of the restaurant interior. McDonald's attempts to meet the needs of families, children, and adults with birthday parties, Happy Meals, and in-built play zones.

Maximization

How does McDonald's increase the average order value?

The question referenced earlier, 'do you want fries with that?', is the most fundamental factor in how McDonald's achieves maximization. Customers are encouraged, with very great success, to add products, and increase the size of those products, through clever product bundling, Happy Meal, Big Mac Meal, etc.

When fast food businesses came under scrutiny a few years ago, for the perceived unhealthy quality of their food, McDonald's responded by adding healthier options, such as salads, to its menu, maximizing the options available to customers.

How does McDonald's increase the average order frequency?

Increasing the average order frequency leverages the strategies played out in our two previous questions: how to increase the number of customers, and how to increase their order value: maximum convenience of location, diverse menu, product bundles, auxiliary services – Wi-Fi, birthday parties, play zones. Whilst there may be a finite number of visits any one person could make to a McDonald's in a week or month, the key is ensuring it's your business they visit when they crave what you offer.

Retention

How does McDonald's increase the retention of customers?

The biggest retention strategy McDonald's has mastered is the relentless pursuit of consistency. Though there may be nuances to its menus around the world – in Japan there is a Teriyaki Mac Burger, in Germany a three bratwurst McNürnburger, and in Russia you can order a side of breaded shrimp instead of fries – McDonald's customers will be able to find their favourites wherever they are.

Added to this, many McDonald's customers experienced the brand first as a child following a visit with family, the taste of a Happy Meal, the celebration of a children's birthday party, and have remained customers into adulthood. McDonald's sustained business growth is not an accident, but a strategy honed, polished, and designed with deliberate intent.

Case study 2: LEGO®

LEGO® is universally recognized both for its products and for its brand and offers another masterful example of how to deliver accelerated, sustained, and profitable business growth through an effective AMR strategy. The perception of LEGO® in most people's minds is high quality, innovation, and lots and lots of fun. However, it hasn't always been that way for this privately held Danish company that was founded in 1932.

In 2003, Jørgen Vig Knudstorp, today the company's CEO, noted the precarious state of this company that had diversified too much (remember LEGO® wristwatches) and lost its way, describing it as '. . . a burning platform, losing money with negative cash flow and a real risk of debt default which could lead to a break up of the company'.

Fast forward to 2014, and the company posted record results of $4.5 billion in revenue, with an enviable operating margin of 33% before tax, making it the second largest toymaker in the world, second only to Mattel. So what did LEGO® do to turn things around? Well, among the changes were new financial and manufacturing processes, which gave it the control it had begun to lack. While it fixed its operational base, however, it turned to deep analysis of its AMR strategy and the Four BIG questions.

Acquisition

How does LEGO® *increase the number of customers?*

LEGO®, using its core product, the LEGO® brick, attracts new customers through its product range and bundling, its brand endorsements, and the LEGO® experience. LEGO® aims to satisfy the needs of its customers irrespective of their stage of life. They have the human lifecycle, early childhood to late adulthood, catered for.

They have a very clear segmented target market, with specific product strategies for each segment: from simple DUPLO block sets for young children, to the Ultimate Collectors Millennium Falcon from *Star Wars*, which contained 5,197 pieces. Special edition sets, developed around movie franchises with big fan bases, like *Star Wars* and *Harry Potter* for adults of all ages, and *Bob the Builder* DUPLO sets for young children.

Maximization

How does LEGO® *increase the average order value?*

LEGO®'s maximization strategy has been one of the most compelling of any company in history. The tie-ins discussed under Acquisition with the biggest movie franchises have enabled it to develop hundreds of premium-priced themed products with a defined end result: they make something specific as opposed to being open-ended. Those sets are designed to complement one another for example, *Star Wars* fans will purchase several of them in order to create a collection.

How does LEGO® *increase the average order frequency?*

By tying in to movie franchises, LEGO® has evolved a clever strategy because just as fans eagerly await the next instalment in the *Star Wars* series, there will be a brand new range of products to buy. Currently, *Star Wars* fans have more than 400 to choose from, ranging from those with as few as 25 pieces to those with thousands. As the franchises expand, LEGO® creates a fresh desire for its brick sets on a constant basis.

Its successful association with movie tie-ins has led in the past decade to the LEGO® movies, in which both the LEGO® bricks and the iconic LEGO® characters with their claw-like hands, are the heroes. Not only are the movies entertaining to the kids that watch them, they present a whole world of new ideas about how to play with LEGO®, new scenarios to create and, of course, which new kits are required purchases if the kids in the audience are to have the most possible fun with their LEGO®.

Added to that are the seven LEGOLAND® theme parks in Denmark, UK, California, Germany, Florida, Malaysia, and Dubai (three more are planned for Korea, Japan, and China), which represent a great marketing opportunity for sales of LEGO® bricks.

Retention

How does LEGO® *increase the retention of customers?*

By aggregating the Acquisition and Maximization components of LEGO®'s AMR strategy, it has developed an impenetrable Retention capability, constantly bringing customers back for a repeat purchase.

To boost that, Knudstorp's focus on retention led the company to turn its attention to greater customer interaction through focus groups, as it develops new products, and interestingly, a deeper interaction with what it calls AFOLs, the Adult Fans of LEGO®. As a result, customers are more involved in product development than ever before.

LEGO® has also embraced the use of technology, to make it easy for customers to buy again. Internet sales through LEGO® Direct enable customers to make purchasing decisions when and where they want, and buy new products quickly.

The LEGO® numbers speak for themselves:

- LEGO® products are on sale in **130** countries
- The LEGO® club has approximately **4.7 million** members
- There are currently **7** LEGOLAND® Resorts worldwide
- On average every person on earth owns **86** LEGO® bricks
- **10** LEGO® sets are sold each second. During the Christmas season **34** sets are sold each second

- Laid end to end, the number of LEGO® bricks sold in 2012 would reach more than **18** times round the world
- **2.5 million** LEGO® DUPLO elements are moulded daily at the factory in Hungary
- Over the years **650 billion** LEGO® elements have been manufactured
- If you built a column of about **40 billion** LEGO® bricks, it would reach the moon
- In 2012 approximately **22 billion** LEGO® elements were made at the factory in Denmark; equivalent to approximately **2.5 million** elements an hour
- In 2012 approximately **400 million** mini figures were produced. If you put them next to each other in a line, it would stretch approximately **10,000km** – equivalent to the distance from Denmark to Singapore
- **45 billion** elements: the number the LEGO® group achieved in global production
- **457.7 million** dollars taken at the worldwide box office for *The LEGO® Movie*
- **110.5 million** dollars raised from domestic video sales of *The LEGO® Movie*.

In an ever-changing world LEGO® has maintained its relevance not only to survive but also to thrive as one of the most popular toys of all time.

Making this real for your business: Is it AMR or RMA?

Now, one other interesting dynamic I would like you to think about is that AMR can be approached from two very different perspectives, depending on the maturity of your business.

If you're in the early stages of your business lifecycle, then your focus might be weighted towards AMR and acquiring new customers. If this is the case, then great. Just make sure from day one that you have strategies in play to maximize and retain the customers you bring in and don't fall into the trap of becoming stuck in the acquisition stage. You will never build a high performing sustained business by just being focused on the 'A'. What you bring in through the front door will only compensate for what you're losing out the back door if you're not looking after your existing customers and realizing the value they can bring to you.

If your business is more mature, it might serve you to turn AMR on its head. Start with retention, run an audit of how well you're doing in maximization and finally, aligned to your business growth ambitions, make up any shortfall in retention and maximization through targeted acquisition activity.

The great thing about your AMR strategy is that it is agile, designed and tailored to fit your business, not the other way around.

Developing Multiple Strategies

We've talked about the power of AMR working in unison within the business growth formula. The fun part is to brainstorm ideas against each of the Four BIG questions that underpin AMR:

1. How do you increase the number of customers?
2. How do you increase the average order value?
3. How do you increase the average order frequency?
4. How do you increase the retention of customers?

One of my clients has AMR on their monthly sales agenda and one exercise the sales director does every quarter involves four flipcharts and the Four BIG questions of AMR. The sales team splits into four groups and they have 10 minutes to share their AMR ideas from the last three months. Perhaps it comes as no surprise to hear that within 24 months of the sales director leading their UK business they moved from no. 5 to no. 1 in the global territories league table, delivering double digit growth month on month. AMR simply works!

How many ideas can you generate when you brainstorm all the different strategies you could use against each of the Four BIG questions, aligned to your overarching AMR strategy?

Become Really Curious

Curiosity is a great trait. There are examples of AMR strategy in action in abundance, and I would urge you to become curious about them. I'm talking about TV ads, newspaper ads, online banner ads, and clickable links – even the flyers that come through your morning post. Read them and take note.

Your normal response may be to ignore them, or fast-forward through them, or even think of them as junk mail. Yet each of those marketing messages contains a clue to how the business behind them, thinks about AMR. If you change your response and become curious about them, you might uncover a good idea or an insight that you would otherwise miss.

Some of the best ideas come from what others are doing in completely unrelated markets and sectors to you. The trick is to consciously and constantly think about how you can adapt, adopt, personalize, and apply ideas from elsewhere to your own business growth strategy.

Supermarkets offer loyalty cards and special offers that compel you to make a special visit outside your normal weekly shopping trip, or to make additional purchases that you wouldn't ordinarily make.

An emerging trend, which has turned industries on its head and which is gaining momentum: companies that make money as a middleman, while incurring no costs at all. Think of Uber as a current example: it owns no cars and hires no drivers, but makes money by linking drivers (who have made the capital investment in a vehicle) with customers through a simple app. Airbnb follows the same model: it owns no properties but charges a fee to link millions of accommodation seekers with property owners who have a room or a flat to spare. In the UK, notonthehighstreet has built a business by providing an e-commerce hub to small product manufacturers who otherwise wouldn't have access to large marketing and retail opportunities.

These businesses have acquired large customer bases by building nothing more than an interface and aim to maximize and retain those customers by managing the quality of their suppliers. A ranking of peer review ratings created by the customer themselves often drives this quality review. That's a game changing idea, and it offers a challenge to every business with a big investment in people head-count and infrastructure.

Summary

So now that you have a basic understanding of AMR and the Four BIG questions that underpin the strategy, I want you to consider the personalization for your business. Since we're just getting to know one another, I'd like to start you off with the sort of exercise that is going to be asked of you repeatedly in this book as we get to grips with the principles that will drive your accelerated, sustained and profitable business growth.

Think about the opening statement of this chapter, and then take some time to answer the questions that follow. You may have to research some of the answers, but I guarantee it will be time well invested.

'Strategically, the primary purpose of a business is to Acquire, Maximize, and Retain the right customers. Everything that contributes to this is an investment; anything which doesn't, is a cost.'

1. How do you increase the number of customers?
2. How do you increase the average order value?
3. How do you increase the average order frequency?
4. How do you increase the retention of customers?
5. Which activities are an investment and which are a cost?
6. What's the lifetime value of a customer to your business?
7. Having understood your customer LTV, what's the acceptable acquisition cost of a customer?
8. What's the cost to serve? What does your multi/omni channel solution need to look like?
9. What's your profitability by customer, taking into account acquisition cost, cost to serve, product mix, and lifetime value?
10. Do you have different strategies centred on Acquiring, Maximizing, and Retaining customers?
11. Are they all wrapped together into your business growth/AMR strategy in action?

Chapter 2

Your Business Growth Transformation Framework® (BGTF)

> 'It takes a wise man to learn from his mistakes, but an even wiser man to learn from others.'
> —ZEN PROVERB

When it comes to doing anything new, you have two choices: the first is to put in the hard yards, learning through trial and error as you reinvent the wheel; the second is to learn from those who have already navigated a pathway to success.

I personally know many business owners, business leaders and entrepreneurs that have started businesses, achieved phenomenal success, perhaps even sold their business, but have failed to embed the lessons they learnt. They've spent the next decade frustrated, setting up numerous new ventures, which never delivered the same levels of success. Why does this happen? Because they never had a replicable framework that allowed them to deliver consistent, repeatable, predictable results every time!

I learned early in my career that observing and emulating the habits, processes, and attitudes of successful people was a reliable way to fast track my own success. On reflection, this was one of my most important life lessons and it has stayed with me ever since.

Leaving school at 16, I was keen to get into the real world and start earning money, and my first opportunity was an apprenticeship at a construction company where I completed a four-year rotation through each department of the business. That could have been a long process of trial and error for me, but instead, my very wise site manager advised me that as I moved into the various departments, I should ask the three best people in each area what they thought I needed to know in order to be successful from day 1. When I joined the planning department, I asked the three best planners, who shared tips and tricks I would otherwise have had to learn the hard way. When I joined the quantity-surveying department, I did the same.

Adopt a Success Modelling Approach

If there is one idea that can 'fast track' your success: personally, professionally, and in your business, it's this: success modelling! You can either develop yourself and your business the hard way or the easy way . . . which pathway are you currently on?

The first pathway is the hard way: learning through your mistakes, trial and error and constantly re-inventing the wheel. This road can be long, winding, and a painful experience! Sometimes we become so locked in our own world, so inwardly focused on thinking we can do it all ourselves and we know best, that we simply miss the opportunity to learn from others' experiences.

Is there an easier way? Yes, and top achievers follow this second pathway. They have an insatiable need and thirst for discovery, tapping into the success formula of those who have already been there and done it. Knowing that if they learn from their lessons, they might just accelerate their own journey, and in the process, avoid some of the common pitfalls which can easily derail and sabotage their success.

It doesn't mean there isn't some trial and error involved. When a child learns to walk, they start by modelling the people around them, but they still fall over constantly to begin with. Why does a second sibling generally develop faster than the first? Because they have a role model to emulate and copy, they are 'success modelling' from an early age.

The optimum solution therefore is a blend of pathway two – modelling other people's success – and pathway one – trial and error – testing out some of your thinking and ideas, making some healthy mistakes, and learning from them fast.

What if you could 'fast track' your success and reduce the timeline in delivering accelerated, sustained and profitable business growth in your business?

Your Business Growth Transformation Framework®

Therein lies the thinking behind the Business Growth Transformation Framework® (BGTF): A framework to future proof your business and unlock opportunities for accelerated, sustained and profitable business growth.

It can work for you, regardless of the industry you're in, or the business you run. I want to stress that point because I often hear business owners, business leaders, and entrepreneurs say: 'That may be great for some businesses, but mine is really different.' Believe me when I tell you, it is not. I'll show you why as we work through this chapter.

It's worth explaining to start with the context to the word 'growth' as it may have a number of connotations. The obvious one is a small business growing into a big one. It could also simply be growing your customer experience or growing one or two of the nine interlocking strategy areas of the Business Growth Transformation Framework®. It could be maximizing profitability and margin growth or it could even be about *standing still* in terms of your turnover and revenue. If you historically had a high year-on-year customer attrition or churn, replacing that attrition to remain at revenue neutral at the end of the year is 'growth'.

The definitions are infinite and determined by the maturity of your business, the sector you operate in, and your vision, aspirational goals and ambitions for your business.

Your Recipe for Success

I like to think of the Business Growth Transformation Framework® as a recipe, giving you the ingredients you require, the quantities of those ingredients, and the sequence in which you add them together, with the outcome of accelerated, sustained and profitable business growth.

Let me elaborate. I really enjoy cooking and I am a fan of TV cooking shows. One such show, *MasterChef*, has a global franchise you might have heard of or watched. If you haven't, I'm sure you're aware of similar shows. In *MasterChef*, there are two cooking challenges each week, in which amateur chefs have the chance to impress the panel of professional judges, which include a famous food critic and a famous restaurateur.

In the first challenge (consider this pathway one: trial and error), the amateur chefs are asked to create a dish they have never cooked before and here the pressure builds. Half the time, even though they understand food and are capable of producing some special dishes, they crumble when faced with the unknown. Without a recipe to follow, there is too much guesswork involved and that's . . . well, it's a recipe for disaster.

In the second challenge (consider this pathway two: success modelling), the amateur chefs aim to impress the judges with a recipe they know well; one they have cooked many times before and know intimately. Those that are prepared for the challenge can usually produce something really good. They know how to do it, and it works.

This analogy is so strong that when I'm speaking at conferences or working with leadership teams, I have some fun by asking: 'who sees themselves as a potential *MasterChef* winner?' There's always one. So I lead them into what is usually a fascinating conversation:

I'll ask them: 'What's your signature dish? The one all your friends and family tell you you're great at?'

They'll respond with something like: 'Spaghetti Bolognaise.'

I'll then ask them how they make it?

'Well, I put olive oil in a pan and heat it up. I know how many people I am cooking for and I've got all the ingredients so that I can do the prep work (usually with a bottle of red wine open . . . chef's special treat). When I start cooking I throw chopped onions in first, followed by some garlic and then add and brown off the mince. I then add mushrooms, brown these off for a few minutes followed by chopped tomatoes and peppers. Finally, I'll add some tomato purée, some Italian seasoning, black pepper and red wine, place the lid on the pan, let it simmer on a medium heat, giving it a quick stir every five minutes so that it doesn't stick to the pan. Once that's done, I mix the garlic butter and make my own garlic bread using a fresh baguette, and then 10 minutes before the bolognaise is ready I put the fresh pasta in boiling water and pull the whole thing together.'

'Okay,' I'll say. 'But how do you know it's any good?'

'Well I love it and I always get a lot of praise for it. The best way to answer I suppose, is that there's never any left over.'

'Great,' I'll say. 'Tell me, do you ever put the tomato puree in the pan first?'

'No, of course not.'

'Why not?'

'Because the onions always go first.'

'Interesting comment. Hold that thought. What if you missed a key ingredient? Say, for example, you forgot the mushrooms?'

'Well it just doesn't taste the same.'

And so the conversation will flow back and forth with my probing questions. You may be able to guess where I am heading with this: whether it's making Spaghetti Bolognaise or building a business, if you want the outcome to be predictable, it's best to follow a proven recipe, which has already been developed through trial and error and success modelling to make it bulletproof.

If it matters in cooking, it matters all the more in your business. Your business is about your life and your entire personal and professional success. Are you prepared to leave it to chance or do you think it makes sense to tap into a framework . . . a recipe . . . a blueprint . . . which is proven to deliver results, every time?

We call it the Business Growth Transformation Framework® (BGTF) (Figure 2.1). It's specifically a framework as opposed to a rigid plan, because every business is different.

Business Growth Transformation Framework® (BGTF) – a-e represent the 5 components

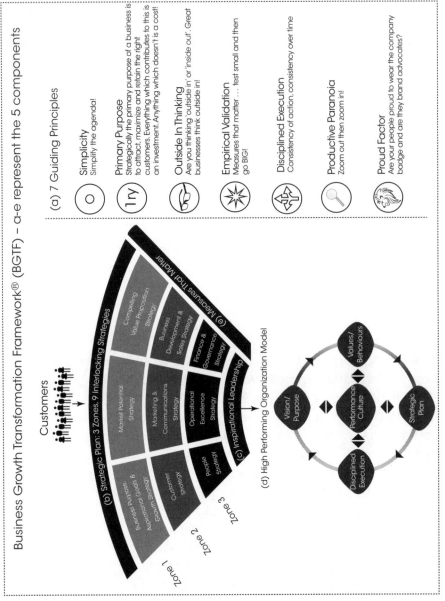

(a) 7 Guiding Principles

Simplicity
Simplify the agenda!

Primary Purpose
Strategically the primary purpose of a business is to attract, maximize and retain the right customers. Everything which contributes to this is an investment. Anything which doesn't is a cost!

Outside In Thinking
Are you thinking 'outside in' or 'inside out'. Great businesses think outside in!

Empirical Validation
Measures that matter … test small and then go BIG!

Disciplined Execution
Consistency of action, consistency over time

Productive Paranoia
Zoom out then zoom in!

Proud Factor
Are your people proud to wear the company badge and are they brand advocates?

Customers

(b) Strategic Plan: 3 Zones, 9 Interlocking Strategies

Compelling Value Proposition Strategy

Business Development & Sales Strategy

Finance & Governance Strategy

Market Potential Strategy

Marketing & Communications Strategy

Operational Excellence Strategy

Business Purpose, Aspirational Goals & Growth Strategy

Customer Strategy

People Strategy

(e) Measures that Matter

(c) Inspirational Leadership

Zone 1

Zone 2

Zone 3

(d) High Performing Organization Model

Values/Behaviours

Vision/Purpose

Performance Culture

Strategic Plan

Disciplined Execution

Figure 2.1

As I've already demonstrated through the concept of success modelling, there is a recipe and formula for delivering accelerated, sustained and profitable business growth. As you will see in Figure 2.1, there are five critical components of the Business Growth Transformation Framework®:

a: 7 Guiding Principles
b: Strategic Plan
c: Inspirational Leadership
d: High Performing Organization Model
e: Measures that Matter.

The Business Growth Transformation Framework® empowers business owners, business leaders, and entrepreneurs to build a high performing, sustainable, legacy organization through the creation of an all-encompassing business growth strategy. This strategy can be cascaded into functional and departmental plans ensuring individuals understand the part they play in turning the organizational vision and purpose into reality.

It also enables colleagues to understand the interdependencies, cross functions and where collaboration, teamwork, and clarity of communication are required to:

- Leverage the power of the 'whole' business behind a common vision, purpose, and set of strategic priorities
- Avoid duplication of activity costing time and money
- Allow your business to be fast, agile, and proactive in driving the business forward
- Create the capacity and structure to grow, future proof, and easily diagnose where blockers might be in the business growth strategy
- Build a high performing, sustainable, legacy organization, which you can be PROUD of!

By the end of this book, I will have guided you step by step through each component of the Business Growth Transformation Framework® and shown you how to personalize it for your business. Now let's look at the five major components in more detail:

7 Guiding Principles

The 7 Guiding Principles have been developed through my 20 years of experience in working with thousands of organizations. Their purpose is to stimulate your thinking about the critical challenges and opportunities in growing your business and how you can avoid some of the trial and error which otherwise might stifle your growth potential or, worse, derail your ambitions.

As you read through the Seven Guiding Principles, score the current performance of your business against each on a scale of 1–10: 1 being 10% of the time and 10 being 100% of the time. How does your business shape up?

1. Simplicity

We have an innate ability to over complicate and over engineer life and this certainly applies in business. A question I frequently ask to bring the principle of simplicity to life is this: would you describe your business as being like a tugboat or an oil tanker? In the early stages of the life of a business it is fast, agile, responsive, and able to move quickly (the tug boat). The challenge is that over time we start to introduce complexity: additional layers of people in the organizational design, multiple sign-off processes and procedures, key performance indicator overload, an unhealthy obsession for governance, reports for the sake of reports, decision-making by committee, and – perhaps worst of all – bureaucracy that makes it difficult for a customer to do business with you (the oil tanker). Is your business a tugboat or an oil tanker? Perhaps utopia is to have the scale and size of an oil tanker, yet have the mentality and agility of the tugboat! Great businesses and their leaders are great simplifiers; they seek to uncomplicate and de-clutter as a primary objective.

2. Primary purpose

Strategically the primary purpose of a business is to Acquire, Maximize and Retain the right customers. Everything that contributes to this is an investment. Anything that doesn't is a cost! We covered this in detail in Chapter 1 and it is the key principle that underpins your entire business growth model. Aligning all your available resources (people, financial investment etc.) to this principle will create the focus and momentum for accelerated growth.

Just imagine if you completed an audit of every process, system, and procedure in your business and as part of the exercise asked the following question: 'Strategically the primary purpose of a business is to Acquire, Maximize and Retain the right customers. What's an investment and what's a cost in our business? What's helping us to deliver this goal and what is detracting our focus and derailing us?' This process alone will help you simplify your business and ensure you maintain 'tugboat status'.

3. 'Outside in' thinking

Are you thinking 'inside out' or 'outside in'? Great businesses think 'outside in', the customer is the focal point of everything they do and how they do it. They are fanatical about looking at themselves through their customers' lens and culturally are self-challenging, asking probing questions: How easy are we to do business with? Are we truly delivering a world-class customer experience? What are our customers' real needs and wants now and in the future? Are we fulfilling them? What will our business need to look like, feel like, and act like in 5 or 10 years' time in order to be relevant, market leading, and a trust brand? Where are we on the journey towards provider of choice status? It is no accident that the customer sits at the pinnacle of the Business Growth Transformation Framework®. It's because of this key Guiding Principle! In your business are you thinking 'inside out' or 'outside in'?

4. Empirical validation

Thinking beyond and testing small before going BIG. Measuring the *right* detail allows you to make proactive, informed, well-educated, empirically validated decisions about how you can deliver accelerated, sustained, and profitable business growth. The challenge for most businesses is threefold. First, some businesses just don't have performance measures in the first place, second they are measuring the wrong things, or third they are not paying enough attention to what the measures are telling them and how this subsequently informs their decision-making on strategy and driving the business forward.

As we work through *Built to Grow*, we'll focus on the measures that matter, and just like your AMR strategy and business growth formula, small changes in each area will have an exponential uplift in your overall business growth. Are you measuring the right things currently in your business?

5. Disciplined execution

Consistency of action, consistency over time. This is the difference that makes the difference for high performing organizations. You can spend an eternity creating the best strategy in the world and on paper you should be a phenomenal business, however you fall down on disciplined execution. I've seen so many businesses achieve *accelerated* growth, but delivering *sustained* and *profitable* growth requires a whole new set of skills and disciplines. It requires focus, it requires rigour, and it requires boundless levels of energy, commitment, and resilience. Perhaps most importantly it requires alignment of all individuals behind a common purpose and ambition. How good are you and your business in the discipline of disciplined execution?

6. Productive paranoia

Zoom out then zoom in! What if you lose your biggest customer? What if a competitor makes a game-changing move that affects your potential to grow? What if a key person in your business leaves? What is your plan B? Your plan C? Or even your plan D? Great leaders have the ability to zoom out and take a helicopter view of their business and when required, zoom in to the detail. Mohammed Ali said, 'The fight is won or lost far away from witnesses. It's won behind the lines, in the gym, and out there on the road, long before I dance under those lights.' Productive paranoia is preparing for the unforeseen, and running scenarios, however improbable, to combat possible roadblocks and curve balls, which suddenly appear out of left field. Are you spending too much time working 'in' your business or are you making time to work 'on' your business?

7. Proud factor

Are your people proud to wear the company badge and are they brand advocates? This should be the number one question on every single employee survey. When your people are out on a Friday evening with friends, and the friends are all griping about work, do your people say 'you know what, I'm sorry you're in that position because I work for a great business and I am really proud of working for them'? That's the proud factor in action and we'll be talking about this principle in more detail in Chapter 11: People Strategy.

So, that's component 'a' of your BGTF. How did you score against each of the guiding principles?

Strategic Plan

Failing to plan is like planning to fail. *Built to Grow* is about making sure you are in the driver's seat of your business with a clear vision of where it is you want to get to, why you want to go there, and how you're going to turn your vision into reality.

In order to do this, you need a Strategic Plan. Before I share the nine interlocking strategies with you, the starting point is aligned thinking about precisely what strategy is.

What is strategy?

Having spent two decades working with business owners, business leaders, and entrepreneurs, one question I frequently ask is: 'What is your definition of strategy?' My experience is that everyone has a different definition; even members of the same leadership team and business.

How would you define strategy? The definition we are going to use in *Built to Grow* is this:

> 'A strategy is a changeable set of implementable actions that we frequently revisit and redefine according to shifting market conditions in order to achieve the long term aspiration of the organisation.'

Now, that's a pretty detailed statement, with lots of moving parts, so let's dissect it in order to bring it to life.

Strategy is *changeable.* One thing is for certain: your strategy must be fluid because it's constantly exposed to changing external and internal market conditions. We live in a world where the norm is a relentless pace of change, and strategy, by its nature, cannot be rigid.

It is about *implementable actions.* It's no good creating a high level strategy that is so complex in the wording you use and the way you translate it, that it creates confusion. Implementable actions are critical if you want strategy to live within your business. Every single person in the organization must have alignment and know the part they play every day in delivering the overall business strategy.

We must *frequently revisit and redefine.* The whole point about success modelling is learning both what is working, and what is not, so it is really important that we revisit and redefine on a regular basis. You shouldn't find yourself setting off on your strategy at the start of the year and then come to the end and realize you've failed to reach your goals, thinking how on earth did that happen? Frequent reality checks enable you to make timely adjustments along the way and adjust course where needed.

Shifting market conditions are linked to the word changeable. The market is constantly shifting and we must be proactive and reactive in addressing changes to ensure we're ahead of the curve. These changes can be both internal and external. External changes can relate to micro or macro economic conditions, new regulations, and new competitors entering the market. Internal changes include key people or organizational changes, refinement of processes, a shift in focus or priorities.

Finally, the *long-term aspiration of the organization* is hotwired to your business purpose, vision, ambition, and goals.

Now we have a common definition of strategy let's look at the key areas within your Strategic Plan.

Exploring the three 'Zones' within your Strategic Plan

A robust Strategic Plan built on the Business Growth Transformation Framework® consists of nine interlocking strategies, organized into three Zones. Combined, these nine interlocking strategies form the overall Strategic Plan for your business.

The reality is that most organizations tend to be good in one or two of the interlocking strategies, but weak in others. Any business that can truly call itself built to grow, must achieve excellence in all nine, acknowledging that each one is equally important and constantly impacted by every other one, in real time, 24/7.

Each interlocking strategy is explained in rich detail in a chapter of its own, giving you specific insight, tools, and techniques applicable to that given strategy. Here, I'm going to talk briefly about the three 'Zones' of the Strategic Plan and their purpose.

Zone One

There is a specific reason why the Business Growth Transformation Framework® is visually represented using a funnel shape. Zone One, which is at the widest point, is all about 'big picture thinking' around your business purpose, analysing the market potential to realize your growth ambitions, and creating tangible differentiation through your compelling value proposition. Zone One contains the following interlocking strategies:

1. Business Purpose, Aspirational Goals, and Growth Strategy
2. Market Potential Strategy
3. Compelling Value Proposition Strategy.

Zone Two

Zone Two is the core of your Strategic Plan, the centre of the funnel, sandwiched between Zones One and Three and is your 'go-to-market' plan including:

4. Customer Strategy
5. Marketing and Communications Strategy
6. Business Development and Sales Strategy.

How can you create real differentiation through your compelling end-to-end customer experience? What part does marketing and communications play? What are the key components of a world-class business development and sales strategy? Just some of the questions we'll be answering in these chapters.

And finally, Zone Three

This zone is about enabling success. The reality is you can create clarity on your business purpose and aspirational goals; understand your market potential through a detailed analysis of your target customer profile; design and build a compelling value proposition; and develop a detailed end-to-end, go-to-market strategy. Then . . . the business falls over because you didn't pay enough attention to Zone Three, which includes the following interlocking strategies:

7. People Strategy
8. Operational Excellence Strategy
9. Finance and Governance Strategy.

For most businesses people are usually a key differentiator. Having the right people in the right seats, inspired and doing the right things, is a critical success factor. Likewise, it is essential your business is operationally enabled to deliver on customers' needs and wants. Operational excellence is the goal to which most businesses aspire, but few achieve. I'll show you how you can get there.

Finance and governance is the final inter-locking strategy, which binds your entire Strategic Plan together. Revenue growth, profitability, and cash management are the fuel to deliver accelerated, sustained, and profitable business growth. Governance, when working well, ensures the business is protected and doing things the right way.

Whatever your proposition and commitments to the marketplace, you've got to be able to follow through and deliver on the promise.

An undeniable challenge

You could be feeling the effects of a lack of clear strategy in your business today. Or perhaps, having read up to this point, you're thinking there are critical areas that I've touched on which are missing in your plan or receiving insufficient focus and attention.

One of the common challenges faced by businesses without a clear strategy is a leader building their own empire. The Head of Marketing may be a wizard at his or her craft and produce high volumes of excellent work, but if he or she isn't aligned to the needs of the sales force, it could work against you, rather than for you. The Head of Operations may have an excellent eye for rock-solid back-end systems that enable the efficient flow of information but if those systems demand a new way of working that isn't aligned with the customer service team, the same thing applies.

A clear strategy doesn't just clarify roles inside silos. It clarifies interdependencies between business areas so the business, acting as a cohesive multi-part whole, moves and is aligned in the same direction.

It's because of a lack of clear strategy that many business leaders, business owners, and entrepreneurs get sucked almost exclusively into Zone Three, having their time dominated by constant tactical delivery and crisis management.

The timeline for your Strategic Plan

A great deal of work underpins a comprehensive and well thought out Strategic Plan, therefore my timeline recommendation is:

- Three-year line of sight: target financial goals, revenue and profitability for Years 3 and 2
- Twelve-month detailed plan: strategic priorities, deliverables, budgets with measures that matter
- Ninety-day/quarterly 'bite size' priorities, deliverables, and measures that matter.

Our aligned definition of strategy included: 'frequently revisit and redefine according to shifting market conditions'. My recommended timeline builds in regular reality checks to evaluate what's working and what isn't, ultimately giving you the opportunity to make the necessary adjustments to your 12-month plan.

To help in the creation of your personalized Strategic Plan I have developed a Strategic Plan template for you to use in your business. Download details are available at the end of this chapter.

Inspirational Leadership

A key competitive advantage for businesses today is their ability to grow, nurture, and develop their leadership and management capability faster than the competition. Future business success depends on it.

A high performing organization recognizes its leadership strength and capability throughout the business, not just at the top of the organization. Unfortunately, high performing organizations with leadership bench strength at every level are the exception rather than the norm.

You don't need to look far to understand the extent of the challenge in developing leadership capability. The UK Government Department for Business, Innovation and Skills published a paper titled: 'Leadership & Management in the UK – The Key to Sustainable Growth', which highlighted some telling numbers:

- Ineffective management is estimated to be costing UK businesses over £19 billion per year in lost working hours
- 43% of UK managers rate their own line manager as ineffective – and only one in five are qualified
- Incompetence or bad management of company directors causes 56% of corporate failures.

Developing leadership capability is imperative for a growing business. The entire focus of Chapter 3 is dedicated to how you can build a leadership culture within your business and identifying the seven essential traits of an inspirational leader.

High Performing Organization Model

A Strategic Plan and inspired leaders alone are not enough. A high performing team has a feel about it – a sort of 'teamness'. The secret to building a high performing organization is knowing how to build the 'teamness', how to bottle the ingredients and, most importantly, how to replicate it.

One of the best examples of a high performing team which has 'teamness' is the Red Arrows, officially known as the Royal Air Force Aerobatic Team. They are a global brand and when discussions arise about excellence in flying, without exception the Red Arrows will enter the conversation as an exemplar of best practice.

All nine Red Arrows display pilots are fast jet pilots from frontline Royal Air Force squadrons. Once they have finished their three-year tour with the team they will return to their Royal Air Force duties.

As Red Arrows display pilots join directly from the RAF they are already perceived as having 'elite status', the best of the best. However, talk to any of the pilots who have completed a tour and they will openly admit that, just as in life, sometimes you just don't know what you don't know and working in the Red Arrows is another gear shift in performance and what it means to be part of a high performing elite team.

Where are you on your journey in building a high performing team and business? A compelling vision and purpose, aligned values, agreed behavioural standards of excellence, and a performance culture are just some of the key ingredients that allow the Red Arrows to own a space in the upper echelons of high performance that others aspire to achieve.

High performing organizations are not created by accident, and even organizations that are excellent in some areas rarely become excellent overall, without creative design. Since your high performing organization is a product of purposeful design, Chapter 4 is dedicated to this subject.

Measures that Matter

How are you going to know if your Strategic Plan is working? Over time, businesses often fall into the trap of over measuring and over analysing, get caught up in form filling, and lose their ability to extract meaningful insight. Regaining those important insights is about shifting your focus from measuring everything and becoming KPI-overwhelmed, to focusing only on those things that enable you to make informed, educated, empirically validated decisions. By focusing on the Measures that really Matter!

What's on your dashboard?

A great analogy for determining which measures are important and which are not, is your car's dashboard. Right in front of you, when you start your engine, are the three or four things you absolutely need to know in order to have a successful journey.

Your first key dial is your speedometer, a critical performance measure for driving safely and legally. The second: the amount of fuel you have on board. Imagine if you had to guess at that! Third: your satellite navigation system. The days of the physical map are long gone for most people. I think there are some people who couldn't actually get to their destination without this performance tool!

If you had to guess at how fast you were going, whether you'd got any fuel left, and whether you were travelling in the right direction on the right road it would certainly impact your desired outcome of getting to your destination safely, legally, and on time. You can also press buttons on your dashboard and access data such as your fuel efficiency, the outside temperature and so on, but that isn't critical data in the way your fuel gauge is.

I like to think of businesses as having dashboards just like the one in your car. Many companies over engineer their measurements and often find themselves to be experts on the temperature, but fail to notice they're running low on gas. To simplify matters, I believe three high level strategic measures should matter most to any business (Figure 2.2).

As you would expect, a series of performance metrics sit beneath each measure and, as mentioned earlier in this chapter, as we work through each of the nine interlocking strategies within the Strategic Plan, we'll look at specific measures that matter for each.

At this stage in *Built to Grow* I just want you to start thinking about the following questions:

- Are you the provider of choice for your customers?
- Are you the employer of choice for your employees? In the spirit of openness and transparency, what would they really say?

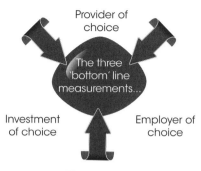

Figure 2.2

And finally, if you focus 'outside in', are obsessed with being the provider of choice, passionately care about and look after your people and create the optimum environment for them to feel inspired and do their best work every day, you will become an investment of choice.

If you need funding for your business, banks, private and venture capital investors, and other funding lines will look at you favourably. Your competition will be nervous and watching their backs. Suppliers and strategic partners will want to support you. You will truly be seen as an investment of choice!

Summary: Setting a Foundation of Great Habits

A few years back, Bill Gates and Warren Buffett gave an address at a Harvard graduation ceremony and in the Q&A session at the end, Buffett was asked: 'If you could share one lesson that above all would increase the chances of success, what would it be?' His response: 'It's simple: get your habits right, while you're young.'

Are the habits you have in your business today enabling your success or derailing you from realizing the goals and ambitions you have for your business?

Buffett's point is absolutely correct because it is far easier to change bad habits and embed the right ones when you're young. If your business is at an early stage of development, auditing it at every level using the ideas in *Built to Grow* will allow you to put in place the right habits, processes, and systems now.

However, even mature businesses can benefit from Buffett's logic. There is a saying that the best time to plant a tree was 20 years ago; the second best time is right now. There is no such thing as a closed window of opportunity when it comes to embedding habits that serve you and your business well.

It's a great opportunity for any business. Even if you're the only person or the only leader in your business, start an audit of all your habits right now and begin to make improvements. If you are a larger business with multiple teams, I encourage each team to take a chapter of *Built to Grow* and complete an audit of their business area.

You'll then have a strong platform for a business purposefully designed to achieve greatness and deliver accelerated, sustained, and profitable business growth. To accelerate your journey in the creation of your own personalized Strategic Plan, download now your Strategic Plan template: **http://pti.world/BTG-Toolkit**.

Chapter 3

Inspirational Leadership

'If your actions inspire others to dream more, learn more, do more, and become more, you are a leader.'
—John Quincy Adams

There are many stories of inspirational leadership throughout this book, because it is such an integral part of building any high performing organization. Building winning strategies requires great leaders, who will create and define them, guide and shape their implementation, and win the hearts and minds of their people to deliver with passion and commitment, not because they have to, but because they want to.

So in this chapter, we're going to cover two key things: first, the correlation between leadership capability and building a high performing sustainable business, and second, the key traits of inspirational leaders.

Here's a positioning statement to get us started:

> *One of the single most competitive advantages for businesses today is their ability to grow, nurture, and develop leadership and management capability faster than the competition . . . future business success depends on it.*

That's a bold statement to make, but I passionately believe in it, and more importantly, I have seen it have a profound impact in thousands of businesses of all shapes and sizes. If you want to accelerate and fast track the success of your business, and build sustained high performance, developing your leadership culture is among your biggest priorities.

Where are you on your journey in building leadership and management capability and developing a leadership culture in your business? If you're a sole trader, leadership and management responsibility probably sits with you. If you've got a small team, it is more important than ever as you need every single one of your people aligned and performing at their peak. If you run a much bigger organization, creating consistency and building strength at every level is critical to succession planning, creating the stretch, and the capacity to grow your business.

Leadership is the enabler to turn your vision and goals into reality! If you have ambitions to grow your business, then it cannot be all about you. Jack Welch really understood this principle when he said: 'Before you are a leader, success is all about growing yourself. When you become a leader, success is all about growing others.' He was chairman and CEO of General Electric between 1981 and 2001, the youngest CEO in the company's history. During his tenure, GE's value rose 4,000% and when he retired, he received a severance payment of $417 million, the largest such payment in history.

Now what was impressive about this? Was it that he ran a global business for 20 years (an impressive feat in itself when you think about turnover of CEOs today)? Was it the 4,000% increase in the share price over that period? Was it the huge pay-out on retirement? Actually, what was really impressive was what he did in his first 90 days in office – he set up a Leadership Academy. Welch had a core philosophy: for the business to be successful it needed the best leadership capability, and he was prepared to attach part of his legacy to this philosophy. Welch became known for growing and teaching leaders.

From day one, a marker of success for Welch was how many leaders who served under his tenure at GE would go on to run Fortune 500 businesses or become CEOs of major organizations.

His success was no accident. The success of the organization, particularly the 4,000% increase in the share price, was the by-product of a relentless and unwavering focus on developing people and leaders. At the last count more than 35 CEOs in today's top companies trained and served under Jack Welch.

And if ever you needed further reinforcement of the importance of leadership capability today, leadership strength is one of the top 10 'value enhancing differentiators' that accountants, private equity, and venture capital specialists utilize in valuing businesses. If you have an aspiration to float or sell your business, your leadership capability will directly affect your multiplier and business valuation.

So, how can you develop a leadership culture in your business?

Developing Your Leadership Culture

Firstly, what do I mean by culture? Your competition will copy your products if they are good. They'll copy your services; they'll copy your branding; they may even try to poach your people!

However, there is one thing they will never be able to copy, and that's your culture! Your culture is the very thing that makes your organization special, distinct, and unique. It's your competitive edge and advantage. Your culture informs your people what's acceptable and what's important.

And it's your culture that lets your people and your customers know what your organizational values are, i.e. honesty, innovation, candour, going that extra mile for customers. In creating that sense of uniqueness, your culture meets a key human need. People want to feel they're part of a community. One of the deepest psychological needs of all human beings is belonging.

We also want to work for a business that values us as individuals. A business that provides personal growth opportunities to be better this year than last year, enabling us to feel we're contributing to something bigger and more meaningful than just the job we're doing.

Developing a leadership culture expands the essence of your organizational culture by adopting an entirely new take on leadership.

A leadership culture operates from a solid core of personal own-ership, each individual taking responsibility and accountability for their actions and results; where everyone thinks, feels, and acts like it's their business, regardless of their job title, office, or place on the hierarchy. It's where individuals:

- Are enterprising, entrepreneurial, and proactive
- Are focused on getting to the solution rather than concentrating on the problem (the glass is definitely half full, not half empty!)
- Do whatever it takes to build a legacy world-class business that is revered by the competition, sets the benchmark for industry stan-dards, and is known as a great place to work
- Are concerned about results and outcomes, and do their part to reduce costs
- Take personal ownership for achieving results that move the busi-ness forward (whether they work in the post room or sit in the boardroom)
- Shape the culture, stay positive, and lead by example.

A book I highly recommend for its many great lessons is *Turn the Ship Around!* by L. David Marquet, a retired US Navy captain. Within its pages, Marquet offers a really interesting definition of leadership straight from the US Navy handbook, which says:

> 'Leadership is the art, science, or gift by which a person is enabled and privileged to direct the thoughts, plans, and actions of others in such a manner as to obtain and command their obedience, their confidence, their respect, and their loyal cooperation.'

It's especially interesting when you dissect and interpret it, because what it is in effect saying is that leadership in the US Navy (and in fact in many organizations) is about controlling people. It divides the world into two distinct groups of people: leaders and followers.

The leader-follower structure has been with us for generations and is perpetuated through organizations to this very day. A hierarchical, command and control structure with decision-making from the top is what we know, and for good reason. Throughout history, a number of great achievements have been accomplished through the leader-follower model, and it has enabled many people to achieve success in their chosen field. It is exactly because the leader-follower way of doing business has been so successful that it is so hard to give up. But it was developed during a period when mankind's primary work was physical and as a result, it's optimized for getting physical work out of people.

Why the Leader-Follower Structure is at Odds With Developing a Leadership Culture

In our modern world, the most important work we do is cognitive, and the leader-follower structure just isn't a very good model for intellectual work. Differing motivations and aspirations, particularly from one generation to the next, only exacerbate the problem and demand an alternative approach.

People who are treated like followers have the expectations of followers and act like followers. That means they have limited decision-making authority and little incentive to give the utmost of their intellect, energy, and passion. Those who take orders usually run at half speed, under-utilizing their imagination and initiative.

In a leader-follower model, all decision-making defaults to the leader and therefore the organization gets squashed, constrained, and contracted, reducing the headspace to grow the organization. It can be particularly challenging when the leader is exceptionally charismatic, or worse, when they're an out-and-out autocrat, because the ability of people to shine is increasingly limited over time.

In a leader-follower structure, the performance of the organization is closely linked to the ability of the key leader at the top, so inevitably there is a natural tendency to develop personality-driven leadership; an approach that might deliver short-term results, but will never allow you to build a high performing, sustainable, legacy organization.

The Solution: Leader-Leader

A leader-leader structure is fundamentally different from the leader-follower model. At its core is the belief that we can all be leaders, and in fact, it's best when we all are. Leadership is not some mystical quality that some possess and others do not. As humans, we all have what it takes to take the lead under specific circumstances.

The leader-leader model not only achieves great improvements in effectiveness and morale but also makes the organization stronger. Critically, these improvements are enduring, decoupled from the leader's personality and presence. Leader-leader structures are significantly more resilient, and they do not act as if the designated leader is always right. Further, leader-leader structures naturally spawn additional leaders throughout the organization. It's a force that can't be stopped.

The faster you can get every single person in your business to embrace and demonstrate leadership behaviours, regardless of their position, the quicker you'll secure your position as a world-class organization. The race is on to grow leaders, team members, and colleagues fast. You must develop a leader-leader structure and a leadership culture before your competitors do!

The Four Types of Leaders

In an organization with a leadership culture, each individual falls into one of four leadership groups, which together create an over-arching leader-leader framework (Figure 3.1):

- Leader of Organization: leads a whole business or function end to end
- Leader of Leaders: leads managers
- Leader of People: leads a team or is a key influencer in leading a business area
- Leader of Self: an individual with no direct reports, who takes responsibility for their own actions and performance and for

Figure 3.1

holding fellow colleagues to account for performance through positive peer pressure.

Implementing a leader-leader structure and developing a leadership culture does not happen overnight. It takes focus and commitment, and requires consistency of thought and action.

Which are you building in your organization? Do you have a leader-follower structure based on short-term results or a leader-leader culture for a high performing, sustained, legacy organization?

Turning Your Organizational Design Upside Down

Here's a disruptive idea for how you can fast track your journey toward a leader-leader culture in your business.

One of my clients is a major global food distribution and manufacturing business. I was running a year-long leadership transformation programme for the executive leadership team and one of the discussions we got into was about leadership capability and how to create the stretch within the organization.

A challenge that one of the leaders posed, was that all the decision-making was still rising to the top and that people further down the organization were still abdicating responsibility and not making decisions. My suggestion to them was one I think all organizations could apply: turn the problem on its head and simply think about it in a different way.

What do I mean by that?

When you think about it, most organizations create organizational charts that position the CEO at the top, the senior executives next and the whole structure filters down to the employees at the bottom of the chart who are often the people on the front line, interfacing with customers every day.

My belief is that businesses should invert their organizational charts or structures, with the CEO at the base, the senior executives above him or her, and the customer-facing people right at the top. Then allow all decision-making to rise to the top. Yes, let me just repeat that part again as it is so important: turn your organizational structure upside down and let all decision-making rise to the top.

That's disruptive thinking, and it represents a step change in how people think culturally when they are encouraged to make decisions, and both empowered and enabled to follow through on that new way of thinking. The senior leaders in that scenario become the foundation and the platform to support the business and the people who do the important customer-facing work. To me, that ultimately defines a leadership culture.

So, now we've covered some key ideas on building and developing your leadership culture our focus shifts to understanding the essential leadership traits of high performing inspirational leaders.

Developing Your Leadership Traits and Style

Having worked with thousands of business leaders, business owners, and entrepreneurs, there is a pattern of thinking, feeling, and acting which put them in a unique category that enables them to write the rules of the game. Of course these are by no means a definitive list, rather seven core principles from which you can build and shape your own leadership style. Are these an integral part of *your* DNA?

1. Think BIG
2. Focus on one thing!
3. Winning mentality
4. Attitude of ACTION
5. Resilience
6. Authenticity
7. A never-ending pursuit of personal mastery

1. Think BIG

If you don't start out by dreaming BIG, you're never going to move beyond mediocrity. Inspirational leaders set the bar high. They think BIG thoughts, and dream BIG dreams. They live their lives as if all their dreams had already come true and challenge reality to catch up. They don't think *of* their goals, they think *from* their goals. What's the difference, you might be thinking? In his book, *Golf my Way*, Jack Nicklaus revealed how he used this technique to become one of the greatest golfers of all time. Before each shot, he created a mental movie of the entire golf shot in his head.

> 'I never hit a shot, even in practice, without having a very sharp, in focus picture of it in my head. It's like a colour movie. First I "see" the ball where I want it to finish, nice and white and sitting up high on the bright green grass. Then the scene quickly changes and I "see" the ball going there; its path, trajectory, and shape; even its behaviour on landing. Then there's sort of a fade out, and the next scene shows me making the kind of swing that will turn the previous images into reality.'

That's the difference between thinking *from* your goals as opposed to thinking *of* your goals.

American gymnast Mary Lou Retton did the same thing, which enabled her to push past the intense pressure on her during the 1984 Los Angeles Olympics. For her, the stakes couldn't have been higher; she had to score a perfect 10, the ultimate mark of flawless execution, or forsake her dreams of a gold medal and entry into the highest of all echelons of gymnastic achievement.

The world held its breath as she took to the mat. You could have heard a pin drop when she closed her eyes before starting. A matter of seconds later, she came off the vault having defined perfection for an entire generation, earning the highest possible score. When asked by reporters afterward what she was thinking when she closed her eyes, she told them she saw herself doing every motion precisely, flawlessly, and achieving a perfect score.

This is a common theme among inspirational leaders. They set goals that are, to others, unattainably high, and then they work out how to reach them. They know something that others do not; that, as the famed Renaissance artist Michelangelo put it: 'the greater danger for most of us is not that our aim is too high and we miss it, but that it is too low and we hit it.'

2. Focus on one thing!

There is a wise Russian proverb that goes: 'If you chase two rabbits, you end up catching neither.' Are you suffering from Rabbit-ism?

Inspirational leaders are able to galvanize their forces around one thing that makes the organization they run most successful. They're able to present that one thing as the North Star; the thing that makes their organization stand out above all others. In so doing, they are able to head off at the pass the constant threat of direction changes that prevents many organizations from really achieving the highest levels of GREATNESS.

There are many compelling examples of the one thing in action:

- Colonel Sanders started Kentucky Fried Chicken, now KFC, with a single secret chicken recipe of eleven herbs and spices
- The small time burger outlet that Ray Kroc acquired in 1954 became the most successful, replicable formula the fast food restaurant world has ever known, namely McDonald's
- Beer maker, The Adolph Coors Company grew 1,500% from 1947 to 1967 with only one product, made in a single brewery

- Chipmaker Intel has for four decades seen the overwhelming majority of its revenue derived from microprocessors
- Starbucks was built 'one cup of coffee at a time'!

The list of businesses that have achieved extraordinary results through the power of one thing is endless. Those organizations of course had many products and services, but the inspirational leaders that ran them never allowed their employees to forget the one thing that they ultimately had to be constantly great at.

Google's one thing is search, which makes its source of revenue, advertising sales, possible. It does other things too, but through the development of those sidelines Google's leaders have never lost sight of its one thing, and neither have its people.

What's your one thing? Your one key product or service? What will it be tomorrow?

Self-help gurus will tell you endlessly that focus is the key to success; that we have altogether too much on our plates at any one time to be assured of success when we attempt it too broadly. That has probably always been true; those who have advocated focus in the past decade have certainly drowned out the proponents of multi-tasking. But focus doesn't alter the importance of embracing change in order to remain relevant into the future. While Ray Kroc's one thing – the replicable model for a franchise which has enabled McDonald's to open over 35,000 fundamentally identical restaurants in nearly 120 countries around the world in the past 60 years – has entirely retained its focus, it has shifted its thinking in recent years to a menu that suits modern demands. That's a big change for McDonald's, but it doesn't represent even the slightest shift in focus from its one thing.

Apple is another great case study in the application of focus even through profound change. Apple's one thing is simplicity and usability, and it has informed the development of every single product, providing answers that consistently earn a standing ovation from Apple fans, to the question 'What is Apple going to do next?' Apple is powered from one era to the next by the iPod, iTunes, the iPhone, the iPad, and now the iWatch, each of which has at its very soul the one thing that defines Apple.

Apple products are designed to perfectly integrate with one another so there are compelling reasons to buy more than one product. With the overlay of iCloud software that automatically synchronizes all devices when it is enabled, Apple has built what it aptly calls an ecosystem that locks users in by making it preferable to have more than one of their products. As each new 'golden gadget' enters the limelight, the products that preceded it find themselves refined and improved in order to maintain brisk sales as natural extensions of all the other products, living out a phenomenon called the halo effect. A clever strategy.

If you and your business don't know what your one thing is, make it your one thing to find out.

3. Winning mentality

The past century has seen endless books written on the subject of the winning mentality; the mindset that enables winners to be absolutely certain they are going to achieve their goals. To many it seems like an elusive concept; as if it's too whimsical to possibly be that simple, yet again and again, we hear from inspirational leaders that their mindset is the most potent delivery system in their arsenal.

It starts with a positive attitude, and the good news is that this is entirely achievable through determination. Inspirational leaders know that the world is full of negativity, which presents a full frontal challenge to anyone trying to be positive, and the one unassailable key to success lies in their ability to shut those messages out.

In thinking about developing your winning mentality the starting point is about being clear on your own definition of a positive attitude. How would you define it? My own personal definition is this: *the way you dedicate yourself to the way you think.* And the key within this definition is that it is a conscious choice.

I would even go as far as to say that the quality of your life is in direct proportion to the quality of choices you choose to make.

Thinking positively is a conscious choice.

Acting positively is a conscious choice.

Reacting positively is a conscious choice.

We've all spent time in the company of negative people who seem to suck the energy and life out of you. After leaving them you almost feel like sticking your finger into the plug socket to recharge. I call these people 'Life's EVs': emotional vacuums. The challenge is that negative people are worse than negative experiences. Why? Because the experience can be over in 10 minutes, whereas the person may hang around for years!

There is a really important life lesson here and it is simply this: who you spend time with is who you become. Spending time and surrounding yourself with inspirational leaders and inspired people and their attitude, their mentality, and their mindset will rub off on you. It's the easiest and best choice you'll ever make.

Inspirational leaders know this.

One story that floors me every time is that of two times Formula One World Champion Lewis Hamilton, who won his first ever Grand Prix in his rookie season back in 2007. That first victory was in the Canadian Grand Prix, and the newspaper headline the next day read: Canada High Lewis: I knew I'd win.

That's quite a statement, but read the story that supported that headline and there was a fascinating insight: Hamilton said: 'I always knew I was going to win; it was just a question of when and where.' Think about that for a moment. If you have wired yourself with that level of certainty and belief, not just in terms of mindset, but also in terms of your whole being, your whole physiology right to your core, what's going to happen? You're going to win!

Hamilton's story also has another fascinating twist to it. When he won that first race, he was driving for the McLaren Formula One team. Years before he was a kart racer and after one particular event he attended an evening dinner and the guest speaker was Ron Dennis, the team principal of McLaren Formula One. After dinner, Hamilton went up to Dennis and introduced himself, saying that he had really enjoyed the presentation and that he just wanted to put Dennis on notice that at some point in the future, he was going to win a Formula One Grand Prix driving for McLaren.

He was 10 years of age. Now what made Lewis Hamilton special? Was it because he had encouraging parents? Yes, certainly he did.

Was it because he had driving skills etched in his DNA? Perhaps. But what really made him special was the way he dedicated himself to the way he thought, the way he programmed his winning mentality, even from the age of 10.

Once again, we come to the concept of not thinking *of* your goals, but *from* your goals. Even before he won that first race, Hamilton had already been on that podium; had already looked out over the crowd and heard the voices chanting his name. All he had been doing since the age of 10 was living out the script of the movie he had already created.

What's the script for your movie, for your life and your business, and what are you doing to turn that script into reality right now?

4. Attitude of ACTION

Another trait of inspirational leaders is the ability to translate positive intentions into tangible results. If you've had any sort of scepticism about positivity, if you believe that it demands a suspension of disbelief, then you'll struggle to really embrace it. Positivity isn't about dreaming and then hoping for an outcome; it's about dreaming and then working out a plan and then *working that plan* to get to the dream. It's an Attitude of ACTION.

We've all heard the expression 'knowledge is power', but for me, that idea is incomplete. '*Applied*' knowledge is power! I'm fortunate in my life to have met some really knowledgeable people, but I can tell you that often, their knowledge hasn't always correlated to a high level of success. Why? Because it's all about the *application* of the knowledge. These individuals talk a good game; they constantly talk about what they're going to do, and on paper they should be achieving even greater levels of success. The challenge is they're missing the critical part – 'applied knowledge' and taking MASSIVE ACTION!

Inspirational leaders are people of action. They constantly push themselves to find better and faster ways to merge the present with the future, and realize their goals. They understand the 'Law of Diminishing Intent' and make sure it doesn't happen to them. What is this law? It's simply that the longer you wait to implement a new idea or strategy, the less enthusiasm you will have for it.

You and I have probably both had that feeling of rushing out of a motivational seminar, full of great ideas that will change key aspects of our lives . . . and then doing nothing with it. Why? Well, the demands of the day compete for our attention, and all of our good intentions and personal promises for change get pushed to one side. The longer we put them off, the lower the probability that we will ever actually fulfil them. That's how great ideas earn an untimely death, and you may find yourself one day in the frustrating position of discovering that your great idea has been done by someone else who is living the dream you should have led.

An Attitude of ACTION is about acting daily on your strategy and ideas before life snuffs them out, taking your future goals and vision with them. As the German philosopher Johann von Goethe said many years ago: 'Whatever you can dream, you can do, begin it. Boldness has genius, power and magic.'

Ninety percent of success lies in implementation and execution. Do you have the Attitude of ACTION?

5. Resilience

Resilience is an essential trait, especially in the face of failure, but also in terms of daily life as a business leader, business owner, or entrepreneur. Even armed with your Attitude of ACTION and a reputation for making things happen, things will sometimes go wrong. That's life.

For example, Lewis Hamilton, with all his certainty and vision and talent and experience, sometimes makes an error that he kicks himself for. Sometimes he doesn't get the result he wants and it may have nothing to do with him at all, for example succumbing to the chance error of another driver while driving an otherwise perfect race.

You will make mistakes, you will come off the rails, and if you don't, it begs the question of whether you're really pushing the boundaries of possibility. Inspirational leaders aren't immune from mistakes or runs of bad luck; what they have learned to do however is recover from them quickly. They pick themselves up, bounce back, and refuse to carry any additional and unnecessary baggage from the experience.

Ask any of the 'greatest failures' in the world.

Arguably the greatest American basketball star in the history of the game, Michael Jordan went home, locked himself in his room, and cried after being cut from his high school team. In his later career, he missed as many shots as he made, but he consistently recovered and made another attempt; enough attempts, as it happens, to make him a legend of the sport.

At the beginning of their career, The Beatles, still one of the most successful musical acts of all time and absolutely the kings of popular music when they were around, were rejected by Decca Records, which declared: 'We don't like their sound. They have no future in show business.' In fact, they had the greatest future in musical history.

When Apple founder Steve Jobs was just 30 years old, he was left devastated and depressed after being unceremoniously forced out of the company he started. When he picked himself up, he started NeXT, bought Toy Story maker Pixar Studios, and continued as he had intended, changing the world. When Apple invited him back, it was a company on its knees.

Walt Disney, of all people, was fired from a newspaper at which he worked, for 'lacking imagination' and 'having no original ideas'. His ideas have remained among the most iconic in the world for the best part of a century.

And what would you say of an American man who was defeated in his bid for election to his state legislature, then went bankrupt in business, then was defeated in his run for election to be the speaker of the same state legislature, was defeated in his run for the United States Congress, then was elected, but lost his re-election, was defeated in his run for the United States Senate, then defeated in his bid to become Vice President and again defeated in his second run for the Senate? Time to give up? *Wouldn't you?* That run of failures beset the same man between 1832 and 1858, but the fact that he got up and tried again . . . and again . . . makes a clear statement about his resilience. In hindsight, it's not surprising. The man was Abraham Lincoln, a president that many Americans herald as one of the most significant of them all.

One of my personal favourite stories is that of Sylvester Gardenzio Stallone, the man who gave us Rocky, Rambo, and a number of the most celebrated movie characters of all time. Stallone not only played the eponymous character in each of those movies, he also wrote every script and directed some of them.

Today he is Hollywood royalty; a man whose name opens doors and who commands respect. But life wasn't always so kind to him. His slurry speech and droopy visage are the result of a forceps accident at birth, and though they've become trademarks for him, they were extremely challenging obstacles for a younger Stallone. His parents fought, he spent part of his childhood in foster care, and was expelled repeatedly from schools as a result of what was deemed a difficult attitude.

In later years, having turned his hand to acting, he found himself constantly rejected causing him (thankfully, as fate would have it), to turn his hand to writing scripts. Not that it helped him at the time. His scripts initially received no greater enthusiasm than his acting attempts and he and his family lived in poverty, struggling even to find enough to eat.

Then one day in 1975, Stallone saw a boxing match on TV between Chuck Wepner and the great Muhammed Ali, in which Wepner took a major battering but kept coming back for more. It was just the underdog story Stallone was looking for, and he began to dream up his signature character: Rocky Balboa.

Twenty-four hours of focused writing gave him the script that is so beloved today . . . but once again, absolutely nobody wanted it. By this time, he was so poor he had to sell his best friend . . . he stood outside a liquor store with his beloved dog and offered it for sale for $50, giving him some very temporary relief.

And then it happened! Or almost, anyway.

The poor, hungry, desperate Stallone was offered a massive (for its time) $100,000 for the script, potentially solving all his problems in one fell swoop. He insisted that he wanted to play the role however, and when they declined, this man, with his back against the wall, turned it down. Yes, you read that right.

A few weeks later, they came back with a higher offer. He insisted once again that he act out the role and once again, the offer was rescinded. The offer came back again and again, and eventually topped $400,000, but Stallone refused to sell it unless he could also play the part of Rocky. Eventually, the investors relented but with one very stiff caveat: they would offer only $25,000 if Stallone played the lead role because they didn't want to take the risk. He accepted and went straight back to the liquor store to re-acquire his dog.

I know, you're thinking that this can't be real, but I assure you it is. Wait for it though, it's going to get even crazier. Stallone waited outside that liquor store for three days before he saw the guy who bought his dog. He offered him $150 for it. The guy declined. He offered more and more and more, and eventually he offered the guy $15,000 and a role in the movie. The guy and the dog are in Rocky. The following year, 1977, Rocky won the Academy Award for best picture and at the awards ceremony, Stallone read out all the rejection slips he had received. The film cost $1,000,000 to produce. It grossed $225,000,000 at the worldwide box office.

Stallone's story is one of outrageous levels of commitment to his dream, vision, and goals. Are you that committed? Do you have what it takes to turn your vision, goals, and dreams into reality? I said at the beginning that I love this story, but actually, its just one of literally thousands that I could have picked. Why not make yours one of them in the future?

Too many people live in what I call 'the safe harbour of the known', doing the same things over and over again, and following the same routine and thought processes, thinking that just because it worked in the past, they can keep replicating it into the future.

Some things will. The challenge is that some things won't. Einstein defined insanity as continuing to do the same things and expecting different results. Real joy comes when you put some 'skin in the game' and take some chances. It opens you up to failure, and will test your resilience like nothing in the world, but without it, can you really hope to be a high achiever? What do you think?

6. Authenticity

This trait is one of the most important for me as it is the 'glue' that binds all the other traits together. Or you could think of it as the hub.

Authenticity is about being the real deal. It's about being really clear on what you stand for, the values that drive your thinking, and the filters through which you define your behaviour. It's about having an unwavering determination that no matter what happens you will never compromise your core values and beliefs; that you will remain true to who you are and what you stand for.

I could talk for an age on this trait, but instead I'd like to present you with a poem that I frequently share at my keynote and workshop engagements. It's one of my favourite poems. It's by Peter 'Dale' Wimbrow Sr and first appeared in print in 1934, and it is just as true today:

> 'When you get what you want in your struggle for life
> And the world makes you king for a day,
> Just go to the mirror and look at yourself
> And see what that man has to say
> For it isn't your father or mother or wife
> Whose judgment upon you must pass
> The fellow whose verdict counts most in your life
> Is the one staring back from the glass
> You may be like Jack Horner and pull out a plum
> And think you're a wonderful guy
> But the man in the glass says you're only a bum
> If you can't look him straight in the eye
> He's the fellow to please – never mind all the rest
> For he's with you clear to the end
> And you've passed your most dangerous difficult test
> If the man in the glass is your friend
> You may fool the whole world down the pathway of years
> And get pats on the back as you pass
> But your final reward will be heartache and tears
> If you've cheated the man in the glass.'

I suggest you read the poem a few times and then take a few quiet moments to think about how the message applies to you and your life! Are you the real deal? Is authenticity the bedrock of your being? It is for inspirational leaders. They know that energy spent being something they're not is energy they could better apply to building success on success.

What does your mirror tell you?

7. Finally: A never-ending pursuit of personal mastery

Since part of the goal of *Built to Grow* is that you strive for personal mastery in building your high performing, sustainable legacy organization, I thought it made sense to cover this particular leadership trait at the end of the book. Why? Well because this book details precisely the ideas each of us should strive to become masterful at. Therefore, a summary at the end of the book is an essential checklist to ensure you are on the road to building the organization you have always dreamed of.

I'm really looking forward to sharing this big idea with you once we've explored all aspects of *Built to Grow*, and worked through the entire Business Growth Transformation Framework® and seen how to bring it to life for your business.

Summary

Leadership is practised not so much in words as in attitude and actions. Are you an inspirational leader? Is your leadership culture the heartbeat of your high performing business?

Chapter 4

Building a High Performing Organization

'It is an immutable law in business that words are words, explanations are explanations, promises are promises – but only performance is reality.'

—HAROLD S. GENEEN

It's a certainty that you know a high performing organization when you see one. There are clues all around.

New Zealand All Blacks Rugby Team have won 86% of their games in recent years. Manchester United Football Club in its heyday constantly vexed its opponents by winning games often with a goal scored in extra time. Barcelona Football Club has dominated the game in football-mad Spain, and is considered by many experts to be the greatest football team in the world.

What about Leicester City Football Club, which won the English Premier League in the 2015/2016 season a year after it was facing relegation, creating a legacy widely regarded as one of the greatest sporting achievements of all time?

In business, Disney built a reputation as leader in customer experience, which has remained unchallenged for more than 60 years. LEGO® is the second biggest toymaker in the world, with a respected and loved global brand that has remained popular for nearly 70 years. The department store Harrods has held a reputation, not only

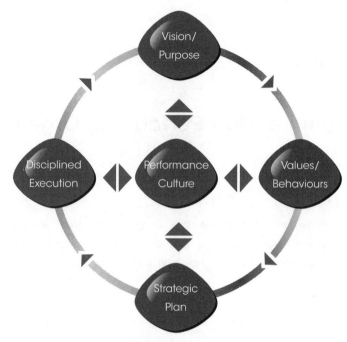

Figure 4.1

as one of the most exclusive shopping destinations in the world but as a London landmark, for more than 180 years.

In this chapter I'm going to share core ideas which these teams and organizations used to ensure their position in history as exemplars of best practice and sustained high performance. As I share with you the five elements of the High Performing Organization Model (Figure 4.1), I'll pose questions to enable you to personalize and apply the ideas to your business.

Vision/Purpose

> *A compelling Vision/Purpose is like infusing work with purpose and meaning!*

If you imagine the High Performing Organization Model as a clock-face, at 12h00 is Vision/Purpose, the starting point of your thinking when building a high performing organization. A compelling Vision/ Purpose describes your unwavering goal for your business and why it exists in the first place:

- Giving employees, partners, suppliers, and customers an emotional and intellectual connection with the business beyond its operational characteristics
- Acting as an important reference point to check every decision you make, before you make it.

In a very real sense, your compelling Vision/Purpose is your North Star; in good times it can focus the business, reinforcing the goal and ambition; in tough times, it offers an inspirational focal point to keep pushing on, in the knowledge that you're pursuing a goal worth achieving.

The ability to focus is critical for success. It's too easy to be distracted by the next opportunity, the next million-pound idea. Most people are better at dreaming up new ideas than making them a reality, and if you're not focused, there is an inherent risk of being known as a great thinker, or even visionary, who never made anything happen.

As the saying goes: Where focus goes energy flows.

Without focus, you're like Alice asking advice of the Cheshire Cat in Lewis Carroll's *Alice's Adventures in Wonderland:*

> 'Would you tell me, please, which way I ought to go from here?' asked Alice.
>
> 'That depends a good deal on where you want to get to,' said the Cat.
>
> 'I don't much care where,' said Alice.
>
> 'Then it doesn't matter which way you go,' said the Cat.
>
> '– so long as I get SOMEWHERE,' Alice added as an explanation.
>
> 'Oh, you're sure to do that,' said the Cat, 'if you only walk long enough.'

In simple terms, too many businesses set off on a journey into the future without first painting a clear picture of where it is they want to get to. They end up taking a route rather like the squiggly line in Figure 4.2.

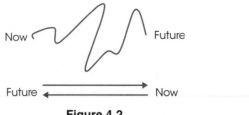

Figure 4.2

However, visionary leaders have the ability to transport themselves into the future in their mind, create clarity on what it looks like, feels like, and acts like, and then, coming back to today, translate their vision into a meaningful story for their people. And in the process, they define a fast track pathway in order to get there.

Their pathway is defined like the second image in Figure 4.2. A set of railway tracks, knowing that if they do veer off course, with a clear destination point they can quickly take corrective action. A compelling Vision/Purpose allows them to deliver accelerated, sustained, and profitable business growth.

The Chief Storyteller

A critical part of your role as a business leader, business owner, or entrepreneur is the Chief Storyteller. Among your responsibilities is to connect your people with your story, your vision and purpose for your business. In doing so, you create meaning to what they do and how they do it, so they can find their own compelling reason to feel inspired, energized, and motivated to deliver their best work.

In the early 1960s, during a visit to NASA by President John F. Kennedy, an interaction between the President and a janitor took place that really illustrates the power of this. As Kennedy was led on a tour of Cape Canaveral, he greeted each person he passed and asked them what they did.

The first one, a man in overalls responded without enthusiasm, 'I'm earning a living, Mr President.' A second one had a similar response: 'I clear away the garbage, Mr President.' However, a third man in overalls put a big smile on his face and replied: 'Mr President, I'm helping to put a man on the moon.'

That man understood the Vision/Purpose of NASA and recognized that everyone, at every level, had a part to play. He could see that keeping the floors clean was an important part of the overall operation; that without his services, other aspects of the programme would suffer. He could see beyond his daily wage, beyond his position. He could see that every role in NASA's quest for the moon was important and he was proud to be part of it.

What's your story? Is it compelling?

Creating the Vision/Purpose for *your* organization?

If you asked a cross-section of your team to describe the Vision/ Purpose of your organization, would they be able to articulate it? What if you asked them the part they played in turning that Vision/Purpose into reality? What would their answer be?

A compelling Vision/Purpose must accomplish three things:

- Specify **Aspiration**: a long-term achievement that the organization is striving for
- Offer **Inspiration**: captivating the organization onward and upward
- Invite **Perspiration**: showing colleagues how their contribution turns the Vision/Purpose into reality.

Some of the most iconic, most successful organizations are built on a strong, compelling Vision/Purpose:

- Nike: 'To bring inspiration and innovation to every athlete* in the world'
  *If you have a body, you are an athlete.
- Google: 'Changing the way the world communicates one click at a time!'
- DHL: 'The logistics company for the world'
- United Nations: 'Meeting the needs of the present without compromising the ability of future generations to meet their own needs'
- New Zealand All Blacks: 'Inspiring and Unifying New Zealanders'
- LEGO®: 'Inventing the future of play'.

What do all the above Vision/Purpose statements have in common?

1. They belong to phenomenally successful organizations which have stood the test of time and delivered both accelerated, sustained and profitable business growth.
2. They all started as an idea. No matter how big or small your business is today, it has the potential to achieve enduring greatness.
3. They pass the test of specifying aspiration, offering inspiration, and inviting perspiration.
4. They are short, use dynamic, active language, and are memorable.

Once created, your role as the Chief Storyteller is to safeguard your Vision/Purpose. Protect it from becoming passive; promote it so that it becomes active and truly living in your organization, through your people. I call this your Vision/Purpose in ACTION.

Your Vision/Purpose in ACTION

The Vision/Purpose is usually displayed in foyers behind reception and provides the first impression of what you stand for. Leaders can walk around the office and ask any colleague what part they have played today in turning the Vision/Purpose into reality and receive an instant compelling answer.

It's the signature template on your emails. It's the home page of your website, your shop window to the world. It's referenced at the start of every internal meeting as part of the rules of engagement. It's central to every performance conversation with colleagues and employees.

It's positively reinforced through the empirical validation of what you do every day to bring your Vision/Purpose to life. What do I mean by that?

Countrywide Group is the largest estate agency and lettings business in the UK. It has more than 12,000 people across the group and 50+ brands on the high street.

On the website it talks about the various businesses which sit within the group, their market position and credentials which are all impressive. However, it's the key facts that really jump off the page and bring to life their Vision/Purpose:

- We agree a sale every 1.6 minutes
- We let a property every 4 minutes
- We sold £18.6 billion worth of property in 2014
- We completed £10.3 billion of mortgages in 2014 which would make us the 7th largest mortgage lender in the UK and the 2nd largest building society
- We complete 150 surveys or valuations every hour.

As you were reading those numbers, what words, phrases and thoughts sprung into your conscious mind? 'Impressive stats'? 'They must be good at what they do'? 'Credibility'? 'Trust'?

Just imagine how proud you would be working at Countrywide, knowing the part you play every day in fulfilling the dreams of new house purchasers across the country.

You see where I am heading with this. It's no good just creating a compelling Vision/Purpose and thinking 'job done, what's next?' In your pursuit of excellence and your vision of building a high performing, sustained, legacy organization, you must be tireless about positive reinforcement, articulation, and alignment of everything the organization does every day. Your compelling Vision/Purpose is everything!

The challenge for most organizations is that they are not using the empirical numbers they have in their armoury in this way to bring to life and positively reinforce what they do and how they do it: their Vision/Purpose in ACTION.

Values/Behaviours

> 'If Vision/Purpose determines where you're going, your Values/Behaviours determine precisely how you're going to get there!'

A common set of Values and defined Behaviours create clarity on what excellence looks like, feels like, and acts like.

This is important from a team perspective and critical to commercial success. Customers today will look beyond your ability to deliver the product or service you provide, because that's a given. In choosing their partner of choice, they want to know the Values that underpin the organization. Can you be trusted? Are the words, credentials, and story you share up-front backed up by substance and depth in how the organization actually acts?

Do you have a clear set of Values for your business? Are they underpinned by a defined set of Behaviours, which propel you towards your goal of excellence in everything you do?

What is a Value?

The dictionary definition of Values is: the moral principles or accepted standards of a person or a group.

Why is this important? Because people never consistently do who they aren't. That's a clumsy play on words, but it's deliberate. Let me explain . . .

If you ask your people to take action that is not aligned with their Values and beliefs, they might perform in the short term, but never over the long term, as it creates conflict and tension with their personal Values. Ultimately they'll leave the organization. On the other hand, if you ask your people to take actions aligned with their Values and beliefs, they will do it every single day of the week. Why? Because people will consistently do who they are.

Misalignment of personal and organizational Values is actually cited as one of the top three reasons people leave an organization. Leaders misunderstand how Values inflexibly influence behaviour. I've met with many leaders, who are frustrated because objectives are not being met, and I've been engaged to help implement an employee behaviour change programme.

My starting point is always to positively challenge their thinking because they're attempting to get the wrong result. Behaviours aren't whims; they are driven by our core Values. It's no good even trying behaviour change unless we understand each employee's individual Values and how they align with those of the organization.

This principle is why there is a growing trend of Values-based recruitment, to ensure there is alignment and cultural fit between the two parties from day 1.

Can you change someone's Values and beliefs?

If you cannot change behaviour without understanding Values and beliefs, the question you might ask is: can you change the Values and beliefs themselves? It's a broad question and in answering, it's important to recognize that they're actually two different things. Values are deep rooted, often based on religion, traditions, learnt from our parents, and are not necessarily the result of conscious decision. Over time, you may be able to change them, or at least influence them, but it's difficult. It's much easier to find people whose Values align with yours in the first place.

Beliefs on the other hand can be easily changed when they are challenged by factually based information that contradicts them. Beliefs lead us to act in very deliberate ways. Unless your people can make a connection between their actions and their Values and beliefs, they may be incapable of delivering a sustained result.

Let me give you a couple of examples to bring this point to life;

The store card

One of my clients was the Head of Sales for a large retail company. His top salesperson outsold all the other salespeople in his area by a mile. But when the department store chain decided to introduce a store credit card and the sales team were targeted with signing customers up something interesting began to happen. The top salesperson didn't sell a single one. After six months, the manager sat him down and said: 'Look these are part of your objectives. What's going on?'

Being a smart manager, he didn't just insist that the salesperson get on with it; he went looking for an underlying problem. He discovered the top salesperson had been raised by his parents on a core belief to never have debt. Therefore, selling credit cards was completely at odds with his core Values and beliefs.

Now the manager had a choice; micro manage his 'poor performance' in which case he would leave, or alternatively make an intelligent exception to the rule for a high performer who in every other aspect was a model exemplar of behavioural excellence. I'm pleased to say on this occasion he chose the latter option.

A passion for serving customers

Another story that demonstrates the effect of Behaviours is an experiment I carried out with a South African bank, a few years back.

Let me give you some background context. This bank, one of South Africa's big four, had been created through the merger of four smaller banks and building societies, all of which had been built on a culture of customer service, as opposed to sales. A few years later, it benchmarked itself against its two biggest competitors in the key area of customer product holding and realized it was falling behind. Where its customers typically had just 1.3 of its products, customers of its two biggest competitors typically held 2.8 products and 3.4 products respectively (i.e. they had a cheque account, a credit card, and a car loan or home loan).

Recognizing a missed opportunity, it asked its branches to cross-sell products to existing customers, but without success. The branches just didn't react in the way expected. So the bank launched a lengthy behaviour change project. Again, no luck. When I was called in, it was obvious something fundamental was wrong.

I invited a dozen branch managers to lunch, took them to McDonald's where I sat them down in a booth and said 'lunch is on me today'. I bought 12 basic hamburgers and handed one to each manager. It didn't take long for the questions to start flying.

Where are the chips and the Coke?

Who said I wanted a hamburger? I don't eat them.

I am vegetarian. I can't eat this.

If I'd been given the option, I'd have gone supersize.

And so on.

So I said okay, tell me what you really want, and wrote down their specific orders. There were chicken sandwiches and fish burgers, Big Macs and chips, Cokes and milkshakes; the complete spectrum of the McDonald's menu; all orders individual and personalized.

Back at the office, I listed all the experiences they had encountered when I had been assumptive, for example, giving them a burger when they wanted a chicken sandwich. Then I compared it to the experiences they offer their customers. I asked how many opportunities their customers were missing because they assumed customers only wanted the basic product rather than the choice to go large, or to individualize their choice. The penny dropped. Once they recognized how their Behaviours were getting in their own way, within three months, their product holding with customers had doubled.

Their behaviour changed when I demonstrated sales and service were not mutually exclusive. The moment I challenged one of their deepest, core beliefs and the fundamental reason why they came to work every day – to serve customers – it was like lighting the touch paper.

The bank had focused too heavily on cross-selling and sales rather than providing customers with a better experience. By reshaping their focus on the latter, the bank aligned its goals to the personal Values and beliefs of its people resulting in a great experience for their customers.

Aligning your people's personal Values and beliefs with those of the organization is critical to unlocking their latent potential. The flip of the expression: 'people never consistently do who they aren't' is 'people will consistently do who they are!'

Considerations when creating your Values

How many Values should your organization have? There isn't an empirical number, but generally today there is a shift in thinking to less is more. Your Values should be the guiding principles that absolutely define you. Most business owners, business leaders, and entrepreneurs set Values without thinking enough about their real passion and deep-seated beliefs.

Too often, they list Values that should actually be a given. For example, in 2015, the Harvard Business Review said that 55% of companies in the Fortune 100 list 'Integrity' as a Value and described it as a 'permission to play' Value that any business should have, by default.

One company that really stands out for me as an exemplar of best practice in this area is Santander, a global financial services business. Its Values are: Simple, Personal, and Fair. Those are three words that really roll off the tongue and are memorable. Santander has used the meaning, catchiness, and simplicity of its Values to connect with customers as well as internal colleagues with phenomenal results.

Most organizations generally major on Values for internal use, though admittedly there is a shift in this thinking. Santander, after 18 months of embedding Values and creating alignment in the hearts and minds of its people, began to use them in its customer marketing. That really puts them to the test; nothing will make your people live up to the promise quite like the Values being played back to you by customers as the expected standards.

Values in ACTION

Just like with your Vision/Purpose, Values are not designed to be passive and should be clearly displayed. Values are also fundamental in your performance review process as a key tool for empirical validation and measurement of behavioural performance.

Particularly when they are underpinned by winning and derailing behaviours; winning behaviours focus on excellence in action and are the model standard of best practice, and derailing behaviours raise conscious awareness of the behaviours that will not be accepted.

Individuals are able to take ownership of living those behaviours and hold others accountable for doing the same. Peer pressure can be a powerful force that supports the efforts led by leaders and managers to embed the Values.

Strategic Plan

'Failing to plan is like planning to fail!'

I introduced the three Zones and nine interlocking strategies that make up your Strategic Plan in Chapter 2. Each interlocking strategy has a dedicated chapter in *Built to Grow*, so I won't repeat here. What I am going to share is a fascinating story about how a strong Strategic Plan can make all the difference between an awesome victory and a tragic loss.

Amundsen vs. Scott

It can be seen clearly in the stark differences between the successful expedition led by Norwegian explorer Roald Amundsen, and the failed one led by Robert Falcon Scott as they raced to be the first to the South Pole in 1911.

On paper, it was a perfectly matched competition: Amundsen and Scott were of similar ages and each could boast plenty of experience in daring polar exploration. They set off within days of each other and it was reasonable to assume they might arrive simultaneously; such was their mutual reputation. But that's not what happened at all.

Before I continue, let's consider some of the hardships they would face: gale force winds, temperatures of -20F, even during the warmest months, and a round-trip journey of more than 1,400 miles. That would be a serious challenge today, even with all our modern equipment and expertise; it's hard to comprehend how much harder it was in 1911.

Amundsen had been preparing for years however. He adopted an intensive and long-term fitness regime. When he travelled more than 2,000 miles from Norway to Spain to earn a master's certificate in sailing, he didn't go by ship or train, but by bicycle. He planned for scenarios he might only face once in a lifetime, such as testing the usefulness of raw dolphin as a source of nutrition. He studied the Inuit people in the north of Canada and discovered how it was better to move slowly in frozen conditions so sweat couldn't form and turn to ice. He was 39 when he set off on his journey to the South Pole, but he had already been on a journey to personal mastery from a tender age.

Scott's preparation paled in comparison.

Among the significant differences between their Strategic Plans:

- Amundsen learned that dogs thrive in Antarctic conditions and spent time with the Inuit people in the north of Canada to learn

dogsledding. Scott selected a mixture of ponies, which are completely unsuited to Antarctic conditions and motor sledges, which
were brand new, untested, and quickly failed. The result: while
the Amundsen party ran their teams of dogs all the way to the
pole and back, the men on Scott's team had to pull their sleds
themselves, moving far more slowly and exhausting themselves
along the way.

- Amundsen laid down supply caches along the route, and marked
  them with black flags so they would be visible for miles on their
  way back. Scott did not.
- Amundsen stored three tons of supplies for five men starting out.
  Scott stored one ton for 17 men.
- Amundsen carried enough extra supplies that he would be able to
  miss every one of his stock supplies and still complete the journey.
  If Scott missed even one of his stock supplies it would be the end
  for him and his team.
- Amundsen brought four thermometers. Scott brought one, which
  broke.

While both men knew there was no way to remove all of the risk,
Amundsen prepared for the very worst weather, unexpected geo-
graphical challenges and other hurdles, where Scott appears to
have operated on hope that everything would work out all right. In his
journal, discovered with his frozen body years later, Scott complained
about his bad luck.

On 15 December 1911, Amundsen and his team planted the Norwegian flag in the South Pole. It would probably have stunned him
to know that the Scott expedition was still 360 miles from the pole,
man-hauling their sleds and would take another 34 days to get there.
By the time they did, the Amundsen team was just eight days from
their home base. They reached it precisely on the day they planned.

Amundsen was already sailing back to Norway when Scott's team
finally gave up hope, exhausted, depressed, frostbitten, and near starvation. Their frozen bodies were discovered in a tent, eight months later.

It's a tragic tale for those brave men, but it's also a cautionary tale.
If Amundsen had reviewed Scott's plans before he set out, he would

probably have urged him not to go at all. Scott set himself up for failure. Amundsen set himself up for success through a compelling Strategic Plan, which was future proofed, through 'what if' scenarios and a plan B, C, and D. They each got a predictable result aligned to the quality of their planning.

A cultural pitfall to be wary of

There is one cultural challenge to be conscious of in building your high performing organization. We've talked about change as a constant and our agreed definition of strategy accounts for this:

> 'A strategy is a changeable set of implementable actions that we frequently revisit and redefine according to shifting market conditions in order to achieve the long term aspiration of the organisation.'

However, whenever change occurs in a business you often hear generalized comments like: 'here we go again; everything is changing'. Not everything is changing and as a leader it is important to head off this cultural pitfall before it arises. The way to do that is to create a distinction between your strategy (which should be fluid, agile) and your Vision/Purpose which is fixed, acting as your North Star.

Amundsen's preparation reflected his understanding of this point. Scott's preparation on the other hand suggests his strategy was flawed in inflexibility. However, both men had a Vision/Purpose, which never changed: to reach the South Pole.

Disciplined Execution

> 'Perfection is not attainable, but if we chase perfection then we can catch excellence!'

The story of Amundsen and Scott could be seen through the lens of disciplined execution. Not only did Amundsen have a great strategy, he was flawless and disciplined in its execution.

Disciplined execution makes the difference when delivering accelerated, sustained and profitable business growth. Yes, I advocate allocating time for thinking and for creating your strategy, but culturally you also need to build a personal brand as an action focused individual that makes things happen. Gaps in the market or opportunities are there one minute and gone the next. Your moment to capitalize and steal the edge requires decisiveness, agility, and conscious deliberate intent.

Disciplined execution is about having a plan and being flawless in its execution. It's about frequently revisiting and refining your plan based on empirical validation; what is working (keep doing it) and what isn't (change it). It's about testing small before going BIG. It's about having the measures that matter in play, interpreting the insight, and acting accordingly. It's about having a defining question, which keeps you focused, and on track.

Will it make the boat go faster?

It was a simple defining question that propelled the British Olympic rowing team to world champions at the end of the 1990s. The British rowing team had been in the wilderness for decades, typically coming 6th, 7th, or 8th in races and had been written off as real contenders. When Ben Hunt-Davis joined the team in 1991, very little changed at first. For the next seven years in fact, to 1998, the results remained the same: 6th, 7th, or 8th at World Championships, Regattas, and Olympics.

Finally, after another 7th place at the 1998 Cologne Regatta, the team was utterly fed up. They realized that if they wanted different results they would have to do things differently. They started to test every decision they made by asking one simple question: 'Will it make the boat go faster?' and action only the things that would.

In 1999, things began to change. The team took 2nd place in four races. In 2000, the team was placed 2nd in its first race of the year and 1st in the next three. On Sunday, 24 September 2000 at 10h30, the team rowed to victory at the Sydney Olympics, winning the gold medal.

Making the boat go faster was all that mattered if they were to achieve their Vision/Purpose of 5 minutes and 18 seconds over

2,000m. With a clear understanding of their goal, they had a defining question to test all their decisions: 'Will it make the boat go faster?' They were focused, they were disciplined, and they avoided distractions, activities, or blind alleyways which took them off course from realizing their goals, dreams, and ambitions.

What is your defining question? How effective are you and your business in the discipline of disciplined execution?

Performance Culture

> 'Our culture, our heritage, our language are the foundations upon which we build our identity. Culture is everything!'

At the heart of your high performing organization is your performance culture, which can often be a misunderstood concept. Take Google as a leading example, known for its unique approach to mixing work and play. But Google's strong performance culture has nothing to do with playground offices; in fact, it is the strong performance culture that makes those playgrounds possible, not the other way around. Google is widely held to be an organization where high performing individuals undertake work that is 'important' and has 'meaning' and for that reason has always attracted an unusually high calibre of high performing individual.

In organizations where culture is strong, people either fit in or they don't. It's as simple as that. It's a very effective filter. The ultimate success measure in whether you have developed the right culture will be how proud your people are to wear your company badge and be brand ambassadors and advocates for you. Culture is the 'thing' that gives two companies in the same industry, with similar services and products, and similar pricing, distinctly different flavours.

Consider the differences between Virgin Atlantic and British Airways, for example. Both are excellent organizations, flying modern aircraft on competing routes, aiming for the same customer demographic. But step on board an aircraft operated by each of them, and the feeling is quite different. Where one is aiming for high energy, and a modern, fun, innovative experience, the other expresses traditional British Values of reliability, sturdiness, professionalism, and politeness.

Those elements reveal the essence of their culture, which is undoubtedly evident in their hiring criteria, their training, their internal language, and the way their people think, feel, and act.

A common mistake is thinking of culture as a 'nice to have', rather than a potent competitive advantage. Culture may earn companies a strong showing on annual 'best companies to work for' lists, but its greatest strength is the achievement of high levels of performance through shared Vision/Purpose, Values, and beliefs. That's why performance culture sits firmly at the epicentre of the High Performing Organization Model. Think of it as the central nervous system for your entire organization. All the roads lead back to culture.

Making it real for your business

To make this real for your business, let me share an exercise with you, which I do when running workshops, coaching, or consulting with a client. I ask the leaders the following question;

'Write an executive summary capturing the essence of the "to be" performance culture in your business; what would it look like, feel like and act like?'

The reaction to this question amazes me. Some people will hit the ground running and enter a stream of consciousness as they scribble down their ideas. Others find the exercise difficult and struggle to articulate the key characteristics and traits. What's even more fascinating is when I complete this exercise with the Senior Leadership team of the same business. Guess what? 99.9% of the time the answers are all different.

If the Senior Leadership team are not on page with one version of the truth what chance do employees, customers, strategic partners, and other key stakeholder groups have in understanding what you're about and what you stand for?

What would your executive summary say? Would all the leaders and people in your business describe the 'to be' performance culture in the same way?

Summary

Management guru Peter Drucker is credited with one of the most often repeated statements about business: 'Culture eats strategy for breakfast every time.'

In a business which is Built to Grow, Vision/Purpose, Values/Behaviours, Strategic Plan, Disciplined Execution, and Performance Culture all work together, leading, leveraging, and supporting each other. The power is in the 'whole', demonstrating that all are equally important. One cannot overpower the other if you are truly committed to building a high performing organization.

The five elements working in unison will ensure accelerated, sustained and profitable business growth and high performance will become your reality!

Chapter 5

Business Purpose, Aspirational Goals, and Growth Strategy

'If the WHY is compelling and strong enough, then you'll figure out the what and the how.'

Every person experiences important moments in their lives, but in business, there is one that stands out above all others: the moment a person changes from someone with a *job* to someone with a *purpose*. While the motivation to do so must come from within, the triggers that compel them to make the switch are ones the organization and its leaders can create.

The reality is that most people have difficulty making a commitment to *anything*. They spend their whole lives jumping from one thing to another, looking for a quick and easy way to success, or else they just settle for something less than their dreams. Many people make a half-hearted commitment to something, and tell themselves they are making a total commitment. Then they see something better somewhere else; the grass looks greener in a new business or job. They commit for a while to something new, and then they get tired of that too, and they're off again to something else.

The challenge for the organization is obvious; an endless cycle of rehiring, retraining, lost opportunity, the loss of perfectly good people to the competition, and a constant feeling of disruption. Furthermore, if people are leaving your organization, it gives others a reason to consider the exit door too. A lack of a compelling WHY can have a huge knock-on effect in your people strategy.

While people have difficulty making commitments, however, I don't believe they are necessarily nomads by preference. Organizations with a strong WHY prove the point with much lower rates of attrition. Why? Because we realize at some point in our lives that we've got to stop looking over the fence and decide to maximize the potential of what we already have. We've got to look at the opportunity before us and find what is good in it. A compelling WHY gives us the best reason of all to do just that.

The Power of Your WHY

Think for a moment about why you do what you do? Most people, when asked WHAT they do, can speak about it at length. They might have a quick answer, and when pressed, will give you tons of details about the logical, technical, and procedural aspects of their job or business. You are probably the same. We don't have any difficulty at all with our WHAT.

But let me ask you something different: WHY do you do it? What's the purpose behind it? What made you decide to do it in the first place? What made doing WHAT you do, so compelling that you *had* to do it? The problem with answering those questions for many people is that either they aren't sure, or they've completely lost touch with their reasons over the years.

In adulthood, we lose the idealism that drove us when we were younger; the illogical excitement of doing something just because we're really excited by it. There's good and bad in that, of course. Idealism isn't the best platform upon which to make big decisions, in the real world. However, the spirit and passion that drove that idealism are very real and whether we admit it or not, it still forms part of our decision-making today.

We are moved by significance. When you're able to answer not just WHAT you do, but elaborate the reasons WHY you do it, feel a rush of excitement, passion, and deep-rooted emotional connection as you speak about it, that's one of the most compelling feelings of all. If you take a look through history at some of the biggest personalities who have shaped our world, their WHY was strong enough for people to align behind them, even though the demands they made and sacrifices they required were often enormous.

Think of Winston Churchill during World War II. His WHAT was defeating an enemy; his WHY was that he was fiercely proud to be British and would rather have died than allow British culture, the British people, and Britain's reputation be subjugated or damaged in any way. Mother Teresa's WHAT was taking care of the homeless and the sick in India's cities. Her WHY: she felt it was her calling. Steve Jobs' WHAT was building digital devices that challenged the status quo. His WHY was that he believed the world had become too complicated, too inaccessible, and too ugly and he wanted to find a better way.

Bill Gates' compelling WHY was a computer in every home enabled with the Microsoft Windows operating system. In Chapter 3: Inspirational Leadership, we discussed how Sylvester Stallone was driven to write a great script because he wanted more than anything to be an actor, and initially even turned down the spoils of success as a scriptwriter so that he could fulfil his dream and play the lead role in *Rocky*.

Remember how Formula One driver Lewis Hamilton was driven from a young age to become Formula One World Champion and visualized it so clearly that it was just a matter of when and where?

But is a compelling WHY *really* that important?

The third most watched TED talk of all time, with more than 25 million views at the time of writing, is on the very subject of finding your WHY. Called 'How great leaders inspire action', management expert Simon Sinek speaks exclusively about the importance of finding your WHY, and he illustrates this point using the Steve Jobs way of thinking:

> 'The way we think, the way we act, and the way we communicate is backwards . . . I use Apple as an example because it's easy to understand: if Apple were like everyone else, their marketing message might be:
>
> WHAT: We make great computers
>
> HOW: They're beautifully designed, simple to use and user friendly.

Want to buy one?

That's how most of us communicate; that's how most marketing is done. We say what we do, we say how we are different and how we're better and we expect some sort of behaviour; a purchase or a vote. But here's how Apple actually communicates:

WHY: In everything we do, we believe in challenging the status quo; we believe in thinking differently.

HOW: The way we challenge the status quo is making our products beautifully designed and user friendly.

WHAT: We just happen to make computers.

Want to buy one?'

Sinek goes on to say that 'people don't buy what you do; they buy why you do it'. Relate this to our earlier examples: British people rallied around Churchill's call to sacrifice not because they enjoyed sacrificing, but because they bought into his WHY. People supported Mother Teresa for the same reason.

Finding your WHY, or reconnecting and reaffirming your WHY, is the most important journey you can undertake. It requires you to be fully awake to the desires that drive you. When Peter Jones, one of the wealthy investors on BBC's *Dragons' Den*, was a boy, he used to go to work with his dad and listen to the conversations and play in his dad's office while he was in meetings. As a result of those conversations and play, he knew early on that he wanted to be in business. He got a rush from building things and solving problems and knew that he could do something great if he pursued his WHY. Note that he didn't necessarily find his WHAT for many years after that, but he found it by pursuing and never losing his passion for WHY.

I had a similar journey in business; my dad had a specialist construction company and, growing up, many of my holidays and Saturday mornings were spent there. So it was no surprise that my first job on leaving school at the age of 16 was an apprenticeship in a construction company on a rotational management programme. I caught the business bug, coupled with a never-ending thirst for learning and trying new things.

We all have the need to be a part of something; to do something that has some bigger meaning. We all need to find our WHY.

When you find it, I guarantee it will change the way you think about everything you do in life. It will change the way you make decisions and the value you place on things. Finding your WHY is a life-changing moment because it denotes the point at which you acquire real purpose. You have something that is worth putting every ounce of your energy into. Your WHAT is nothing but a means of delivering on your WHY.

Caution: Two Pitfalls to Avoid in Finding Your WHY

There are two major pitfalls to avoid when thinking about your WHY: the first is confusing your WHAT with your WHY and the second is believing your WHY is solely about making money. Let's look at each closely.

Sometimes we confuse a WHAT with a WHY, and the business landscape is littered with failed entrepreneurs who did precisely that.

Management guru Michael Gerber speaks of one common phenomenon, *the technician with an entrepreneurial seizure*; an employee with a high degree of technical skill who believes they could do as well or even better if they started a business offering services that capitalized on those skills. On the surface, it seems like sound thinking, but you don't have to dig very far to discover a fundamental problem: the world of business and the application of technical skills are very different things.

It's also common to underestimate how hard it is to build a business. Where motivational gurus will tell you that going out on your own is about freedom and control and commanding your own destiny, many entrepreneurs discover the initial stages are about loneliness, anxiety, sleepless nights, pressure, and perhaps even keeping a growing collection of debt collectors at bay. The broad and diverse facets of building and running a business can be brutal and unless there is a compelling reason to put yourself through it, it may be impossible to stay the distance.

The second pitfall to avoid is believing that making money is your primary WHY. Making money should be a measure of success as a by-product of what you do (the output). However, if it is your primary motivation, it may be impossible to provide the sort of authentic, customer experience focused product or service (the inputs) that ultimately will result in the financial rewards.

This leads on to a core philosophy and integral part of my moral compass, which I passionately believe is key in delivering accelerated, sustained and profitable business growth:

Life is Like a Boomerang

I am CEO of a business consultancy & people development organization, and this outward value-adding philosophy is embedded in the company's DNA and culture. When a new member of the team joins, no matter what their role, they receive a boomerang. Our business purpose is growing businesses and unlocking people potential and the boomerang symbolizes that when we are truly living an outwardly focused value-adding philosophy, the rewards of success will come back to us.

We know that if we focus on rewards as our purpose, they'll be harder to find, but if we throw our boomerangs and add more value than any of our clients ever dreamed they would get, we'll earn the returns.

One of my fundamental beliefs is that the very things you want to see more of in your life are the very things you need to give away. Want more credit for all you do and who you are? Be the one who gives credit and praise to others. Want more understanding from others? Be a more understanding person. Want more loyalty? Be the most loyal person you know. Want more respect? Give more respect. None of us have a given right to this one. You have to earn it.

Life wants you to win. Most people just get in their own way and sabotage their own success. To realize all you want from life, apply the boomerang principle and do great things first. Most people have their focus the wrong way round.

Never forget; life is a boomerang.

Translating Your Personal WHY into Your Business's WHY

For many business owners, business leaders, and entrepreneurs, their own personal WHY becomes the WHY of the organization. They have a calling, a vision, an epiphany, and they create an organization with the goal of turning their vision into reality. Most successful businesses can trace their early roots and reason for being back to a similar starting point, and those that continue to pursue it as their North Star have a compelling means of motivating their people to do the same.

Every leader in business should make it an unarguable goal to connect with, and remain connected to, the organization's WHY. The journey to reinforce, embed, and constantly check your people's alignment with WHY is never ending.

Your organization's WHY has the power to give your people a reason to get motivated and connected. If there is one thing we know about the mysterious science of motivation, it's that you and I cannot motivate anyone but ourselves, and even that is sometimes a hard enough task in itself. Motivation is an inside job; it's a personal choice. There are no 'outside in' solutions, only 'inside out'. People do things for their own reasons, not *your* reasons, and you can't motivate anyone to do something they don't want to do.

However, if we are effective communicators of our organization's WHY, we arm ourselves with the motivational triggers to ignite an individual's self-motivation, desire, and will to consciously choose to motivate themselves and connect with the WHY. The challenge is that human psychology will always default to the WIIFM factor . . . *what's in it for me*. The business's WHY, if positioned correctly, addresses the WIIFM factor. It gives your people something to believe in, a set of emotional anchor points to connect to. Those that believe in the cause, the big idea, the reason we're doing this, and who believe not only that it is a worthwhile thing to do, but that we are the right people to be doing it, have a reason to get motivated.

Aligning Your Business's WHY With Your People's Personal WHY

Through communication and alignment of your WHY with your people's WHY, coupled with their own personal motivations, you can ensure people have skin in the game and a deep-rooted motivation to help you succeed. Let's look at a real world example.

You're working with your sales team and running a series of one-on-one sessions at the start of the year, perhaps to go through the sales targets (your WHAT), and that's where the discussion stops. In some instances, you might move on and explore some ideas on HOW you can do it, but all too regularly that step never takes place. The result, unfortunately, is a team that understands the objective, and possibly some ways to go about achieving that objective, but which has no compelling personal reason to care.

But what if, at the start of the process, you decided to look at what truly motivated them, so that you could align the business objectives with their own personal goals? Their own WHY? In practical terms it's about asking some relatively easy questions:

- What are your personal goals for the year?
- What is it you want to achieve?
- Why do you want to achieve it?
- How can I help you achieve those goals?
- What do you want to earn in financial terms?
- Why do you want to earn it?

One of the keys to unlocking a motivational environment is to clearly understand your people's personal goals and how being successful at work can be one of the vehicles and enablers in helping them realize their goals. The moment we create the bridge in their mind – the link between their personal goals and business goals – self-motivation kicks in.

One of my clients was so excited by this idea he went back to his team and sat with them individually to understand their personal goals and their WHY. During one conversation, he discovered that a member of the team wanted to earn a £10,000 bonus in order to take his wife and two children to Disney World. That's important to note. He didn't want the money for its own sake, which is a very poor motivational driver; he wanted it for something specific. He wanted Disney World for his family, and the money was simply his way to deliver them their dream holiday.

Once his manager knew his WHY, he could have a much more meaningful conversation about the WHAT and the HOW. It also enabled him to go one step further. He went to a Disney shop and actually purchased a mini Mickey Mouse and positioned it on the corner of his desk, creating an anchor; a motivational trigger. When the guy was doing well and on his game, the manager would go to his desk, point to the Mickey Mouse and say well done; you're another week closer to Mickey and Disney World.

When he was not performing, off his game, or had a difficult week, he would go over and point to Mickey and say 'Your activity needs to improve if you're going to get to Disney World', and then proceed to run a coaching session, refreshing the WHY, the WHAT, and the HOW. At the end of the year, that salesperson was a hero to his family when he walked through the door with his bonus cheque and he was able to take them on the holiday of a lifetime.

The people working with you are important in helping you to achieve your vision and goals; do you truly understand their personal WHY; what really makes them tick and WHY they come to work every day? Have you aligned their personal WHY with the business WHY so they know precisely what part they play in the big picture and how the work they do on a daily basis has real purpose and meaning?

As Andrew Carnegie, one of the most successful businessmen of all time, observed: 'Teamwork is the ability to work together toward a common vision. The ability to direct individual accomplishments toward organisational objectives. It is the fuel that allows common people to attain uncommon results.'

French writer Antoine de Saint-Exupéry came at it from another angle when he said: 'If you want to build a ship, don't drum up people together to collect wood and don't assign them tasks and work, but rather teach them to long for the endless immensity of the sea.'

Creating alignment between the personal WHY and business WHY is where business leaders, business owners, and entrepreneurs should be investing quality time. Returning to Simon Sinek's observation about Apple, and its obsession with the WHY, it's not hard to understand why its people get excited about working there and push themselves to do great things.

So how do you unlock the business WHY and use it to galvanize your people to achieve both business and personal goals? By asking one fundamental question that will forever change the course of your thinking and open your business to its true purpose: What business are you *really* in?

What Business Are You *Really* in?

If I could give you one question to ask that will provide the most fundamental shift in your business, this would be it. I've seen it over and over, in businesses of all sizes over the past twenty years. When you understand the answer to this question, it can completely transform what you do, how you think about your business, and how you engage with employees, customers, shareholders, partners, and all key internal and external stakeholders.

So, if you have a pad and pen or electronic device I'd like you to write down your answer to the question: what business are you in? Don't over analyse or over think your answer; it is not a trick question. Just capture your immediate response in black or white or worst case, imprint the answer firmly in your conscious mind. We'll come back to how you responded later in this chapter.

Here's the kicker to start with: in my experience most people answer that question from one of three angles. First, they think they're in the business dictated by the name of their business; second, the industry in which they operate; or third, the products or services they provide.

But actually for all three, nothing could be further from the truth. You see, I don't think most people know what business they are really in. Now, I know that is a bold statement to make and you might already be challenging me on it, however stay the course and let me build and demonstrate my business case through some real world examples.

PizzaExpress is a global chain of over 500 restaurants, founded by a guy named Peter Boizot in 1965. If you were to ask anyone at the company what business they are in, the response might well be selling pizzas. At a logical level this is correct. However, as part of their induction, new colleagues are educated on the history, heritage, culture, and purpose of PizzaExpress – guess what business they say they are 'really' in . . . 'Feeding great conversations since 1965.'

The product or service, which in this case is pizza, is just the prop to engage the customer in the memorable experience. The fact that a pizza restaurant makes great pizzas should simply be a given; your product is merely your licence to trade and it has to be great because in a competitive world, mediocre products quickly give way to better ones.

The profound difference 'really' can make

Notice what impact the addition of one word has when you change 'what business are you in?' to 'what business are you "really" in?' Your response to the first question will drive you down the road of answering the question from a logical perspective aligned to your industry or products and services you provide.

Your response to the second question creates an entirely different dynamic: great businesses think differently. The starting point is seeing through the eyes of the customer . . . what do they want and need now and in the future? They think 'outside in' as opposed to inside out. The one word 'really' added to the question challenges you to go beyond the physical product or service you provide and delve deeper into the benefits your customer receives by choosing your products and services. Let's explore a couple more examples to really bring this concept to life.

In his book *Bottled for Business*, Karan Bilimoria, the founder of Cobra beer, talks about the importance of being able to define what business he was *really* in. Bilimoria created Cobra as a smooth lager for drinking with Indian meals. Many lagers were gassy and left him bloated and full before he could finish his meal and he wanted to create one that did the opposite.

The beer he produced wasn't without its challenges: he chose to only provide it in 660ml bottles, when restaurant owners were used to the 330ml bottles; insisted on selling a minimum of five cases; and each case was slightly more expensive than the competition.

Bilimoria tackled those objections by moving the perception of Cobra from being in the beer business, to being something quite different. The secret of his product was in its smoothness and drink-ability. The uniqueness was the key selling point he presented to would-be customers – Indian restaurants in the southern counties of the UK – when he started out. He would literally knock on the doors of restaurants, ask for the owner, and place one of his beers in front of them, explaining that it was less gassy and therefore less filling, which meant customers would be more likely to order extra rice and naan bread with their curries, or have three beers instead of two. This different approach turned the conversation away from the potential objections, to how much more curry the restaurant would be able to sell.

Bilimoria achieved success by understanding what business he was *really* in; not beer, but helping Indian restaurant owners sell more curries, increase their profits, and put more money in their pockets.

There's a long list of companies that have been able to refine their product and service offerings and to create great new commercial opportunities for themselves by answering the all important question; what business are they really in?

What business is Google in? The logical answer would be search, but the real business: changing the way the world communicates, one click at a time. You may logically think that Shell is in the petrol business, but it sees itself as helping customers get from point A to point B in the smoothest possible way. Singapore Airlines sees itself as being in the entertainment business, not the airline business.

One further example that I absolutely love is how the New Zealand rugby team, the awesome All Blacks, define themselves. They speak about the need for Whanau, which is a Maori word for the extended family, and how All Blacks are held accountable by one another for their commitment to the family. In recent times, they have won 86% of the games they have played, which is a stunning achievement, yet they consider their greater purpose not to be that of playing rugby, but rather of inspiring and unifying New Zealanders.

You can apply this concept to any organization . . .

Asking what business are you 'really' in can be applied to any organization to understand the WHY of that business. I have been asking this question for over a decade now, and this single concept alone is responsible for over £500 million worth of value creation.

It is not just at an organizational level where you can make the profound difference. It is when every single person in your business knows precisely what business they are really in and this thinking drives consistency in the alignment of their values, behaviours, and the work they do every day. For example, the retail assistant at a clothing store could be in the business of selling clothes, or they could be in the business of making their customers look and feel good. The business of confidence and self-esteem; the business of personal branding. The holiday company customer advisors could be in the business of selling holidays or they could be in the business of turning families' dreams into reality. The list is endless.

. . . or to any function or department

You can internalize the concept and apply it to the functions and departments within your business. Let me give you an example of what it could look like when a department gets to grips with what business it's really in. Let's use the IT department, and to set the scene, let's put the CIO in a board meeting in which IT is the hot topic of the day. As he or she launches into their 15-minute presentation of their findings on the implementation of a new system, the conversation can go one of two possible ways.

They could start talking in IT language about main frames, outlets, and number of users; how much it will cost; how long it's going to take to do and the disruption it's going to cause to business, or . . .

the conversation could focus on how the new solution is going to accelerate the business growth strategy, help the business to acquire and retain more customers, and provide deeper understanding of customer buying trends so that the business will be able to satisfy their requirements better by aligning the appropriate products and services. The business benefit: return on investment is reduced to just 24 months and will have been recouped twice over within 36 months.

Which is more compelling?

I am sure you agree that the second version is, but what is the fundamental difference? In the first instance, the CIO believes he or she is in the IT business, and that delivering IT performance is their most important role, despite the fact that it exists only as a part of a bigger organization. In the second, the CIO believes he or she is in the business of delivering business performance aligned to customer service and satisfaction and the overall strategic goals and vision of the business.

You can apply this thinking across your entire organization. Is your HR department in the business of developing processes and procedures or is it in the business of unlocking people potential? Is your finance department in the business of crunching numbers, or delivering insight and expertise beyond the numbers that allows the business to make more informed, educated, and empirically validated financial decisions aligned to the overarching business growth strategy?

You can look at any department in any business in terms of the pure functional services they provide, or in terms of the underlying benefits of those services. Only doing the latter enables you to galvanize the people who provide those services to get behind them with enthusiasm and excitement.

Your Goal Before You Move on

The challenge for all businesses, and especially those that have been around for a long time is that they become processors of products and services, focused on the WHAT and the HOW. They lose touch with their WHY, and as a result, they lose the ability to see the world through the customer lens.

For the business starting up or at the early stages of growth, this concept is key as it drives your thinking and how you set your entire business up for success from day 1 – particularly around all the other components of the Business Growth Transformation Framework® which we're going to move onto next. Your goal before you move on is to find or reconnect with your purpose and your WHY from an 'outside in' perspective through answering the question: What business are you *really* in?

Now, I have dedicated a significant amount of this chapter to explaining how you can find your purpose because it is such an important subject. However, it would be remiss of me not to give attention to two other key components. Firstly, your aspirational goals and exploring the sense of possibilities of where you can take your business and what you can achieve, and secondly, starting with the end in mind, thinking about your business growth and potential exit strategy.

Your aspirational goals

I'm sure it's clear by now that the overarching guiding principle of *Built to Grow* is delivering accelerated, sustained and profitable business growth. I'll reiterate this throughout this book because I don't want you to ever lose sight of it.

Great businesses are driven by aspirational goals that really stretch them to achieve big results. When John F. Kennedy challenged NASA to put a man on the moon within seven years, the goal galvanized the organization to develop technologies and ideas and to find people that could drive the project forward and turn the vision into reality. Without the goal, it's likely NASA would still have advanced throughout the 1960s, but it may never have reached as far or as fast as it actually did.

Aspirational goals are the 'game changers' that can propel your business to an entirely different level of achievement. It immediately calls to mind one of the most meaningful quotes related to aspiration by success guru Anthony Robbins: 'Most people overestimate what they can achieve in a year, but underestimate what they can achieve in a decade.'

What will you achieve in the next decade with a really BIG aspirational goal?

In Chapter 3: Inspirational Leadership, I shared some of the traits of inspirational leaders and I'll recap a few of them here in the context of achieving big aspirational goals:

1. Think BIG: have the courage and the ambition to set a big long-term goal and inspire your people to reach for it. You can't achieve big things by thinking small.
2. Focus on ONE Thing: NASA didn't simultaneously attempt a Moon mission and a Mars mission; it focused on one thing and by focusing, it achieved it.
3. Winning mentality: if you think you can or think you can't you're probably right! Believe you can do it and look for reasons to make it happen, not reasons that it can't.
4. Attitude of ACTION: achieving goals requires constant activity to move you forward. There's no substitute for taking massive action and being known as one of those individuals who just makes things happen.
5. Resilience: aspirational goals are for the long term and since they require stretch, there is the threat of a setback at every step. NASA experienced several on the path to glory.
6. Authenticity: your goals must be aligned to your Vision/ Purpose.

Starting with the end in mind: Your possible exit strategy

There is one final consideration when you're thinking about your aspirational goals, and that is your exit strategy. What are you building your business for? What purpose do you ultimately want it to fulfil? What is your end game? Answering these questions will help you shape your overarching business growth strategy.

There are a number of reasons to grow a business: to have something to leave to your children, for example, or to sell for a profit once it achieves a target value. Alternatively, perhaps your intention is to take it all the way to an IPO (initial public offering) and list it on the stock exchange to really give it some scale and possibly even take it global.

All of these are important considerations when you're applying the lessons of *Built to Grow* to set your business up for growth, because unless you're absolutely clear about your exit strategy, you could make decisions that limit your options later on, or lead you off in a direction that makes it impossible to repurpose your business in alignment with your goals.

Many business owners, business leaders, and entrepreneurs find themselves in a sort of prison as time goes by because the business they have built is so tightly wrapped around their personality that it has little value without them. Where their intention was to start or lead a business, they find that they have instead created a demanding job that keeps them working 24/7. Irrespective of the maturity of your business growth strategy or your business journey, if you haven't consciously planned your exit strategy, now is the time to give it serious consideration.

Summary

This chapter is full of key thoughts and ideas to equip you with techniques to help shape your business growth strategy. The natural default position for businesses is to focus on their WHAT and their HOW and this approach may have served you relatively well. However, being clear about your WHY, the golden thread running through everything you do, defining what business you are really in and thinking aspirationally about what you want to achieve along the way to a clearly defined exit strategy, will set you up for success in the following chapters of your journey.

Chapter 6

Market Potential Strategy

'A spray and pray approach will not cut it in today's market!'

The game of chess is interesting to watch. Chess masters are experts in almost every conceivable move and counter-move so they're able to think many moves ahead. They control the game from the outset. The expectation of success requires a clear understanding of the potential that exists from the moment the game begins, and with every single move that follows.

An amateur, on the other hand, can be sure of losing, almost every time. They randomly move pieces that may or may not have an impact, and they celebrate when luck leads them to a momentary victory. There is no intelligent way for them to predict an outcome at any stage of the game, it's all just 'spray and pray'.

Now, interestingly, should a chess master choose to abandon their logic and simply move pieces randomly, it is entirely conceivable that they could lose to a first-time player; the sort of amateur that has to have the correct movement of the rook or bishop explained to them every time they put their hand on it.

That last scenario is how most companies approach market potential: as a random series of moves that may or may not pay off, entirely dependent on whether competitors misjudge the market or the market happens to come towards them.

Could that be your business?

Everything in *Built to Grow* involves being the architect of your own destiny; the chess master in your own game; deliberate, considered, and intelligent in the pursuit of creating and delivering your own strategic plan. Spray and pray just doesn't cut it for an organization that is Built to Grow.

So the big question we're focusing on in this chapter is: do you know the market potential for your products or services (each could have different potential) that will enable you to deliver accelerated, sustained, and profitable business growth? Does the market exist? Do you understand the extent, or indeed the limits, of the market that is available to you? Are you set up to capture those markets and extend the reach of your product and service propositions?

A new business might have more modest goals when it comes to market potential in year one and year two than a mature business, so the scale is likely to be very different. However, for each business, understanding and applying the fundamentals of market potential are identical.

Alignment of Your Aspirational Goals With the Market Potential

A key first step is to ensure alignment of your business purpose, your aspirational goals, and growth strategy with the market potential.

A starting point is to determine the basis of your market positioning, usually against two axes: competitor positioning and price (see Figure 6.1). Are you operating in the high-end market with a differentiated product or service and a premium price? Or the low-end market with an undifferentiated product or service and low price? Are you somewhere in the middle? What is the 'white space' opportunity you've identified? The space with fewer competitors, an under-served customer, or a new way of doing something?

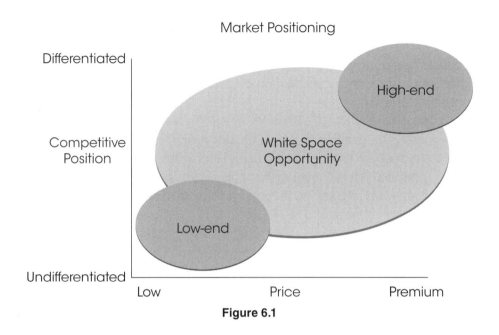

Figure 6.1

The 'white space' in UK supermarkets . . .

In the past decade, British shoppers have seen first hand how super-market giants Tesco, Asda, Sainsbury's, and Morrisons have been disrupted by German brands Aldi and Lidl, who paid little attention to their competitors' strategies, and pursued their own.

During the financial crisis commencing in 2008, the German supermarket retailers took the view that shopping patterns were changing and consumers were looking to shop less frequently, buy more, and take advantage of bulk discounts. Added to that, they based their entire strategy, from store layout to the limited product range (Aldi typically stocks around 1,200 items compared to the 50,000 stocked by Tesco just a few years ago) on the emerging consumer preference of sticking to the basics, rather than luxurious extras. Their products were rarely premium brands, but offered a sufficiently high quality to appeal to consumers across a broad economic spectrum.

They did this while the traditional big four simply hunkered down against the bracing wind.

It would be easy to consider the UK supermarket space as over-saturated and impossible to break into. Aldi and Lidl examined the changing patterns of consumer buying from both a demographic and psychographic point of view, and turned the existing market into something entirely new.

At the time of writing, as the UK economy was markedly swinging consistently up, the big four had reported an increase in sales once again for the first time in years, but the cost has nevertheless been high: Aldi and Lidl are now entrenched as competitors in a marketplace they were allowed to invent, and the landscape has changed forever.

. . . and budget airlines

Similar disruptive thinking turned the short-hop European airline market on its head in the mid-1990s with the arrival of easyJet and Ryanair. Their business model sought to appeal to the one thing that large numbers of passengers wanted more than anything else: a cheap flight.

Whilst other airlines charged up-front for the provision of services such as in-flight refreshments, the discount airlines decided to strip out such services and leave them to the discretion of the consumer. As a payoff, the airlines were assured of more full cabins, optimizing load capacity in a way that traditional airlines hadn't managed to.

Whichever part of the market you have chosen to serve or white space you have chosen to operate in, the key is in aligning your goals to the market potential.

What are the measures that matter?

- X number of sales in a particular product or service area
- X percentage of growth
- A market share of X
- A market position of X.

Perhaps you want a thousand sales of a particular product. Does the market support that? Could it realistically deliver that number of sales? If one in ten people buy from you, you'll need to have a guaranteed audience of ten thousand to achieve sales success. Can you identify who they are? Are they accessible?

Starting with your aspirational goals compels you to ask deep, probing questions about whether or not those goals are achievable with your current focus. Spending quality time dissecting your goals might save you wasted time, energy, and resources chasing an aspiration, which the market simply cannot support.

Now, having validated the existence of the market and recognized it is yours for the taking, you must turn your attention to quantifying, segmenting, and profiling the opportunity.

Defining the Size of Opportunity

The first requirement is to define the size of the opportunity. In other words what is the overall size of the market? To gather this insight, you will need to reach out to secondary sources of information: census reports, government statistics, industry specialists who will have provided reputable quantifiable data on your market.

Let's use an example of the domestic pet market, since one of my clients operates in this space and the pet grooming business is a market with an upward trajectory. The Pet Food Manufacturers Association (PFMA) produces a yearly pet population report that looks in detail at pet ownership trends. In 2015, it estimated that 46% (12 million) of UK households have pets and the pet population stood at 58 million. Dog ownership was by far the largest with 24% of UK households owning a dog – a canine population of 8.5 million. Regional concentrations are apparent, with the North East of England having the largest dog population and London having the smallest.

Euromonitor estimates total UK consumer spending of £4.7 billion on pet care of which £1 billion is on non-edible items such as grooming, clothes, and toys.

So how would this data help me if I were looking to set up or grow a pet grooming business? Firstly, it has confirmed the scale of pet ownership and that dogs are the most popular pet. It has confirmed that pet grooming is a viable market with UK consumers happy to spend on commercial pet services and products. It has also shown me that regional differences exist. I could now investigate further the size of the pet grooming opportunity, or make some high level assumptions. For example, 10% of dog owners will want to benefit from pet grooming services. You keep defining and refining until you have identified the size of the opportunity in your chosen field.

Empirical validation here is key. In this example I researched only one data source but I would recommend a number of go-to sources, cross-referencing their similarities and differences to obtain a complete understanding of the market.

Segmenting and Profiling the Opportunity

Having defined the size of the opportunity, the next requirement is to develop a segmentation framework to identify your core target segments. What do I mean by segmentation?

'. . . the process of defining and subdividing a large homogenous market into clearly identifiable segments with similar needs or wants.'

Take my pet grooming business example. Having validated the size of the homogenous market, i.e. dog ownership, my next task is to subdivide this into a number of segments with similar needs or wants. The key here is similar needs or wants. So you may be asking 'Royston, we are talking about a dog here, surely they all have the same needs; food, water, shelter and exercise?' Yes, of course. But thinking in the context of my pet grooming example there are a number of ways to approach this.

One approach could be to sub-divide the market into segments based on dog owner types and the reasons why they would need a dog grooming service. Think, for example, of the elderly, the impaired, full-time workers, etc. An alternative approach could use the industry classification of seven dog groups: sporting, hound, working, terrier, toy, non-sporting, and herding, with each dog group having specific characteristics based on personality, temperament, and grooming requirements dependent upon the breed.

So why is this important? Irrespective of *how* you choose to segment the market, the key is that you *have* segmented the market. Identifying distinct target segments will ensure your product, service, and experiential proposition addresses the specific needs of a particular segment.

Customer profiling and pen portraits

To fully understand your market potential for any product or service, a useful exercise is to create a key customer profile. Many successful authors have considered it to be a critical component in the development of some of their most successful books. Writing for a general idea of their readership, which may number in the millions across a broad range of demographics, would be an impossible task. So many authors write with just one reader in mind. One person. Perhaps someone they know well. That person, being the ideal reader for their story, informs everything they put into it, from character names, to plot twists, and helps them to develop a laser beam focus in the pursuit of their story. The thinking goes that if that one ideal person loves the book, others like him or her will too. It may sound like an odd thing to do: what if they write a story for the wrong person? Well, to avoid that, the author would have spent a considerable amount of time obtaining a deep understanding of their target reader; who they are and what makes them tick.

In business, the marketing term for such a person is a pen portrait; an ideal customer that enables you to practically answer questions such as: Who are they? What do they buy? Why do they buy?

Whenever I am working with clients and we talk about market potential, one of my key questions is always: Can you describe the ideal profile of your key target customer? To give some broader context and help frame this question I suggest two additional sub-questions aligned to demographics (Who are they?) and psychographics (Why do they buy?)

Now, let me deal with the most common objection I get, which is possibly at the forefront of your mind right now: 'Yes, but Royston you don't understand; our business is different and narrowing our target market is really hard as our target market is literally everyone.' If you're thinking that, you're not alone. I assure you though, that each product and service has an ideal target market and you really can define them. Yes, businesses are different, but the principles underpinning *Built to Grow* are universal, have stood the test of time, and have been applied in a variety of market sectors. Not convinced? Let's analyse what a pen portrait actually is, and how to build one.

Pen portraits are both specific and generic. While you can't describe every single aspect of every single customer, you can be very specific about customer segments. Your pen portrait may cover age and other hard variables, but will focus on softer dimensions such as attitudes, appearance, and lifestyle. This may be part of the outcome of a piece of qualitative research you have commissioned or undertaken by yourself.

Continuing the theme of the pet grooming business, let's look at a couple of pen portraits, each of which describes a category of person who would be ideal for a particular product or service.

Pen portrait #1

Elderly couple with limited mobility. Wants to ensure their beloved pet is well groomed at all times and feels pampered. Their visit to the salon acts as a social outing and makes them feel part of the community. Whilst they may not use the service often, they are extremely loyal.

Pen portrait #2

38-year-old man or woman, in a professional services environment, on a partnership track. Time poor and asset rich, happy to pay a premium for convenience, availability, and speed of service. Looking for a regular service as the local dog walking area can be a muddy terrain.

Reviewing the pen portrait examples should highlight how different products and services would appeal to a particular target segment and how, if you were the owner of this business, you would develop your proposition to meet the needs of these different segments (more about developing your compelling value proposition in the next chapter).

To emphasize pen portraits, many companies will go as far as creating visuals of that ideal person, and decorating their offices with them, on life-sized cardboard cutout stands so that they are 'top of mind' for employees. The pen portrait technique builds a clear impression of who it is that buys. The next step in establishing your market potential is to understand why they buy.

Why Consumers Buy and How the Competition Can Impact Your Market Potential

At a basic level, customers make purchases to satisfy needs. In our pet grooming example the basic need is 'convenient pet pampering from pet loving stylists'. If you can meet this need, you have a good starting point to win their business. Clearly nothing is this simple and therefore you take account of other factors: price, location, quality of product, service, competition.

Whilst all these factors can favourably or unfavourably alter your market potential, the competitor landscape can also have a major impact on your market potential. I have two views when it comes to the subject of competitors. We like to say in business that competition is good. It keeps us on our toes and ensures we challenge ourselves to achieve the three bottom line measures that matter, referenced earlier in the book:

- Are you the provider of choice for your customers?
- Are you the employer of choice for skilled and talented people?
- Are you the investment of choice?

If it were possible to eliminate the stress of competition with a magic wand, it's true that many organizations would prefer to be alone in a market they could dominate. There's nothing wrong with that. Competition can bite, can hinder, and it can be a real distraction, so it's probably natural to wish it away. Doing so, however, won't make the blindest bit of difference, because in a free commercial market, competition is a given, and you need to find a way to deal with it.

That brings me to the first of my two points: keeping an eye on the competition is a worthwhile exercise because it's useful to see what they're up to, what ideas they may have that are worth modelling (remember, *Built to Grow* is all about success modelling), and noting any new moves they make to see if they offer niche opportunities or gaps that you may want to own.

However, my second point is that you can obsess too much about the competition and lose sight of your own mission, all too easily. History is littered with once great companies that did that; even mighty Apple found itself in that position in the mid-1990s, before the return of Steve Jobs, when it attempted to compete purely on features with Windows-based laptops from Dell, HP, and Compaq. Apple's obsession with beating its competitors distracted it from being a unique organization with a unique view of the world and challenging products that forged an army of Apple-or-die disciples, headlong into a competitor furnace, which nearly ended it. It's absurd to think of it. It was only with the return of Steve Jobs in 1997 that Apple began to find its way again, and it's no surprise that with the development of tablet devices, smartphones, music players, a legal music and movie download service and so on, Apple went on to become the most valuable company in history.

Where competition is rich and you're 'in the pack' with everyone around you, allowing your competitors to drive part or even all of your strategy, the chances are high that you'll become a me-too organization without the real differentiators and competitive advantage that deliver double-digit growth. Inevitably, it will be your competitors, not your customers, who are at the core of your strategy and as a result, you focus your time and attention on benchmarking your rivals and responding to their strategic moves rather than understanding how to deliver a leap in value to your customers.

Companies that are Built to Grow don't obsess with competitors. They innovate, deliver value, and let the competition worry about themselves. More importantly, it is innovation and value that are the focal points. A truly Built to Grow company may be unaware of how many sleepless nights their competitors are having because they're so focused on their own next big thing that they haven't had time to notice.

Remember the supermarket and airline examples earlier? The new entrants focused on innovation and value rather than existing barriers to entry or the possible market saturation. They found a new 'white space' to compete in and created market potential based on their offering.

Market Potential and 'The Four Seasons Calendar'

One idea I love, which is simple and incredibly effective, is to identify those times in your business when customers should be in abundance; when the market should be flooded with individuals wanting what you offer. In any industry, there are always significant times or moments.

Toy makers know that being ready for the Christmas rush makes good sense. Successful toy makers don't miss the opportunity to boost sales and achieve their goals at this time of year when customer demand is at its highest. If, as a toy maker, you set your strategy to achieve your greatest number of sales during July, and fail to capitalize on December, you're likely misunderstanding your market potential.

Companies selling services to other businesses should know the most important times of year for them too, such as when their customers and potential customers are planning next year's budgeting cycle. If they're not capitalizing on those opportunities, their aspirational goals may be unrealizable because they'll have to wait for the next budgeting season, often 12 months into the future.

In the flower business, the key moments are more transparent. Valentine's Day, for example, is number one. Other important dates are Easter and Christmas and these form the big seasonal events when any florist should be able to expect high volumes of sales. They are on the calendar every year and are high points that demand certain activities in order to maximize their potential. The second set of important days is more individual and may include birthdays and anniversaries. Let's not forget, these significant times or moments apply equally to our pet grooming business!

Capturing customer information at these key data points will enable you to take specific actions such as sending previous customers a text message or an email to remind them of an event coming up. This targeted, personalized approach moves you into customer relationship management, which is a real competitive advantage.

Reaching out to customers at significant times can have a huge impact in terms of maximization: getting them to buy more, or more frequently; and retention: reminding them that you are still here and that they can easily have a repeat of the great experience they had in purchasing from you before. The more insight you have, the more targeted, systematic, and focused you can be, which in turn will create certainty in your business growth model.

Failing to do this means you have to rely on customers to think of you, which is risky no matter how much they have enjoyed using you in the past, because many will simply make a convenience purchase from the supplier nearest to them. The potential size of your market therefore is either enhanced or limited by your ability, or inability, to understand who could buy from you, when they are most likely to buy, and what they will buy when they do.

Summary

Competing in a saturated market can be a daunting task, but what Aldi and Lidl can teach us, and what the big four supermarkets will have learnt to their cost, is the sheer overriding power of aligning your aspirational goals to market potential. Understanding this strategic view of your business cuts straight to the heart of the three questions we have been discussing in this chapter:

1. Who are your customers?
2. What do they buy?
3. Why do they buy it?

In simple terms, you may ask yourself, where are we going to compete: the high end of the market, or the low end? Without a clear answer to this question, we have seen tremendous companies throughout history lose their way and try to be everything to everybody and end up being nothing to anyone.

For the big four UK supermarkets, competing with Aldi and Lidl on price may be tempting, because that appears to be the newest game in town, but it would likely prove fatal to one or more of them. The reason: that's not what their customers care about. They could choose instead to focus on attacking one another in a bid to dominate a saturated market sector, but that just keeps them focused on the competition, not the customer. Even in the changed landscape, there is opportunity for each of those businesses to focus on their specific strengths, and therefore to differentiate themselves.

In the next chapter we'll clarify this further by drilling into what makes a compelling value proposition. Before we move on, let me offer a final word on market potential. What consistently separates winners from losers in creating a compelling market potential strategy is the ability of winners to refuse to get caught up in the losing idea of building a defensible position within an existing order.

Winners, instead, seek to deliver value innovation; the act not of grappling with competitors, but of creating a giant leap in value for customers so that the competition is made irrelevant. In so doing, they open up a new and uncontested market space. Value innovation places equal emphasis on value and innovation. Value without innovation tends to focus on value creation on an incremental scale. Something that improves value but is not sufficient to make you stand out in the marketplace. Innovation without value tends to be technology driven, market pioneering, or futuristic – often shooting beyond what buyers are ready to accept and pay for.

Value innovation is the new way of thinking about and executing strategy. In the next chapter, I'll show you how to achieve this.

Chapter 7

Compelling Value Proposition Strategy

'Why should I buy from you?'

This is a question that every business leader, business owner, and entrepreneur must ask every day across their entire customer lifecycle: starting with customer acquisition, through maximization, and finally retention.

Why? Because in a fiercely competitive world, your competition is trying to poach your customers; competitors that you could know well, new entrants appearing from nowhere, and old rivals who suddenly seem to have got their act together and are on the offensive. It is ultra competitive, and complacency is not an option.

Having a good product or service won't cut it. You've got to have a *great* product and service. Educating your potential, new, and existing customers about your products and services must be an integral part of your Compelling Value Proposition (CVP), making you stand out from the crowd and contributing to your distinct competitive advantage.

So . . . how *compelling* is your compelling value proposition?

What Customers Really Care About

Do you think your value proposition is powerful? Would your existing customers and prospects agree? Usually when I ask business leaders, owners, and entrepreneurs those same questions their CVP is anything but compelling. They have difficulty articulating their proposition in a clear, concise way, which means they tend to launch into a lengthy description of their business model.

But that's not what customers care about. Customers not only want to know 'What's in it for me?' but also 'Why should I buy from you?' The challenge today is that they want answers to those questions quickly and in terms they understand. Unfortunately, most businesses struggle to answer the first question, let alone the second. My goal in this chapter is to arm you with a way of thinking that will enable you to tackle this fundamental opportunity, really honing in and being clear about what your CVP is. Not only am I going to present a new way of thinking, I'm going to share with you ideas, tools, and strategies which will fast track your journey.

Essentials of a Compelling Value Proposition

A good starting point is to separate compelling value proposition into three individual words. Each word has its own clear defined meaning which can be used in any number of ways, but when combined together they create three BIG words which explain what benefits you provide, to whom, and how you do it uniquely well.

Our first BIG word defined: Compelling

The definition of compelling: 'tending to compel; overpowering: compelling reasons; having a powerful and irresistible effect; requiring acute admiration, attention, or respect: a man of compelling integrity; a compelling drama'.

What key words jump off the page in the context of your compelling value proposition? For me, it's *irresistible effect*. Does your proposition have an *irresistible effect* on your customers so that it becomes a *no brainer* for them to buy from you? We'll explore this more throughout the chapter.

Our second BIG word: Value

Value can mean different things to different people and varies depending on your business model: B2B, B2C, a strategic partner, a reseller – essentially the model you adopt which defines the commercial relationship you have with your customer. However you define *Value*, your customers must perceive it in the same way, in their own minds, whether *logically* or *emotionally*.

The logical viewpoint

- What can I expect as a tangible benefit?
- What's my return for investing?
- How are my needs going to be met?

The emotional viewpoint

- What can I expect as an intangible benefit?
- What's my return on expectation?
- How are my needs going to be met?

Our third BIG word: Proposition

In the context of your CVP, think of your proposition as being the core product or service that you offer. Defining your core proposition and establishing its fit for purpose is your entry point onto the business playing field. Identifying and understanding what business you are really in is very much about identifying and understanding the key benefits of your products or services, 'outside in' through your customers' eyes. Viewing it from this perspective will make you and your business a key player on the field.

Remember:

A **feature** is what the product has or what a product is.

An **advantage** is what the product does.

A **benefit** is how the product improves the customer experience or solves a problem.

Features and advantages of your proposition should become apparent *after* the benefits have been communicated, absorbed, and acknowledged by the customer. If they themselves have been able to answer 'What's in it for me?' and 'Why should I buy it from you?' they'll be the ones leading the features and advantages conversation ('So how does it work?', 'How do you achieve that?', 'How would we get to that result?'). It's an 'outside in' conversation, not 'inside out'.

Pulling it all together and defining your compelling value proposition

Whether you're a business leader, business owner, entrepreneur, in sales, customer service, or management, you're probably passionate about what you do. You're enthusiastic about your products and services, you believe they're better than your competitors' and understandably want to tell as many people as possible about them; how your food is tastier, how your clothes are more fashionable, or how your software has more and better functions.

The challenge when communicating in this style is that the features or advantages of the product are most prominent. The core message is centred on your view of your products, which may not always reflect your customer's view or motivations. When communicating your products and services in this tone, your customers often hear: 'This is what I sell, and this is a list of reasons why I think you should buy it.'

What your customers want to hear is a clear statement which demonstrates that you understand their situation and their needs. They want to know that you recognize the challenge they wish to solve, or the outcome they wish to achieve, and they want to hear how you are going to help them address that situation. Ideally, your CVP will not only explain how owning your product or using your service will help them achieve a desired outcome; it will also explain why your business is uniquely positioned to create that outcome.

Think back to those two questions: customers not only want to know 'What's in it for me?' but 'Why should I buy from you?' One of the most important guiding principles for creating a compelling, customer-focused value proposition is that it focuses on your customer's needs, not on the features of the product or service.

Do not explain the product or service that you are selling, or embellish its features. *Instead*, detail the benefits to the customer of owning your product or using your service. This is one of the biggest mistakes that organizations make. Not only do business leaders, business owners, entrepreneurs, and individuals throughout the organization fall into the trap of building their product and service offerings inside out, as opposed to outside in – build based on the perceptions the organization holds, as opposed to researched customer wants and needs – they also fall into the trap of explaining it in the style of the internal audience.

It happens all the time, and it completely defeats the primary object of communicating with the customer. If your customers do not understand immediately what you're saying, they start to check out and all you're faced with is another opportunity missed. If you were a fly on the wall in the sales leader's office after a salesperson had failed to connect with a customer because they had been communicating in the internal language, you can be sure it wouldn't be the salesperson's fault.

The customer was stupid.

They just didn't get it.

It wasn't what they were looking for.

Wrong, wrong, and wrong. This sales call failed because you were not speaking to the customer in their world about how your product or service could benefit them.

Introducing the Benefits Track

A useful technique I adopt to capture benefit descriptions and avoid the use of internal jargon is called the Benefits Track (see Figure 7.1).

A simple inventory, in tabulation form, which drills into your CVP:

- What's the customer need or want?
- What's our solution?
- What are the customer benefits?
- How is the solution aligned to the customer need?
- What stories/case studies validate this?

Benefits track!

What's the issue? What does the customer need/want?	What's our product/service solution?	'So what?' & 'What that means is . . .'	What are your stories case studies and testimonials to support this?

Figure 7.1

To understand how the Benefits Track works in practice, let me set a scene. Suppose you work for Unilever and are responsible for the Persil washing powder product line. If I asked what you did, you might answer 'I sell automatic washing powder' and the conversation could go:

Me: Okay. So why would a customer want that?

Them: Because it keeps their clothes clean.

Me: Okay. And what does that mean for them?

Them: Well, it enables them to feel good about themselves.

Me: And if they feel good about themselves, what does that mean for them?

Them: It means they'll be able to be more confident in both social and professional situations.

Me: Good. And what does that mean? What does it mean in a social situation, first?

Them: Perhaps it will make them more likely to speak to people and maybe they'll find a partner and start a great new relationship.

Me: Sounds fantastic. What about in a professional situation?

Them: Well, if I was a salesperson and I felt more confident, perhaps I'd be better in front of customers and convert more opportunities and give my career a real boost . . .

You can see where I'm going with this, right? As we have headed down the Benefits Track, what started out as selling washing powder turned into something else entirely. The benefit statements we can draw out of the conversation include:

• Feel good about themselves.
• Be more confident.
• Start a great new relationship.
• Give my career a real boost.

Let's review a couple of other hypothetical examples which have been designed using the outputs of the Benefit Track, i.e. benefit statement driven.

Example I:
Customer: So what can you do for me?
You: Well, you know how you depend on the internet for your business, but are frequently frustrated by low connectivity and high costs?
Customer: Yes . . .
You: Well, what we do is prevent you from ever having to worry about that again.
Customer: So you can provide a better internet experience?
You: More than that. We hear all the time that the biggest frustration IT managers face is that they can't consistently provide the service that their users demand. We're like the most effective headache tablet ever developed, because we stop that pain in its tracks.
Customer: So you're telling me I wouldn't have to deal with that any more, is that it?
You: Yes. And because of that, the associated costs of downtime will be reduced which usually makes a pleasant change for the IT managers we deal with, when the finance department comes around with their usual questions, next quarter.

Customer: Okay, I'm listening. How are you going to do that for us?

You: Rock solid reliability, latest technology, new features, etc.

Example II:

Customer: You've got two minutes. Wow me.

You: Thank you. The reason for my call is to tell you that I've got a brilliant new way to further enhance your hotel chain's reputation for absolute luxury and leave a really sweet taste in your customers' mouths.

Customer: Oh yeah? What are you selling?

You: The basic answer would be complimentary hot chocolate for you to place in your rooms for your guests, but the reason I thought you'd appreciate knowing about it, is that it double ticks all the boxes for elevating your customer experience. It's gourmet, it's beautiful to look at, and our research tells us that it is the most frequently taken-away product by guests at five star hotels because it just makes them happy.

Customer: But it's hot chocolate, right? We've already got that in our guest rooms.

You: No doubt you have. I'd be surprised if you didn't already cater for that. Let me ask you though, in terms of your focus on quality, elegance, and all round sumptuousness, does your current hot chocolate offering add to that and build on that, or is it merely an extra thing?

Customer: I didn't realize hot chocolate did that, to be frank.

You: Normally it doesn't. But you know better than anyone how the tiny details are the things that customers rave about, and what I've got to offer is precisely one of those exceptional, thoughtful, tiny details.

Customer: So what's so good about it?

You: Organically grown, handpicked cocoa beans from Ghana, packaging designed by a famous artist, etc.

In each example, the one thing that I hope stands out is that the product offered is positioned initially in terms of its benefit, not its features. In the first example, the salesperson isn't selling technology; he's selling the most effective headache tablet ever developed. In the second, the salesperson is selling a way to further enhance a hotel chain's quality, elegance, and all round sumptuousness. By the time they get to the features, the customer has already understood why they should consider it, and how it would make their lives better if they had it.

This is ultimately a marketing craft that can apply to any product. If the salesperson in Example II hadn't run his hot chocolate offering down the Benefits Track first, his opening line might have gone like this:

Customer: You've got two minutes. Wow me.
You: Thank you. The reason for my call is to tell you that I represent a brand of hot chocolate, which is made from xyz ingredients and comes in sachets for you to place in your rooms.
Customer: No thanks. We've already got one of those.
You: Er . . .

How much interest do you think that would create in the customer's mind? Not very much. The first question that came to mind was: 'What's in it for me?', and there was nothing in the initial statement that answered that.

In the UK, an electronics and appliance chain store have a wonderful example how a Benefits Track approach can enhance your positioning. In the electronics and appliance market, it's typical for customers to visit a store, buy an appliance, and pay for home delivery. It's fundamentally fine, but fraught with inconvenience. Retailers usually set delivery times according to their own schedules as opposed to the customer's schedule (thinking inside out, note) and offer no additional benefits.

Currys, perhaps in recognition of this, fulfils this requirement a little differently. Now as you read this, see the Benefits Track in action and how it makes your proposition more compelling as it delves deeper:
We offer guaranteed delivery slots.
(This is pretty common, so a fairly neutral benefit)
If you order before 15h00, we'll deliver the next day.
(This is less common, so a little better, but perhaps still not a major benefit)

The next day, could be any day, because we deliver seven days per week.

(This is much more unusual, and actually, that sounds really convenient for me)

On the day that suits you best, we'll also deliver within a two-hour time slot.

(Most of the time, you're given a morning or afternoon time slot and have to stay at home waiting, so this is really helpful)

Our delivery people will call you 30 minutes before they arrive to make sure you're home.

(If I have to step out to go to the shops or something, I can. Meaning I can get on with my day)

We'll also deliver to the room of your choice, remove all packaging, install your new appliance, and remove the old one.

(So all the extra work is done for me, all the inconvenience of disposing of the old appliance is taken off my hands)

It means you have complete flexibility to arrange the delivery to suit you. We will save you time and make your life easier; instant installation to your chosen room, removal of all packaging, and disposal of the old appliance.

Benefit, benefit, benefit, all the way. Very simple, yet very effective.

Zooming In and Zooming Out

One of the seven guiding principles of the Business Growth Transformation Framework® is Productive Paranoia; being able to examine your business in terms of its smallest details, and then zoom out, to take a macro view. In that context, how broad or how focused can you go with the concept of a compelling value proposition? The answer is, there is no limit.

The CVP of planet Earth is that it has a life-supporting atmosphere, liquid water, a comfortable temperature, and all the natural resources required to make life both functional and comfortable. In the context of the other planets in our solar system, that's wildly compelling! The CVP of individual countries could be measured by their ease of doing business, the amount of red tape, or the quality of regulation and compliance. In fact, each department or business unit in an organization should have its own CVP. Each leader in the business should have one. And so should each employee.

When Technology Impacts Your Compelling Value Proposition

Technology by its very nature is at the centre of advancement in every conceivable field and that has been evident in business since the dawn of the computer age. As much as technology has the ability to modernize in progressive steps, it also has the capability to overturn industries with dizzying speed.

One obvious example where technology impacted the compelling value proposition significantly is book retail, which Amazon.com entered into in 1994. In 2015, just 21 years later, Amazon.com was the largest retailer in the world by market capitalization, and along the way, it had a profound impact on the traditional bricks and mortar retailers that had dominated the marketplace.

The Amazon story is well known, but what has been vastly under-analysed is the reason for the slow response of those traditional bricks and mortar book retailers. Until Amazon entered the market, there was nothing basically wrong with the business model; a well-stocked retail outlet in a major shopping area, where customers happily spent time inside, browsing and buying. To this day, there is nothing fundamentally wrong with what is often a great shopping experience.

The flaw however is that today's consumer predominantly prefers to browse in an outlet (such as the World Wide Web) where they can pretty much guarantee to be able to purchase the book they want and have it delivered to their door without having to leave home. Nobody could have predicted that, but that's the impact of technology. Technology used to be an *enabler* of your compelling value proposition. Amazon and similar organizations have demonstrated that technology is your platform to deliver your compelling value proposition.

So how does *your* compelling value proposition shape up? Can you describe what you do in terms of customer benefits? Do you have documented success stories? Do you need to do some work to enhance it? If it's not strong and compelling, you probably only need to look a little deeper to find the CVP. Most organizations have one, they just aren't drilling deep enough, and have got themselves caught up in describing *what* they make or *how* they do things.

Don't let another day go by with a weak value proposition. A compelling one can literally open the door to potential customers, while a weak one will keep the door closed.

So, Are You Ready?

In this question lies hidden one of the biggest mistakes business leaders, business owners, and entrepreneurs make: you convince yourself that you have a compelling product or service that the world is waiting for, without undertaking any honest market research, testing, or even simple questioning. Now that may sound harsh, but it happens all the time. Many times I've met aspiring business professionals with big ideas. They have invested their life savings, built up personal debt, and made sacrifices based on a market or customer need they've convinced themselves exists. Even though they can't answer the first, most basic question of whether the market or customers actually want it. It breaks my heart.

The BBC television show *Dragons' Den* demonstrates this point all the time: people present their business idea to a team of investors – the Dragons – and when they've made their very vigorous pitch, they fall over on the first question: 'Who is your ideal customer for your product/service, have you tested their response?' What they have created is so compelling to them they can't believe it won't be compelling to others. Simple market research can prevent that. You think your idea is compelling? Good, you can't get passionate about it otherwise. Ask others if they believe it is too, but don't assume they will.

Market Research Through Your Customer Lens

Now you may say to me: 'Royston, Steve Jobs, one of the most legendary product developers and marketers in the world . . . he never asked customers what they wanted; sometimes a savvy inventor just knows.'

Well, yes and no. Apple actually has undertaken a great deal of market research over the years and continues to do so to this day. The story of Jobs knowing better than his customers refers to the iPad, a totally counter-intuitive product for its day, with no hard drive, no keyboard, no network connections save for a SIM card and the internet.

He is famously quoted as saying: 'If I asked customers if the iPad appealed to them, they would have said no because they didn't know what they didn't know.' It's heralded as a triumph of visionary product development and so it deserves to be. But that's only because it worked. What if it didn't? What if Jobs was wrong? Years before, Apple had tried to develop a mobile product that was the spiritual precursor to the iPad, called the Newton, which utterly failed.

You must be very careful about basing your approach on the one exception to the rule. Jobs was right about the iPad, but most companies understand that market research makes solid, practical, commercial sense.

In your attempt to discover if your big idea is compelling to others, you can take a range of approaches, which suit a range of budgets. If you're a large organization, market research companies can offer research solutions across countries and continents that include; consumer focus groups, face-to-face consumer interviews, and surveys, all to test the broad appeal of your product or service whilst appreciating any local nuances. On the other hand, if you're a smaller company – a solo entrepreneur or small partnership for example – you can and should undertake market research. Ask friends, family, your connections on social media, or any association you belong to . . . just ask them what they think.

If you recall, one of the seven guiding principles of the Business Growth Transformation Framework® is: Are you building your business inside out or outside in? Well, that's exactly what we're talking about here.

Summary

What customers really care about are the tangible and intangible benefits they will receive when using your product or service. How do you ensure you meet the logical and emotional needs? Through your compelling value proposition, your three BIG words.

Do not explain the product or service that you are selling, or embellish its features. *Instead*, detail the benefits to the customer of owning your product or using your service. Use the Benefits Track to sharpen your focus, and help articulate the benefit statements of your product or service.

Build your compelling value proposition through your customers' lens; use benefit statements to articulate what's in it for them, why they should buy from you; test the concept, receive feedback, learn and improve. All traits of a high performing business that delivers accelerated, sustained, and profitable business growth.

Chapter 8

Customer Strategy

'Customers want memorable experiences and organizations must become stagers of great experiences.'

Are you and your business a stager of great customer experiences?

There is a massive philosophical shift happening in the way businesses around the world are having to think about how they acquire, maximize, and retain customers and it's affecting your business right now. Where you have previously been able to focus your energies on building great products and services as a competitive advantage, taking your business to its full potential is going to require something quite different in the future. The difference will be the experiences you can provide for your customers. (Note: to keep it simple I'll refer to the generic term customer throughout but the term client is implicit.)

How significant is this philosophical shift? According to Gartner, one of the leading research firms in the world, 95% of business leaders see customer experience as the key competitive battleground. Keep that number in mind because in this chapter we'll look at why the shift is happening and what you can do to find a leading position and points of differentiation in your business growth strategy.

The Big Idea

Let's start by putting customer experience in context so that we can agree it's not just a faddy idea, but a cast-iron common sense approach to growing your business. What if at the start of your new financial year I said you could employ another ten or a hundred or even a thousand salespeople without expanding your people budget? What if those salespeople had no motivation for promoting you to customers you have never met, other than the fact that they are outright believers in your business, what you do, and how you do it?

Do you think that could make a difference in helping you grow your business? I am assuming the answer would be yes, absolutely.

What if I told you that you already have them, and that they are already primed to hit the ground running and go out and sell for you? Does that sound like sheer wishful thinking?

Actually, it is anything but. It just requires a shift in your mindset as to how you think about your customers. I want you to stop for a moment and think about the number of customers your business has right now, because they are your brand new elite sales force.

If traditional thinking has been 'the purpose of a business is to create customers', the new way of thinking is to 'create customers who create customers'. Now that's a different way of thinking. To create customer advocacy and genuine affiliation; to create raving fans who will go out into the world and tell their friends, neighbours, and colleagues just how good you are; to create customers who become your 24/7 sales force.

Is that a pipe dream or a reality? Well actually, many businesses are doing it successfully, right now. Let's talk precisely about how you can make it a reality in your business.

The Experience Economy

We've seen the demise of the *industrial economy*, which was focused solely on the efficient production of goods, and we're now past the peak of the *service economy*, which wrapped products into bundles of services to make them more attractive to customers. Now we're in a new age of competition . . . the *experience economy!*

The experience economy is the latest manifestation of customer preference, and products and services are simply the props that companies will use to engage customers in the future.

> 'Customers want memorable experiences and orga-
> nizations must *become stagers of great experiences!'*

Customers are more informed, more educated, and have even more choices than ever before. The critical question is: what can you do to make your business the partner of choice for your customers?

'Where dreams come true . . .'

To clarify what a great customer experience looks like on the ground and in the real world, it helps to look at some of the companies at the leading edge of this change. In any new business philosophy, there will always be idea originators followed by early adopters, and in this instance, one company in particular is renowned as one of the originators in creating memorable customer experiences: Disney.

The very idea for Disneyland was germinated during a Sunday trip that Walt Disney made to an amusement park with his two daughters. While he waited for his daughters to finish their rides, the successful animator began to watch the other customers and how they reacted to the park. He asked himself how this experience could be improved.

Walt's answer was to create a new kind of amusement park, and since the beginning, Disneyland and all of the company's parks have been intensely focused on the 'guest' experience. When you talk to Disney cast members (the name given to all Disney employees, who are seen to have a 'role' to play in the grand production of every day experience at Disney) about the parks, you will hear them described as 'living movies', movies in which the guests themselves participate.

As if no elaboration was needed, Walt himself simply said: 'Disneyland is a show.' With the infusion of some practical magic, your business could be too!

It wasn't enough to have the best rides if the rest of the visit wasn't also exhilarating and special. His strategy in creating Disneyland became ultimately what that company is best known for: immersive experiences of joyfulness from the moment guests enter the gates, until the moment they go home. Disney has earned an enviable reputation for turning its customers into its sales force.

Isn't customer experience just good customer service packaged differently?

A question I'm frequently asked is 'OK, I understand conceptually the idea of the customer experience, but what is the difference between a service and an experience?' Let's take a look at this first (Figure 8.1), in order to demonstrate that it's not just a semantic difference.

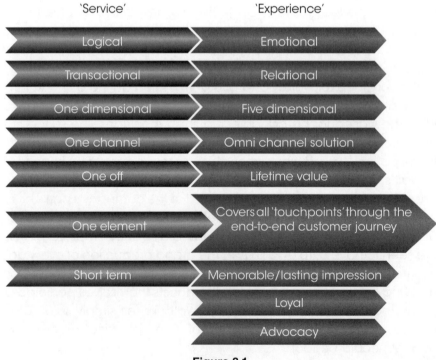

Figure 8.1

The four psychological needs of the customer

Exploring this notion of service versus experience at an even deeper level, there are four specific psychological needs that we must satisfy when creating and delivering world-class customer experiences. So what are these four needs?

1. The tangible needs
2. The informational needs
3. The intangible needs
4. The affiliation needs.

Let's bring these to life with a really simple analogy. Do you have a favourite restaurant you frequent on a regular basis? I do. In my case it's a great Italian called Ristorante Italiano Buschetto.

The first psychological need

If you went there to satisfy your tangible need, what do you think you would you be looking for? A meal, right? The tangible need in this case is food. So the tangible need is the physical product or service that you provide.

But there's a challenge facing Ristorante Italiano Buschetto just like all restaurants, which is this: if you did a Google search of restaurants within a small radius of around three miles, there are 72 other restaurants offering their own tangible needs. There are Chinese, Thai, Indian, French, Greek, Turkish, and at least four other Italian restaurants.

That's a crowded marketplace to compete in, and it's unlikely therefore that the tangible needs alone, however good they may be, will be enough to differentiate it from the competition. In fact, those tangible needs merely give Ristorante Italiano Buschetto the right to exist and to compete, as a baseline.

In the *experience economy* there has to be more!

The second psychological need

Now, imagine that you arrive at Ristorante Italiano Buschetto, are seated, given a menu, and you place your order with your waiter.

You may think this serves the informational needs, and that you've been offered everything you require in order to make your selection.

But then, a waiter walks past with two dishes that look fantastic, and leaves an aroma behind him of garlic and herbs that hits your nose and sends all your senses into overdrive. You call him over and ask what it was, and he tells you that it's fresh lobster served on linguine with the chef's special garlic and herb sauce. It's very popular and utterly delicious.

You comment that you can't believe you missed it when you were reading the menu, and the waiter smiles. 'Ah well you see, that dish isn't on the menu; it's on today's specials board.' Since he never told you about the specials as you were ordering, how do you think you'd feel at that point? Not so positive any more, I'm guessing. I certainly wouldn't be, and all because the waiter missed the opportunity to proactively satisfy my informational needs. Proactively being the operative word!

As a Ristorante Italiano Buschetto regular, you may be generally pleased with your regular choice, because you know it's going to be great, but you're also irritated and feeling a little like you've missed a great opportunity. An hour later, as you're paying the bill, the waiter asks if you enjoyed your food and all you can think to respond is 'Yes, but . . . I wish I'd had the fresh lobster in garlic and herb sauce.' You're a disappointed customer and all because your informational needs were not satisfied in a proactive way. Your previously favourite restaurant has disappointed you.

Out of the four psychological needs, this need is the least satisfied, and yet one of the easiest to fulfil for your customers! And how much extra would it have cost to fulfil the informational need? Nothing! In a world where the BIG things make little difference, it's the little things that make a BIG difference. The little things usually cost very little, but they can be game changers in raising the bar on the overall experience you deliver to your customers.

Putting this in the context of your business, if, after placing an order for a product or service, customers contact you for a status update and to chase where it is, there should be an alarm bell ringing that the informational needs of your customer have not been satisfied in a proactive manner.

Recently, I worked with a team of solicitors who were concerned about the number of customer complaints they received. I was called in to train the front of house staff and found them to be personable, professional, and able to provide a great first impression of the business. The problem, as it turned out, had nothing to do with them. A deeper look into the organization revealed the worrying fact that 80% of the incoming calls were from customers requesting information from the partners who weren't proactive enough in managing their informational needs.

Those calls would say things like: 'I need to speak to Frank. He said he would call me on Monday and it's now Thursday but I have heard nothing' or 'May I please speak to Lorraine? She promised to send through a contract four days ago and I've heard nothing.'

I'm sure you can recall personal experiences where your informational needs have not been satisfied. I know I can. How does it feel to you, to have to chase people to find out what is happening? Are you doing this to your customers?

Informational needs must be satisfied to educate your customers and keep them informed throughout the entire end-to-end customer experience, including:

- The first touch point they have with your business
- During the buying process
- Before delivery of your product or service
- During delivery
- After delivery . . .
- . . . to the ongoing regular contact through your omni channel 'touch point' strategy.

The bottom line is that satisfying their informational needs is key to your customers having the peace of mind to enjoy doing business with you. Informational needs can make the difference between your customers being your brand advocates and your sales force, or quietly slipping out the back door of your business.

So think about this for a moment: on a scale of 1–10 how good are you and your business at satisfying the informational needs of your customers across your end-to-end customer experience? Take some time to think this through. It deserves substantially more than a cursory thought.

The third psychological need

Intangible needs. Let's go back to Ristorante Italiano Buschetto to see how this one works in real life. Imagine you walk in and the waiter says: 'Hi Royston, Hi Jane (they greet you and your partner by name), we haven't seen you for a while. Would you like your usual table in the corner? The couple have paid the bill and are just finishing their coffees. Why don't you go through to the bar and I will prepare the table and come and get you in 10 minutes?'

How would you feel at this point? I think most of us would feel pretty special. However, the waiter goes one step further: 'Can I get you a drink while you're waiting, Royston do you want your usual, a Peroni? Jane a gin and tonic, Bombay gin isn't it?' How are you feeling now? Even more special? That's satisfying your intangible needs in action!

You're probably already imagining how far you can go with this, and it's limitless. What if while you're drinking your Peroni, the waiter points out the specials board to you and takes you through them, describing each one and answering your questions. I'm confident you'd call that a memorable experience, and it's a great example of how intangible needs can be brought to life.

Intangible needs are all about the emotional engagement and connection with the customer, creating a lasting impression and leaving them feeling individual, special, and unique. As Carl W. Beuchnar once famously said: 'They may forget what you said, but they never forget how you made them feel!'

These emotional needs of your customers can be as far-ranging as

- Pride
- Importance
- Excitement
- Peace of mind
- Ego gratification
- Curiosity

- Winning
- Pleasure.

Customers have specific emotional needs that need fulfilling at each stage during the end-to-end customer experience. Great businesses have not only taken the time to understand the emotional needs of their customers at each point in the customer journey, but designed their experience to meet and fulfil these needs.

On a scale of 1–10 how good are you and your business at satisfying the intangible needs of your customers across your end-to-end customer experience?

And finally, the fourth psychological need

Affiliation needs. Picture the following scenario; you go to work on Monday morning and you're talking to one of your colleagues. They're racking their brain to think of a great restaurant to take their family to for a celebration next weekend and they ask you if you can recommend somewhere.

What's the first place that pops into your head? Ristorante Italiano Buschetto, of course. You ask if they like Italian food and when they say yes, you have the enormous pleasure of being able to say: 'Then try Ristorante Italiano Buschetto. When you call, mention my name and they'll give you a great table and look after you.'

That's Affiliation in ACTION!

Affiliation in ACTION

Innocent Smoothies is a brand that has built a fantastic band of loyal fans through relational activity with their online community. They listen to their customers' opinions, answer all personal messages, and have a wall of love in the office showcasing their biggest fans. By investing in their fans, and making all interactions memorable, innocent recognize these individuals as the first to recommend innocent products to their friends, family, and colleagues. Some are so affiliated with the brand they have innocent tattoos!

The entire concept behind fan clubs is that they enable you to develop deep affiliation with followers and supporters. Ask any loyal follower of their sports team whether they would change their allegiance and support another team and they will look at you as if you're insane, regardless of how their club is performing. In good times and in bad, they are affiliated to their team. Loyalty cards are another strategy that organizations use to create affiliation and of course keep you coming back for their products or services (the maximization and retention of the fundamentals of business growth).

Affiliation is all around you; some of it in the form of subtle approaches, some of it much more overt. But there is a common thread running through affiliation techniques: authenticity. People rally around authentic ideas as easily as they will reject those that are not.

One of the main psychological needs humans have is to belong; to feel part of a special group; to achieve a status of importance often based on nothing more than our unique knowledge. Organizations that are able to meet these needs build a band of loyal customers, who buy again and again and again.

That's about creating customers . . . who create customers! That's about turning your customers into your sales force . . . and that's about customers who STAY, SAY, and PAY, and drive the sustainable, commercial success of your business growth model.

On a scale of 1–10 how good are you and your business at building affiliation with your customers across your end-to end customer experience?

The prize of getting this right

This whole notion of the experience as a differentiator is not just the latest fad or buzzword. The prize of getting this strategy right in your business is 'true' differentiation from your competitors, greater advocacy among existing and future customers, and a business culture where your people want to come to work every day and be the best they can be. As a result of this experience differentiation, commercial success and business growth will follow through increased acquisition, maximization, and retention of customers.

Apply the 80/20 rule and focus your efforts

In order to understand where to start applying your efforts, it's helpful to look at your business through the lens of the Pareto Principle, or as you may know it, the 80/20 rule. Consulting firm KPMG revealed in a 1999 study that rather than providing 80% of profits, the top 20% of customers actually generate profit of between 140% to 170%. That's a significant finding that makes a really compelling case for identifying who those top 20% are within your business.

That wasn't all KPMG discovered however; the results also revealed that 80% of losses come from 20% of customers and that the largest number of customers, as many as 60%, range from mildly profitable to unprofitable.

Just imagine the difference it could make to your business growth if you had a clear understanding of which customers were generating profit and more importantly how much. That knowledge would enable you to determine the precise profile of customers within your business who:

- Are profitable
- Are loyal
- Buy all the products and services they can from you and don't 'dual source'
- Place regular orders
- Share your values
- Pay on time
- Tell everyone how great you are!

Or as previously referenced, customers who STAY!, SAY!, and PAY! Of course there is a strong link here to the fundamentals of business growth: your AMR strategy and the Four Big questions that we covered together in Chapter 1. Let's look at these closely to drive home the link.

STAY = ensuring you have the right retention strategies in play and are locking the back door of your business firmly shut! It's also about maximizing the value of your customers to your business and increasing their stickiness through increased product holding and ethically locking them in. It's about truly being known for being a stager of great experiences! And of course get this part right and your customers will . . .

SAY great things about you and become your brand advocates, brand affiliates, and customer sales force!

And finally, they will PAY their bills on time and ensure your business has the key lifeline essential to your sustainable commercial success: CASH!

If you need further convincing, consider the following statistics:

- A typical dissatisfied customer will tell eight to 10 people about their problem
- One in five will tell 20, and it often takes far more positive service incidents – as many as 12 according to some thinking – to make up for one negative incident
- Seven out of 10 dissatisfied customers will do business with you again if you resolve the issue in their favour
- If you resolve it on the spot, 95% will do business with you again
- A typical business only hears from 4% of its dissatisfied customers, while the other 96% quietly go away.

The Digital Age Is Transforming the Game

In the digital age the above statistics are actually conservative. Online, a dissatisfied customer is likely to tell their entire social media network, not just the eight to 10 referenced above. For that very reason, social media in particular has changed the game for your business and for every other business out there, in both good and bad ways. Even great companies have felt the horror of a single bad service incident becoming a viral event across social media and have had to develop a totally new form of response.

Making it Real for Your Business

When you satisfy the tangible, informational, intangible, and affiliation needs of your customers, they become your #1 advocates. They become your sales force; active in the marketplace voluntarily and even joyfully promoting you and your business and the difference you make through providing a truly world-class customer experience.

The principles behind staging memorable customer experiences are not complex, and certainly don't need to be over-engineered. However, it is critical to think deeply about how you can personalize and apply these to your business.

Here are some key ideas to start you on the applied learning and personalization journey for your customer experience:

1. Ban the word 'service' in your business and start talking up the 'experience' you deliver for your customers every day.
2. Make time to map out the end-to-end customer experience across your entire omni channel solution. Your omni channel solution must eliminate the duplication and need for customers to have to repeatedly share their information. For example, in a classic multi channel environment, you may have to go through the same information every time as you're passed from one customer representative to another. Omni channel environments obviate that by being seamless whether you're calling, emailing, or contacting them in any of the other available channels. Omni channel thinking is really about being as easy as possible to do business with.
3. Map the fulfilment of the four psychological needs across your end-to-end customer experience and drill into the detail and specifics of each need at each stage. Hint: a great way to do this is to create a matrix, either electronically, on a white board, or on flip chart paper, across the top of which you capture all the end-to-end stages of the customer journey through your business and associated touch points. This, by the way, can be a genuinely cathartic experience in itself! Then, down the left hand side list the four needs in order; tangible, informational, intangible, and affiliation. You are now ready to start populating your matrix.
4. The disciplined execution of engaging the hearts and minds of your people to live the customer experience, and build a culture where the customer truly is the heart beat of everything you do. If you want your people to deliver a truly exceptional external experience

for your customers then you, as the leader/management team, should actively create a culture and environment within your business where colleagues are treated like internal customers. If you get both the internal experience and the employee value proposition right (we'll talk about this in the People Strategy chapter), your people will deliver a great external customer experience.

5. Be heroic in recovery! You can create the most detailed, world-class customer strategy and still have a bad day. Sometimes things go wrong. When they do, consider the words of the great Martin Luther King, Jr who said: 'The ultimate measure of man is not where he stands in moments of convenience and comfort, but where he stands at times of challenge and controversy.'

It's a great word, heroic, isn't it? It has energy, it disrupts your thinking, and it bursts with great potential. In the context of a customer failure, being heroic is a vibrant idea. Ask yourself this: who are the individuals in your business who naturally fall into this camp and go the extra mile to be *heroic* in recovery? Are you one of those people?

When you truly live this principle and are heroic in recovery you will create even greater loyalty and trust with your customers.

Measures That Matter

The ultimate global measurement tool linked to customer advocacy is known as the Net Promoter Score (NPS). However, there are many online survey tools available for you to create your own questionnaire to solicit feedback on how well customers perceive the experience you provide.

Other Measures that Matter in relation to your customer experience strategy could be:

- Commercial model: retention of customers, maximization of existing relationships, and acquisition of new customers
- Implementation and delivery against the customer contact strategy (more of this in Chapter 10: Business Development and Sales Strategy)

- Delivery against specific service level agreements with customers
- Compliments and Complaints (The two 'C's)
- Spot 'thermometer checks' with customers (calling them!)

Using any number of these measures will help you gauge how well you are staging customer experiences or, more importantly, how well your customers perceive you to be staging memorable experiences.

Summary

There's a lot to think about here. We've covered a number of ideas throughout this chapter and posed many questions for you to consider. Below you'll find a summary of those questions, which you can use as a checklist to carry out a mini audit on your business:

1. Is your organization a stager of great experiences?
2. Do you talk about service or experience in your business? Which do you want to be known for moving forward?
3. What's the *tangible* need you fulfil for customers? Is it truly a world-class proposition, whether a product or a service?
4. On a scale of 1–10 how good are you and your business at satisfying the *informational* needs of your customers across your end-to-end customer experience?
5. On a scale of 1–10 how good are you and your business at satisfying the *intangible* needs of your customers across your end-to-end customer experience?
6. On a scale of 1–10 how good are you and your business at satisfying the *affiliation* needs of your customers across your end-to-end customer experience?
7. What are your next steps and actions to review your customer experience strategy?
8. How are you going to measure it?

'Customers want memorable experiences and organizations *must* become stagers of great experiences!' Are you and your business a stager of great experiences?

Chapter 9

Marketing and Communications Strategy

'In marketing I've seen only one strategy that can't miss, and that is to market to your best customers first, your best prospects second and the rest of the world last.'

—JOHN ROMERO, INVENTOR

If there has been one significant change to the way in which people and brands interact over the past decade, it's social media. The impact of social media has been massive and has brought about such disruptive change that you might well have missed the full scope of it. If Facebook were a country, it would be the third largest one on the planet today, smaller only than China and India in terms of population . . . and not smaller by much. It carries more traffic than Google in the United States and almost 50% of the mobile internet traffic in the UK is Facebook.

That isn't just an interesting fact however; for companies wishing to keep control of their brand reputation, it is both a warning and an opportunity. Since 90% of consumers today trust peer recommendations and only 14% trust your painstakingly developed advertising, this puts substantial power into the hands of the people you're trying to reach. Combine that preference for peer recommendations with the vast number of people on Facebook and you have to ask yourself: are you happy with what they are saying about you?

Those everyday people conversations are taking place all over: 34% of bloggers review products and more than 24 hours of video is uploaded to YouTube every minute of every day, much of it talking about brands and products, starting and spreading rumours and creating brand-related commentary.

There was a day when brands controlled their marketing messages. Not any more. Your marketing is being done for you, even while you sleep. That makes for a very exciting world in which your customer experience strategy, as an example, can be a catalyst for conversations about your brand. It's a new world. From a marketing perspective how will you make it work for you?

The Purpose of Marketing and Communications

Let's take stock and recap the Built to Grow journey we have taken so far. By now you have a clearer understanding of what business you are really in and WHY you have chosen to be in it in the first place. You have analysed the market and identified the 'white space' of market potential and the size of the opportunity that exists. You have described your compelling value proposition explaining why customers should buy from you and what's in it for them, in simple, clear benefit statements. And you have developed your customer profiles and designed a pen portrait of your target customer. So where do we go from here?

The exciting part now is taking all that hard work – the hours you have committed to thinking, analysing, and challenging your business model – and turn that brain ache into your marketing and communications strategy; your plan for communicating and promoting your offer to your target customer in a way that inspires them to connect and ultimately buy from you.

Marketing and communications is one of those areas that most business leaders, business owners, and entrepreneurs get excited by, because we all acknowledge the immense potential of a great marketing campaign. You really won't have to look very far to find examples of marketing campaigns that have got it stunningly right and have not only created an enormous groundswell of goodwill but also increased product sales and brand preference. On the other hand, the business history books are also full of campaigns that have gone very wrong.

So where do we start? First, it is important to draw out what marketing and communications *isn't*. As I said back in Chapter 6: Market Potential Strategy, a spray and pray approach just doesn't cut it any more, and that applies to marketing as well. The first facets you may think of when you're considering marketing strategies for your products and services might be whether to focus online or offline; whether to use email or direct mail; whether to incorporate social media channels (e.g. Facebook, LinkedIn, Twitter); or whether to keep it localized and direct. Each approach offers powerful benefits and most organizations will want to combine these to deliver an integrated strategy, considering the overarching goal of reaching people the way they want to be reached. However, not all channels are created equal at all times for your products and services, your customers, or your budget, so in order to be effective, your marketing efforts will require some proper consideration.

Here are some fundamental questions to get you started:

- What do you want to be known for? How do you want to be positioned in the marketplace?
- How will you communicate with your target customer? What messages do you want to share?
- How will you reach your target customer? What channels will you use?
- What communication style will you use with your customers? What is your business tone of voice?
- How will you know if it's working? What return on investment can you expect?
- How will your customers identify your business; what is your brand or logo?

We'll talk through each of these in detail as we move through the chapter, but it's worth noting at this stage that marketing and communications is not an island. In order to develop a winning marketing and communications strategy, you're going to want to take all the learning and insight you've gained from the previous chapters and apply that thinking here.

Interdependency with Your Other Strategies

The interdependencies between marketing, business purpose, compelling value proposition, customer strategy, and market potential are so tightly woven that the boundaries where one stops and another one starts often become blurred.

It's important to recognize this because in your business if you own and manage the entire Business Growth Transformation Framework® you are in a strong position to apply lessons learned from one strategy to the next; you can easily find the interdependencies and work to make them stronger.

If, on the other hand, you're part of a wider organization that has created a stand-alone department around each strategic area, there is a real risk that those lessons won't be shared unless you take action to ensure they are. Without that bit of thinking (and action), you could end up targeting the wrong customer with the wrong messages using the wrong channel and as a result have little to show for it at the end of a very expensive marketing campaign.

The same thinking applies in terms of how your marketing and communications strategy interlinks with those of business development and sales; operational excellence; and finance and governance. If the goal of your next campaign is to drive traffic to the website, make the phones ring in the sales team, and keep the engine pumping with leads, then you had better share your plans with those other parts of the business so they are operationally ready for this upsurge.

Few things in business can be more wasteful than a poorly primed back end that can't keep up with the flood of new orders won by an effective marketing campaign. You must ensure the experience you have mapped out for your customer (as described under the experience economy heading in Chapter 8: Customer Strategy) reflects what actually happens.

That's not all. Your marketing and communications strategy is heavily influenced by, and influences in kind, your People Strategy. You see, marketing isn't just external; your marketing strategy must also include the important role of marketing internally; usually referenced as your internal communications strategy.

Going back to our three bottom line measurements once again, think about how marketing plays a role in each:

1. Are you the provider of choice for your customer?
2. Are you the employer of choice for skilled and talented people?
3. Are you the investment of choice?

While marketing clearly heavily influences numbers one and three, number two might be considered the sole domain of HR through your People Strategy. However, look a little further into other aspects of People Strategy, and marketing plays a critical role:

- Education for the teams about what business we are really in and why
- Brand guardianship: ensuring your people are an extension of your brand in the way they think, feel, and act
- Keeping colleagues updated with business performance, what is happening, why we are doing what we are doing, and any impact on the vision, goals, and stakeholders
- Consistency between external communications and internal communications: the messages being interpreted and relayed from your people and colleagues to customers.

Trends Shaping the Marketing Landscape

In Chapter 8: Customer Strategy, I talked about the experience economy, how customers want memorable experiences, and how organizations must become stagers of great experiences. Before the technology revolution where the likes of Google and Twitter could have been mistaken for nicknames, marketing was quite a simple, albeit expensive, model:

Step 1: We have a product we need to sell
Step 2: Let's advertise
Step 3: Let's write to all our existing customers telling them about it
Step 4: Let's wait for the phones to ring!

That was *then*, and you don't have to be a marketer to see the many flaws in that thinking. Fast forward to today and marketers are waking up to a new reality, characterized by five trends identified by Professor Richard N. Foster of Yale, who advises all businesses to take note.

Trend one: Always On, changing global consumer behaviour

The Always On global consumer is exactly that, always on. They are the connected customers. This dramatically changes the way a business will design and execute its marketing strategy. For example, Professor Foster's research on retailers found just 12 of 72 created a connection between shopping lists (which are an essential aspect of the shopping experience), and mobile and web channels. Only one retailer completed the loop by offering online access in-store. These types of connected experience are essential in meeting changing behaviours and your marketing and communications strategy must think in terms of how to interact with the Always On global customer.

Trend two: New storytelling tools

As consumers split their attention across multiple devices, channels, and times, marketers are responding with a different communication mix. An example of this is what is known as storyscaping; an evolution from creating advertising to creating stories in a multi-dimensional world where consumers interact with the brand through immersive experiences. Each connection inspires engagement with another and each experience reinforces the brand story.

An excellent example of this at work is the Christmas Experience, a much-anticipated December treat from UK retailer John Lewis. At the heart of the communication mix is a three-minute TV advert that typically shares a heart-warming, visually pleasing story demonstrating the affection in the giving and receiving of gifts. The launch of the John Lewis Christmas advert sets in motion the positioning, communication, and targeting of their entire marketing activity over the Christmas period from in-store design, social media, promotional material, to new product development (usually involving a cuddly toy of some description).

Trend three: Connecting the physical and digital worlds

This comes as no surprise, I'm sure. With businesses delving into the world of social media and navigating their way through new territory, they're realizing the power the internet has over the success of their business. This, coupled with an omni channel approach (more on this in a moment), provides the platform to offer a continuous experience across your brand, across multiple formats and devices, completely targeted at the customer.

Trend four: Enabling experience through technology and data

In Q4 2013, the research group International Data Corporation reported that tablets had overtaken PC shipments for the first time. As a result, savvy businesses are embracing new technology and data insights to communicate with their target customer.

Trend five: An expanding role of marketing leadership

Leading marketers are operating at the intersection between technology and story. Technology, in its numerous guises, is providing the route to market and the story is how your brand engages with customers and ultimately becomes their trusted partner.

So why is this relevant? The external environment is constantly changing; what worked today or yesterday may not work tomorrow. Your role as a marketer is to continually assess the potential macro impacts on your business and sense check your response to them:

1. Do we continue with our strategy (i.e. no change, we are still on course)?
2. Do we evolve our strategy (i.e. let's introduce social media as a new communication tool)? or
3. Do we revolutionize our strategy (i.e. let's introduce e-commence as a new distribution channel)?

Maintaining that 'outside in' laser beam focus ensures you remain in the game as a player and not a bystander.

Defining the Brand

How well defined is your business brand? Think about the great brands in the world, the ones that you would be able to speak about even if you only saw the symbol that represented them for a fleeting second. Those brands tell their customers what to expect from them, how to feel about them, what to believe, and whether or not that brand speaks to them personally, or to an entirely different audience demographic. None of this is an accident. The most important point to make about branding is this: a strong brand makes you think or feel the things *that the expert marketers who have built that brand want you to.*

Think Disney, think 'Memorable experiences.'
Think Coca Cola, think 'Taste the feeling.'
Think sofas, think 'DFS.'
Think innocent, think 'Tastes good, does good.'
Think Nike, think 'Just do it.'

Now, the examples above are all established and mature businesses. However, the same principles apply irrespective of your size, longevity, or history; brand building and brand maintenance should be a significant priority for business leaders. To remove any ambiguity about what your brand stands for you should constantly invest in it, educate consumers about it, and ensure your compelling value proposition is communicated consistently.

To get to grips with this, let me share with you the Brand Identity Map; a very useful tool that drills into the meaning of your brand and guides you through the process of brand discovery.

Brand Identity Map

Work through the following five questions in the order outlined below. Questions 1 to 4 can be completed as simple bullet points. Question

5 will require a little more thought. To help you along I have used LEGO® as an example, adopting its own wording to provide guidance so you can identify yours:

1. Brand Personality: how do we look and behave?
   LEGO® example: safe, high quality, innovative
2. Emotional Benefits: how do our customers feel when using our brand?
   LEGO® example: happy, engaged, creative
3. Rational Benefits: what tangible advantages do our customers receive?
   LEGO® example: inspired learning through play, memories
4. Brand Values: what do we want to stand for?
   LEGO® example: inspiring, creative, development

Note: there's no right or wrong here; there's only a need for authenticity. If you're a company that runs great white shark cage dives in the open ocean, you may still want to use the word 'safe' under your Brand Personality, but it's going to have a much more urgent meaning. At the same time, the most meaningful description will probably focus on being exciting, thrilling, and creating adrenaline.

5. Brand Essence – in a single sentence what do we want to be known for?
   LEGO® example: to inspire and develop the builders of tomorrow

The key to answering question 5 is to be as succinct as possible. It's about identifying your Unique Selling Point/Proposition (USP) that will set you apart from the competition, and articulating it simply and clearly.

A simple framework to start your thought process for your own business could be:

For <target customer> who want to <customer need>, <brand X> is the <product definition> that provides <core brand benefit>, because <essential reasons to believe>

An earlier version of the LEGO® brand essence before it was finely tuned might have been 'For children of all ages who want to build,

LEGO® makes the building blocks that provide fun, engaging and high quality play experiences that develop their essential skills.'

See how it works? You just keep finely tuning it until it is short and to the point. It becomes your elevator positioning pitch, everything you need to get across in one sentence. To illustrate a brand identity map in action, I've taken a consultancy business that focuses on training and people development and applied the five steps. The results look like Figure 9.1.

Your brand essence does one other important thing for you too: it guides your marketing strapline, which describes your brand in as recognizable way as the logo does. Many people in the world would recognize the Nike swoosh on sight; maybe even the majority of the world, it has been such a significant marketer for so long. There is also real kudos to be gained however from the instant recognition and association with the Nike brand through three simple words: 'Just do it'.

That could apply to anything. It's just a sentence. They're three simple words. They don't apply to just anything however; they tell you

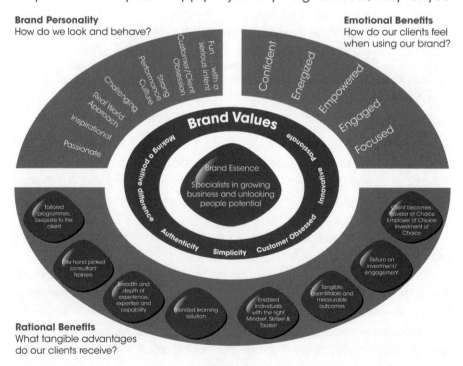

Figure 9.1

the state of mind you should adopt as a Nike owner. They tell you why you want to become a Nike owner. They *are* Nike. 'Just do it' is one of the most successful marketing straplines of all time.

Read the examples below and the chances are very high you'll immediately be able to pick out the brand, just as you did with Nike:

- I'm lovin' it
- Because you're worth it
- The world's local bank
- The best a man can get
- Vorsprung durch Technik
- Reassuringly expensive
- Impossible is nothing.

Now let's see if you got them right. . . .

- McDonalds
- L'Oréal
- HSBC
- Gillette
- Audi
- Stella Artois
- Adidas.

The purpose of your marketing strapline shouldn't be just to create a pithy saying that might be catchy and cool; it's a serious thing. It should become a memory hook for your customers and your potential customers. It should help create affinity with your brand. Rarely will you see Nike advertised without the strapline 'Just do it' deeply interlocking those two concepts.

Once you've defined your Brand Identity Map the next step is your marketing and communications strategy.

Writing Your Marketing and Communications Strategy

One of the easiest things in the world today is to find a book, a website, or a blog about marketing. That's how valuable this strategic field is to any business. I'm not going to talk endlessly about marketing theory here, because as with the Finance and Governance chapter coming up later in the book, I believe there is enormous benefit in learning this subject in-depth, and that would necessitate me writing a whole other book on the subject.

What I do want to do here however is give you some practical ideas to help you write your strategy. In doing so, what you will create is a single document that combines all of your marketing goals and priorities as well as action plans and time frames, all of which align with the strategic objectives of your business.

You've probably heard the principle of spending an hour to save five minutes (those five minutes being saved over and over again, forever, thanks to the hour long investment you have made), and that's precisely the point of a structured marketing strategy. Don't allow these ideas to live in your head, or to be the basis of informal, or even formal discussions; your marketing strategy is one of the most important strategies you will ever develop, and it's worth taking the time to get it right.

The points you're going to want to cover include:

- Section 1 – Executive Summary
- Section 2 – Market Potential & Target Customer
- Section 3 – Compelling Value Proposition & USP
- Section 4 – Product & Service
- Section 5 – Price & Market Positioning
- Section 6 – Distribution (Place)
- Section 7 – Promotion
- Section 8 – People
- Section 9 – Processes (Customer Journey)
- Section 10 – Presence (Physical Evidence)
- Section 11 – Financials
- Section 12 – Marketing & Communications Key Strategic Priorities
- Section 13 – Marketing & Communications Key Performance Indicators/Metrics
- Section 14 – Conclusions/Summary

To add some extra weight to it, I'd really urge you to consider how current and future trends will inform that strategy, so that you can include them. As outlined earlier, an experienced marketer will have their ear to the ground, keeping an eye on new and emerging trends and evaluating them against the marketing strategy, to decide whether they are ideas worth investigating.

Why building your marketing and communications strategy is like building a jigsaw puzzle

As you read through the list of section headers you will realize a number of sections are covered in other chapters of this book. For example, section 2 Market Potential & Target Customer is covered in Chapter 6: Market Potential Strategy, section 3 Compelling Value Proposition & USP is covered in Chapter 7: Compelling Value Proposition Strategy, section 11 Financials is covered in Chapter 13: Finance and Governance, and so forth. All the different pieces of the 'marketing jigsaw' are included either in this chapter or in this book and it is simply a case of bringing the pieces into one place, into your marketing and communications strategy.

To help you build section 4 through to section 10 of your marketing strategy (your jigsaw) there are a number of 'pieces' I want to share with you.

The Marketing Mix

One theoretical model is the Seven Ps of the Marketing Mix, a useful framework to ensure you cover every marketing component. This has been around for a while in an evolving format; it was first proposed to marketers by Edmund Jerome McCarthy, Professor of Marketing at Michigan State University in 1964, as the Four Ps, and has been adapted since then to include three additional components.

Here's what I would like you to do. Using the Seven Ps detailed in Table 9.1, work though each 'P' and look at what you're doing in your business in that area. What are you doing now? What is working? What is not?

Then, consider what you could be doing in each. You may find that your pricing strategy is too one-dimensional to be broadly appealing or to capitalize on opportunistic events. You may find that you're missing a great potential channel or that you're not maximizing a

Table 9.1　Seven Ps of the Marketing Mix

Product	Price	Place	Promotion	People	Processes	Physical Evidence
Features, Availability, Quality, Branding, Image.	Positioning, Discounts, Payment methods.	Channels, Sales support, Distribution.	Direct marketing, Digital marketing, Communication, PR, Branding, Referrals, Strategic partnerships.	Culture, Communication, Recruitment, Reward, Training, Development.	Customer journey, IT, Sales E2E.	Shop, People, Materials, Website, Packaging.

key channel. The purpose of this exercise is to help you identify your strategic marketing priorities and align them to your strategic business goals.

After completing this exercise on your business you may have identified, for example, four marketing and communications strategic priorities as being:

1. Articulate a meaningful brand essence with brand values and action
2. Create a digital marketing presence through the use of social media
3. Re-position technical experts as thought leaders to create a competitive differentiator
4. Create a compelling E2E (end-to-end) customer experience.

By completing the Seven Ps exercise you will have drilled into each 'P' and identified what is working and what is not working; consequently you will have identified where you need to focus. This exploratory insight will form part of your marketing strategy along with the insight you have gained from working through previous chapters in *Built to Grow*. You should now be pulling all these strands together, and it must come as no surprise why marketing and communications strategy is at the centre of the Business Growth Transformation Framework®.

Channel management: Multi channel vs. omni channel

Prior to the technology revolution it was a given that the distribution of your product to your target customers would either be direct (i.e. by mail) or by means of a retail environment. Then of course came the internet. The now firmly established concept of e-commerce took off; a phenomenon only two decades old at the time of writing, but one that has been sufficiently strong to put many retailers on the back foot, and many more out of business entirely because they were too slow to react to this unstoppable force.

This has changed the way you should be thinking about channel management – it's a matter of real urgency that any organization takes this seriously. A traditional 'bricks and mortar' only approach may have reached its sell-by date; the old world multi channel approach, where some things were bought by mail order and others were sold through retail outlets, may be seeing you through, but if you're still getting away with that approach, perhaps you have a particularly niche product set. It's almost a certainty that you too will have to evolve your multi channel approach to an omni channel approach before very long.

I watched a presentation not that long ago with a marketer who highlighted the change in a really interesting, and perhaps alarming, way. One day when he was out shopping with his daughter, he watched as she photographed everything she saw that she liked and would like to purchase, so that she could go back home, look the product up online, learn about it, and search for the cheapest price. Think about that. Though she was in a retail outlet, she was treating it only as a conceptual showroom. Kids today! When her dad asked her about it, she said that was the way everyone she knows in her age group does it. Consider how connected these shoppers are to social media, to blogs, reviews, and so on, and the customer experience they expect you to provide has changed already, whether you know it or not.

It doesn't just apply to teenagers. Many adults have long since reduced their visits to physical supermarkets, bank branches, travel agents and so on, and are simply making their own rules for how they will engage with you. An omni channel approach is therefore one that enables physical shopping, online shopping, and information across various forms of media, and almost anything else you can think of. It's awesome, but it's also dangerous. Finding the right mix, without missing something important or getting too carried away, is a significant function of your marketing strategy.

I cannot reinforce enough the alignment and fusion required between your end-to-end customer experience and marketing strategy. Omni is not just about the media channel and process journey, it is everything to do with the experience and emotional connection with your customer. You cannot afford to look at these in isolation or for there to be a disconnect.

Customers are going from screen to store and store to screen as part of their buying behaviour. Are you factoring this into your plan? Are you mapping customer journeys and experiences adopting an omni channel?

Adding value through thought leadership

We should not underestimate the importance of this, today. Thought leadership is a type of content marketing where you tap into the talent and passion housed in your business to provide solutions to your target audience problems without mentioning your product or company at all. It can be as big as producing a white paper or research report or more simply an 'expert' view on a particular topic. It is often used as a way to create or increase demand for your product or service.

So I hear you say 'OK, Royston. I write something of interest to my target customer and I don't mention our products or the company, but it's going to increase my sales. Have I missed something? How does that work?'

Well, do you recall the boomerang principle I mentioned earlier in this book? If you seek to give more than you get, you'll get more than you give over the long run. Thought leadership is the boomerang principle in action. How much value are you adding? What difference are you really making? If you get these two right, you will have customers who STAY and SAY great things about you to others.

The Customer Buying Zone

One of the main responsibilities of a marketing function is to generate leads, and more importantly the right type of leads. Leads the salespeople can ultimately convert from a prospective sale into an actual sale.

Converting prospects to customers can be a long game especially when potential customers are not ready to buy immediately. This 'lead nurturing' is a process of providing prospects with the information they need to make buying decisions, keep the business brand at the forefront of the customer's mind, and for the salesperson to be ready and available when the customer is ready to commit.

You may ask. 'Why is lead nurturing important? Surely if a prospective customer wants to buy something, they go ahead and buy it.' Yes they go and buy it . . . but from whom? You or your competitor? Lead nurturing enables you to:

- Engage potential customers early and develop a relationship *before* they are ready to buy
- Provide potential customers, or even existing customers making a repeat purchase, guidance and support with their buying decision
- Ensure potential customers understand the value of your product or service and not just the price of the solution
- Differentiate you from your competitors, and start the journey of developing trusted partner status.

So, the BIG question: How do you identify where a potential customer is in their purchasing decision? Are they ready to buy now or are they just browsing for ideas?

The Customer Buying Zone (Figure 9.2) identifies four states of mind a potential customer will move through en route to making a purchasing decision. In parallel, it identifies the opportunities for us to initiate, interrupt, and nurture them towards making their decision.

One: Unconscious state of mind

In this state of mind, the potential customer is unaware that there is a risk or opportunity on the horizon. As a consequence, they are

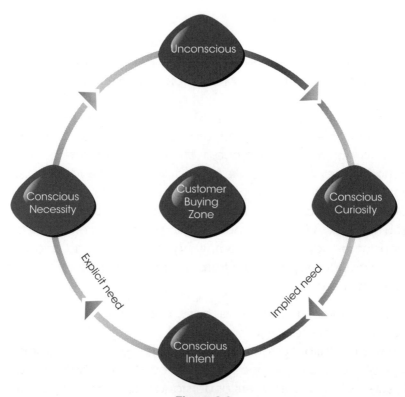

Figure 9.2

oblivious to the potential need for a solution and, more importantly, may be oblivious to *your* solution.

To move the potential customer from an unconscious state of mind into the next state, conscious curiosity, will require specific marketing interventions. This is your opportunity to nurture using the tools and techniques suitable for your business and potential customer, for example, advertising, brand awareness campaigns, direct market-ing (digital or traditional), referral programmes, thought leadership. Raising awareness is your primary objective.

Two: Conscious curiosity

The potential customer is now consciously curious. They are aware of the risk or opportunity on the horizon and are becoming increasingly aware of possible solutions. They may be aware of your product or service (or may not!) and those of your competitors. However, they may be unclear or unconvinced as to why your solution is what they need.

In this state of the mind the potential customer will undertake personal research to understand the solutions available and will reach out to others for opinions or guidance. This part is key and can be a deal breaker even *before* you knew there was a sale to be had.

So imagine the scenario: a potential customer who you don't even know exists has started to research your business and what you can offer. They may go immediately online and view your website, your social media sites, and anything else interesting they can find. They may speak with their friend who recently purchased from you, who may say: 'Well, whilst the product is good, we did have to chase for information on delivery dates and the salesperson we originally spoke to was just trying to sell to us.' Now what is your potential customer starting to do? They are starting to form an opinion and brand perception of you, your product, and your service.

Continuing with our scenario, let's say your potential customer acknowledges her friend's feedback but is still interested to learn more about your business and what you offer. So, they make a visit to your store, or they ring your call centre seeking information, guidance, and assurances that you know what you are doing and can deliver. Clearly this interaction can go one of two ways and you don't need me to illustrate it here. The key point is this: how confident are you that the interactions your potential customers are having with your people are moving them positively into the next state of mind, conscious intent?

Three: Conscious intent

Conscious intent means your potential customer is now informed about the options available to them. They are aware of you, your competitors, and have started to identify preferred providers and solutions. However, they are still unclear and unconvinced as to why they should choose you over your competition.

This is your opportunity to shine. Using all the insight from Chapter 7: Compelling Value Proposition Strategy and having applied the Benefits Track to your products and services, you can WOW this potential customer with your product benefits, not features. In a succinct sentence you can explain your proposition and why they should choose you. You are now one step closer to closing the sale.

Four: Conscious necessity

In conscious necessity, your potential customer is now fully informed, actively seeking to buy, and looking for reasons why they shouldn't buy from you, a state known as buyer's remorse. Don't give them one. Instead give them confidence and assurances and reinforce with action.

Using the insight from the Customer Buying Zone and overlaying the four psychological needs of customers (Chapter 8: Customer Strategy) you can map your key customer touch points. Those interactions, before, during, and after a sale, which can mean the difference between winning and losing a potential customer.

So you have all the jigsaw pieces. You have everything you need to write your marketing and communications strategy. You have the insight, the analysis, the opportunities, and your priorities. It is now simply a matter of making the time and creating the headspace to write it.

Turning Strategy into ACTION Through Your Marketing Plan

If the marketing and communications strategy is your WHAT, the marketing plan is your HOW. In your marketing plan, you'll take the strategic priorities from your strategy and build a detailed tactical plan for achieving them. It will include objectives, action steps, milestones, budget allocation, owners, and specific key performance indicators (KPIs). It may be a yearly overview with a detailed half yearly or quarterly plan sitting alongside.

For example:

Strategic Priority 2

WHAT: Create a digital marketing presence through the use of social media

HOW: Sign up to social media channels ensuring correct usage of the brand and tone of voice

a. WHO: Marketing Manager
b. WHEN: 30th March
c. WHERE: Facebook, Twitter, LinkedIn
d. Key Measures: Fans 100/Followers 100/Visitors 100.

Clearly, in the real world you would have a number of strategic priorities and a number of deliverables against each one. The plan is the detail and should follow the SMART principles (Specific, Measurable, Attainable, Realistic, and Timely).

It is your task list to deliver the marketing and communications strategic priorities, which are the enablers to the business achieving its goals and objectives and ultimately its vision.

Measures That Matter

Your Key Performance Indicators (KPIs) are an imperative element of your business growth strategy. If you don't know what's working how do you know what to change or improve?

There are a number of KPIs that should be on your radar but the most important thing to remember is that you need to be able to measure them. There is no point building a complex dashboard of metrics if you haven't the means to measure the results. Identify the KPIs you absolutely need and want to track and then ensure you have the tools in place to measure the outcomes.

The KPIs I would consider to be vital include:

• Sales growth derived from marketing effort, the mail shot you sent, the event you held, and what actual sales it generated

- Leads and opportunities created from the marketing effort
- Lifetime value of a customer
- Website traffic and lead analysis: unique visitors, impressions, hits, landing page conversions
- Social media reach and engagement: followers on Twitter, likes on Facebook
- Email marketing performance: delivery rate, click through rate, unsubscribe rate
- Inbound link building: when someone links to your website it means you're building credibility within your industry as an authority. Better link building means better search rankings, better search rankings means increased traffic to your website
- Blog posts visits: What do people like to read? Are they staying active with your content? Are you building brand equity as a result?

Tracking your marketing KPIs will help validate everything you do and provide you with transparency in your marketing efforts.

Summary: A Science . . . and an Art

Marketing has the power to take an otherwise unknown entity and launch it into the global marketplace like nothing else can: marketing is an artistic, clever, beautifully creative force. Great marketing ideas can go viral and today we have the peculiar phenomenon of people wilfully choosing to share adverts or ideas they have enjoyed, extending your marketing far wider than you might ever have been able to do yourself.

But if creating beautiful ideas is your sole activity as a marketer, you place yourself in a dangerous position of potentially spending money in all the wrong places. Since user activity is no guarantee, the scientific heart and soul of marketing is important to acknowledge. If you are structured and focused on measurement, return on investment, understanding of optimized channels, demographics, and all the parts of the Marketing Mix, you can often be better off choosing consistency over artistry. Marketing is an art, but it is first and foremost a science. Solely dependent on all the other parts of your organization, perhaps more than any other, your marketing efforts cannot be executed with a silo mentality. Reaching out to others can take you places you may never have considered. For that reason alone, it's worth investing heavily in understanding this further and making it a critical area in your overall business growth strategy.

Chapter 10

Business Development and Sales Strategy

'Sales is the lifeblood of any business.'

There is a direct correlation between sales and revenue, so in delivering accelerated, sustained and profitable business growth, your Business Development and Sales Strategy is critical.

Sales has the ability to transform your business into a profitable organization capable of fulfilling a gap or previously unmet need in the marketplace. This is the reason why all businesses exist: to serve a customer, in some way.

If operational excellence represents the arteries of the organization, sales is the heartbeat that feeds your business.

Internal Brand Positioning of Sales

Now of course, the word 'sales' can carry negative connotations for some people, possibly as a result of ineffective, relentless telemarketers and the wave of 'mis-selling' in recent times.

Despite that association, sales is a profession, an art, and a science. It is a part of the business you should embrace and be truly proud of. It demonstrates your positive intentions through a consultative, relational approach to understanding your customers' needs and aligning the right product and service proposition to meet them.

The ultimate goal of sales is to achieve one of the three bottom line metrics: becoming a provider of choice . . . and the cornerstone to achieve that is: TRUST. As world-renowned sales expert Zig Ziglar so aptly put it: 'If people like you they'll listen to you, if they trust you they'll do business with you.'

Trust doesn't come with a refill. Once it's gone, you probably won't get it back and if you do; it will never be the same. Respect is earned. Honesty is appreciated. Trust is gained. Loyalty is returned. Your sales strategy will be judged by its ethical underpinnings as well as the sincerity of your intentions as a provider of real solutions, which truly address the needs of customers now and in the future.

Who's in Sales in Your Business?

To sense check how a business thinks about sales from a cultural standpoint, I always ask the following question: 'Who's in sales in your business?' For every 100 businesses I ask, only around 1% will provide the right answer to this question.

Leaders will talk about a dedicated sales function. They might reference anyone who interfaces with the customer. They might even say they do some part-time sales through their interactions. However, for me the succinct, focused answer to this question is simply:

'EVERYONE.'

Yes, that's right. Every business professional should be familiar with sales concepts, theories, and techniques. Client support teams, marketing, HR, operations, finance, governance, and any other 'non sales' people in the company who may think they don't need to know about sales need to think again. The direct correlation between sales and revenue should mean everyone has a vested interest and skin in the game in delivering sales.

A significant decrease in sales means a decrease in revenue. What happens when there is a consistent decrease in revenue? You guessed it: potential cut backs and layoffs abound. Fortunately, the opposite also rings true: if you create a great new product, sales increase and your company grows. Each and every employee has the ability to positively impact the company's sales.

Think about the opening quote in Chapter 1: The Fundamentals of Business Growth:

> 'Strategically, the primary purpose of a business is to Acquire, Maximize, and Retain the right customers. Everything that contributes to this is an investment; anything that doesn't, is a cost!'

The essence behind this message is Sales in action!

One of the Seven Guiding Principles of the Business Growth Transformation Framework® is 'outside in thinking'. In sales, an 'outside in' approach is about understanding customer needs and aligning your solution to address that need. That's sales in action too.

When 'outside in' thinking is firmly embedded in your performance culture and your people are aligned to delivering the business growth agenda, you are embarking on the journey to effect accelerated growth.

Now let's unpack the critical ingredients in creating your Business Development and Sales Strategy.

A Scientific Approach

Sales is a science, therefore following a specific sequential series of actions in the creation of your Business Development and Sales Strategy is essential. Think of it as your recipe for selling success. You'll recall the example I shared earlier; *MasterChef* contestants follow tight, sequential recipes in order to realize the specific, predictable results they want.

The same applies to your Business Development and Sales Strategy, which I have broken into six powerful, interlocking, simple ideas and tools:

1. Sales Planning and Forecasting
   How to ensure there are 'no surprises' in your planning and forecasting through a top down and bottom up approach.

2. Your Customer Classification Framework

A bullet-proof method of understanding which customers offer you the greatest potentiality for growth and therefore where you should be focusing your efforts and time in order to maximize and retain them.

3. Your Proposition Matrix – getting customers to buy more

One in three customers do not buy your complete range of products and services simply because they don't know you offer them. Your personalized proposition matrix will allow you to understand your current product penetration and give you a structured approach to maximization and increased retention.

4. Your Customer Contact Strategy

Through a deep-rooted understanding of the cost to serve, and the 'outside in' view of how customers want to be contacted, you can design a commercially viable, proactive, Customer Contact Strategy.

5. Your Sales Map

Your personalized sales map will allow you to track the progress of sales from the point of lead generation right through to the point of conversion. This is critical to forecasting in real time.

6. Your Sales Funnel

Identifying your lead generation activities, which feed your sales pipeline, will help highlight what's working and what isn't. Your sales funnel will also help capture any golden nuggets and ideas you may be missing which could create a torrent of quality opportunities for your business.

That's a snapshot of each of the interlocking ideas and tools. Now let's look at each of them in detail:

1. Sales Planning and Forecasting

We've already highlighted the direct correlation between sales and delivering the revenue goals for your business. In creating your Business Development and Sales Strategy, it makes logical sense for this to be the starting point.

In my experience, most businesses are poor at planning and forecasting. They default to a 'top down' approach based on two factors. First, the historical performance of the business over the last few years ('We've grown roughly 10% year on year over the last three years, so let's target sales with 10% growth again') or second the executive, or senior leadership have lofty growth ambitions for the business aligned to the 3- or 5-year plan and set a target which is cascaded to sales teams with the message 'This is what you need to deliver'.

Now while top down planning is undoubtedly part of the sales planning process, we are missing the other critical part, the scientific element: 'bottom up'.

Your top down/bottom up approach

The key to effective planning and forecasting is to adopt a top down/ bottom up approach, and allow the two ways of thinking to meet in the middle.

Now, there might be a gap or tension in the middle ground between the top down aspirations and what the bottom up approach is say-ing can realistically be delivered. However, it is better to have the discussion at the start of the year as part of a proactive planning discussion, than to have it when it usually happens in a business: three or six months into the year when you're already scarily behind on the numbers, on the back foot, and trying to play catch up.

As I bring the top down/bottom up approach to life in the following example, you will see how AMR is a fundamental ingredient in your ability to forecast accurately.

Top down . . .

Using a top down approach to your sales planning and forecasting, the types of questions you would ask include:

- What does growth look like from both a revenue and profitability perspective over the last three years?
- What are the trends?
- Which products and services are really performing? Which aren't?

- Thinking big picture, what are the growth ambitions and aspirational goals for the business?

Taking into account external factors that will influence your thinking:

- What is happening in the broader economy? What major milestone events are going to take place this year (for example, a general election)?
- What are the trends in the industry or sector in which you operate?
- What are your competitors up to? Specifically; who is growing, who is blowing the market away, what are they doing and what can we learn from them?

A lot of this rich information should be available to you through the analysis undertaken in market potential and marketing strategy and is critical to your effective sales planning. That is your top down approach, and you probably recognize it, because it is by far the most commonly used approach to sales planning and forecasting.

A complete and accurate forecast also requires a bottom up approach.

. . . and bottom up

This is where the formula and science aligned to your AMR comes in and you start to build an accurate picture of what is going to happen in the middle ground of your top down/bottom up approach. Will the two align or is there some further analysis required or expectations to be managed to arrive at aligned thinking from both perspectives?

If I were coaching you as a business owner, business leader, or entrepreneur with *a revenue line last year of £1,000,000*, the first question I would ask, in assessing where your focus should be this year, is: 'What is the natural customer attrition rate in your business?' No matter how good you are at retention, there is always some attrition and that has to be factored in. A low attrition rate demonstrates that you are good at the 'R' part of AMR; a high attrition rate tells you immediately where you have work to do. Let's say attrition is 10%. Right away, you know that of the £1,000,000 you achieved last year, you can only expect around £900,000 this year, based on that rate of attrition.

The second question: 'How much of that revenue is locked in as annuity/recurring revenue, that will reappear this year?' Let's say you have £500,000 locked up in annuity revenue.

Okay, so the next question is: 'What's the potential for growth in the existing customer base?' This speaks straight to the 'M' of AMR. Let's say you acquired some new customers last year who are now going to deliver the full 12 months of revenue from the beginning of this year, and those customers are worth £300,000 in revenue.

Adding £300,000 to your £500,000 in annuity revenue gives you £800,000 in forecasted revenue for this year. With £800,000 in expected revenue from Maximization and Retention, the 'M' and the 'R' of AMR, you know that your Acquisition of new customers, your 'A', has to deliver £200,000 just to stand still as a business and generate the same £1,000,000 revenue as last year.

If your goal is to deliver 10% growth this year on top of last year's revenue achievement, you'll need to bring in £300,000 of business through new customer Acquisitions; £200,000 to close the gap and £100,000 to achieve the 10% growth.

Understanding the numbers is imperative in your planning and forecasting. Table 10.1 summarizes the key numbers in tabular form.

Table 10.1   Sales planning and forecasting aligned to AMR

Key questions aligned to AMR	The numbers (£s) in our example
1. Revenue last year	1,000,000
2. 10% year-on-year attrition	(100,000)
3. Adjusted position	900,000
4. Forecast annuity/recurring revenue for new financial year	500,000
5. Maximization of existing customers	300,000
6. Forecast revenue line (point 4 plus point 5)	800,000
7. Gap to just stand still as a business versus last year	(200,000)
8. Aspirational goal of 10% growth this year	(100,000)
9. Real gap (point 7 plus point 8)	(300,000)
10. New Business Acquisition Target	300,000

If I were coaching the owner of this business there would be a series of questions which spring to mind based on the numbers:

1. Can you reduce your 10% year-on-year attrition in order to retain more of that revenue?
2. Is there an opportunity to maximize your existing customers further in order to unlock more revenue and profit potential from them? I'd also want to see a customer by customer analysis and breakdown of the £300,000 forecast for maximization
3. Is £300,000 for new business realistic? What current pipeline are you carrying into the new financial year and when is this likely to convert?

Through this process, you'll create a clear picture of where you need to find AMR opportunities. To unlock some of those opportunities, let's review the second key idea and tool.

2. Your Customer Classification Framework

Pareto's Principle, more commonly known as the 80/20 rule, is broadly used because of its almost universal applicability. If you're new to it, it's a formula developed by Italian economist Vilfredo Pareto in 1906 to describe the unequal distribution of wealth in his country, observing that 20% of the people owned 80% of the wealth. Over the years, it has been observed that the 80/20 rule can be applied almost anywhere.

For example, it's often the case in organizations that 80% of revenue and profit comes from 20% of customers while the majority of customers (80%) deliver comparatively little revenue and profit. In a second example, 80% of sales may come from 20% of your products and services.

Your business is probably similar. High value customers are great, but it opens you up to risk if you're dependent on a small number of key relationships. If just one leaves it can really hurt your business and growth aspirations.

The Customer Classification Framework is designed to clarify and assess where you have risks and opportunities. It is designed as an internal tool, giving you key insights and intelligence for making informed decisions about how to grow your business. It should not be used externally with your customers.

Using the framework

First, categorize your customers into classification bands: Platinum, Gold, Silver, and Bronze, or Tier 1, 2, 3, and 4. It doesn't matter which method you choose, only that there are clear classification bands. The classification is based on a customer's spend over a 12-month calendar period aligned to the financial year of your business.

It is important you use the 'total spend/value' of the customer.

Why is this a critical point?

Depending on the nature of your business you may have a customer who purchases multiple products and services. For example, I might have my personal account, my joint account with my wife, my business account, our home mortgage, our life insurance policy, and our two children's accounts, all with one financial service provider.

A number of these products and services are probably with different divisions but in the world of Omni and Customer Relationship Management, they should be viewed as my total product holding and my customer classification should reflect this.

You hear so many examples where one part of a business has damaged a relationship with a customer who is a key customer of another division, resulting in them leaving. A holistic view of the customer is critical.

Example to illustrate the framework in action

This example represents a client in the technology industry with 210 clients. The overall revenue for this company is £20 million, of which £13.3 million comes from just 20 customers. Talk about the 80:20 rule in action!

The sales manager in this business has set the classification bands as follows: >£300,000 for a Platinum customer, £125,000 to £300,000 for Gold and so on (see Table 10.2 columns 1 and 2 for classification bands and value).

Table 10.2　Customer Classification Framework

Classification Band	Classification Band value of total annualized revenue	Numbers of customers based on previous year's annualized revenue	Profitability (Average gross profitability by band)	Potentiality what's the potential value through proactive maximization?
Platinum	£300>	10	42%	To be validated
Gold	£125K to £300K	10	63%	To be validated
Silver	£25K to £125K	69	55%	To be validated
Bronze	<£25K	121	28%	To be validated

Mapping the 210 customers into the framework provides a fascinating insight into how many fit into each category. There are 10 Platinum customers, 10 Gold customers, and 69 Silver customers; 121 customers are classified as Bronze, delivering less than £25,000 per annum. That's a significant tail.

In Table 10.2, a profitability column is included, which shows the aggregate profitability for each band. This data provides critical insight and intelligence into who are the most profitable customers. When you apply this insight to your segmentation and customer profiling (Chapter 6: Market Potential Strategy), you'll tighten your focus on your key target market and pen portrait of ideal customers.

Understanding potentiality

Potentiality is your 'acres of diamonds', the potential growth lying dormant or hidden within your existing customer base. You've already invested the time, effort, and money to acquire them; are you maximizing the benefits of that investment through proactively managing and developing the relationship?

I have helped organizations understand the concept of potentiality over the past two decades, and I have never seen a business where their potentiality isn't at least *double the current revenue*. This is especially true for mature businesses. Often it is much higher. Very few companies have maxed out the potentiality of their customers and acquired all of their customers' business.

So, in Table 10.2, column 5, I have introduced a potentiality rating for each customer. You'll see that, in all four categories, I have simply put 'To be validated'. This would be achieved through proactive engagement and annual account reviews with your customers. Once you understand the potentiality of your customers, I guarantee you will have Silver customers who could be converted into Gold and Gold customers who could be converted into Platinum and so on.

For example, you might have a customer who is currently in the Silver band, and through understanding their needs and wants you have unlocked a number of opportunities. With the right focus you could grow them into a Gold or even a Platinum customer.

In this instance, the key design principle is that the 'potentiality' rating overrides the current rating, which was based on last year's revenue. This will become a really important point, and one which we'll cover in more detail, when we loop back to it later in the chapter under Contact Strategy.

Your personalized Customer Classification Framework provides several benefits:

1. It creates clarity and focus on your sales priorities
2. It highlights which customers should get the maximum focus of your retention efforts
3. It enables you to proactively manage and reduce your risk and exposure to your Platinum customers
4. It helps you target the mid-tier Gold and Silver customers in proactive Customer Relationship Management to move them up from Silver to Gold and from Gold to Platinum
5. It helps you understand your revenue 'gap' and what you need to deliver through new customer acquisition
6. It enables you to apply commercial modelling to develop a greater understanding of where you can add most value to which customer, in order to deliver the best revenue and profit.

Having populated your Customer Classification Framework, your next essential insight tool is your Proposition Matrix.

3. Your Proposition Matrix – Getting Customers to Buy More

One in three customers do not buy your complete range of products and services simply because they do not know you offer them! Are you and your business unknowingly part of this statistic?

A thought-provoking question, isn't it?

Some say the problem is even worse, that it's closer to two out of three. Of course it may be different if you have only one product or service. One well-known media company I coached in this area had just four products and services, yet their penetration rate of all four products into their customer base was just 1.27%.

There was a caveat; when we profiled the client base we discovered only 10% were prime for all four products and services, but even so there were still phenomenal growth opportunities lying dormant in their existing customer base.

Bringing this idea to life

If I were coaching you and your team, one of the first exercises I'd ask you to complete would be to write down on a piece of paper, in five seconds, a number that equates to the total number of products and services your customers can buy from you.

In nearly 20 years of doing this exercise, the response – 99.9% of the time – is the same: I have yet to find an organization with more than 20 people and more than 10 products and services where there is instant and unanimous agreement on the total numbers of products and services they offer.

If your team cannot quantify the precise number, who else can't? Your customers! The number one reason customers do not buy ALL of your products and services is that they simply don't know you sell them. Now, whilst being a challenge it also offers one of your greatest opportunities for creating accelerated growth.

Could this be the case in your business?

1. Have you ever come away from a customer meeting and thought, 'I should have asked about . . .'?

2. Have you ever had a customer tell you they've bought a product or service from someone else, which they could have bought from you?
3. Are you missing sales, and cross-selling opportunities of products and services, to current customers?
4. Do you have a process to educate and up-sell to customers your full value proposition of products and services?

If you answered yes to any of the first three questions and a resounding no to the fourth, then you'll find enormous benefit in the Proposition Matrix. The Proposition Matrix is a success formula that guarantees you and your people will consistently educate your customers on your full range of products and services, and it's simple to put into practice.

Imagine a grid, a chess board, like the one in Figure 10.1. List all your customers on the vertical axis and all your products and services on the horizontal axis. Then colour in the meeting square where the customer currently buys your product or service.

The squares that remain uncoloured are your 'acres of diamonds', and through an ongoing process of educating and engaging with your customers on those open spaces, you can start to maximize

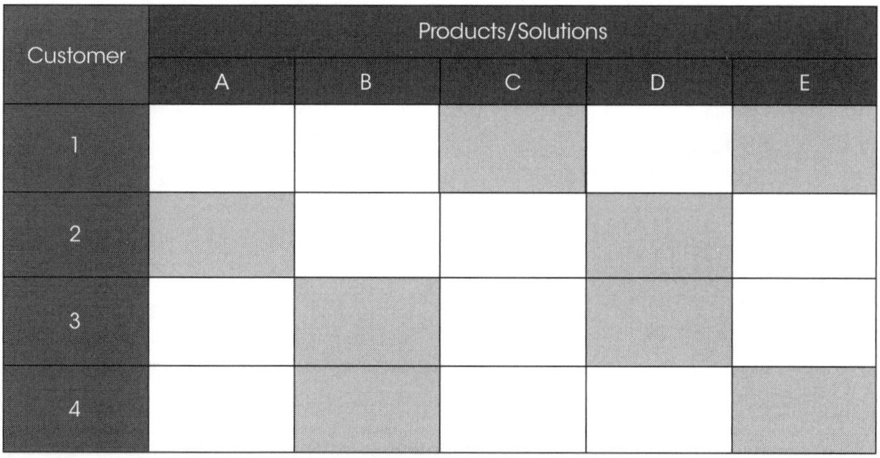

Customer	Products/Solutions				
	A	B	C	D	E
1					
2					
3					
4					

Figure 10.1

and unlock the potential in your existing customer base. Education and engagement can be achieved through face-to-face contact, email marketing, direct mail and telesales, or any number of other media.

There are differing surveys, articles, and expert opinions on the frequency with which customers need to see or hear about your business in varying forms. However, the underlying message is the same: the process of education and engagement never stops.

Measures that Matter: Penetration rates

It is fascinating when you start to measure the penetration rates of your products and services. There are three critical measures to focus on. First, the overall penetration of your products and services into your entire customer base; second, your penetration by product; and third, your penetration by customer (see Figure 10.2).

If you have a dedicated sales team, it is also fascinating to analyse performance by individual. All sales people have favourite products and services, which they prefer to sell. The Proposition Matrix is a great way of identifying skills gaps in knowledge and ability, and

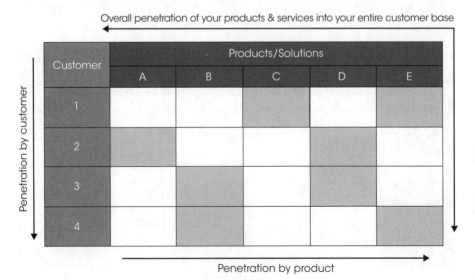

Figure 10.2

understanding which of your salespeople are best at selling which products and services.

The benefits of the Proposition Matrix

What if I told you one business I coached grew from £3 million to over £12 million in just two years by understanding its business better through the Proposition Matrix.

Or that a major media company with over 500,000 customers and just four products and services increased sales to existing customers by 227% on one product line and 183% on another in just six months.

What impact could the implementation of this strategy have on your business?

Personalizing the Proposition Matrix for your business

1. Identify your list of customers and prioritize them on your matrix by classification band. Depending on the number of customers you have, you could have separate matrices for Platinum, Gold, Silver, and Bronze customers. This process will give you in-depth data to inform your market potential strategy for each customer profile.
2. Have a separate matrix for new business, dormant, and prospective customers. Yes, the Proposition Matrix will work just as well for acquisition activity.
3. Create your Matrix either in Excel or linked into your software/CRM system.
4. Identify which customers have bought which products and services and design your education and engagement strategy to target the gaps (your acres of diamonds).
5. Track the Measures that Matter in terms of overall penetration, by customer, and by individual product and service proposition.

As you start to layer your Client Classification Framework with further insight about product and service penetration through your Proposition Matrix, the next thing you need to develop is a strong, proactive Customer Contact Strategy.

4. Your Customer Contact Strategy

There are two key considerations when designing and personalizing your Customer Contact Strategy.

The first: what is your approach to Customer Relationship Management? If you operate B2B, who are the key contacts in the customer business that you need to foster and develop relationships with and vice versa – who are they aligned and backed off against in your business?

This is such a critical part of your Contact Strategy. The breadth and depth of contacts are critical in both businesses. If you only have one contact in the customer organization and that contact leaves, not only do you lose that personal relationship, but also the entire relationship between your two businesses could be at stake.

Similarly, if you only have one person in your business managing all your key customer relationships, you face a major risk if they leave. Especially if they move to a competitor.

The second consideration: ensuring there is an effective schedule of contact between members of your business and your assigned customer contacts, is ensuring you keep up to date about potential changes they may be considering and can work those into your plans. There are few things more wasteful than a customer who silently defects to another supplier entirely without your knowledge, because you didn't have open dialogue.

In Table 10.3, alongside the Client Classification Framework, I've added in two additional columns: Customer Relationship Strategy and Contact Strategy.

A fundamental design principle of your Customer Contact Strategy is having a real understanding of the cost to serve by customer versus their annualized revenue contribution, profitability, potentiality, and lifetime value.

For example, you might have a Platinum customer who requires regular face-to-face meetings, weekly calls, and exchange of emails. From a business perspective their value warrants this level of commitment to the relationship.

Unfortunately, in life he who screams loudest often gets the most attention. In business, the customers who often are the most

Table 10.3 Customer Classification Framework working in conjunction with your Customer Relationship and Contact Strategies

Classification Band	Classification Band value of total annualized revenue	Numbers of customers based on previous years annualized revenue	Profitability (Average gross profitability by band)	Potentiality what's the potential value through proactive maximization?	Customer Relationship Strategy	Contact Strategy
Platinum	£300>	10	42%	To be validated	4 named contacts to include: Director Professional Services, Director Managed Services, CRM and Technical Lead. Where appropriate Executive/Board Sponsor	CRM minimum monthly FtoF/twice monthly benchmark. Director's minimum of quarterly FtoF. Technical Lead as appropriate to Client need.
Gold	£125K to £300K	10	63%	To be validated	4 named contacts to include: Director Professional Services, Director Managed Services, CRM and Technical Lead. Where appropriate Executive/Board Sponsor	CRM minimum bi-monthly FtoF/ monthly benchmark. Director's minimum of half yearly/quarterly FtoF. Technical Lead minimum of half yearly/however appropriate to Client need (Technical Lead portfolio of up to 5 Gold clients).
Silver	£25K to £125K	69	55%	To be validated	3 named contacts to include: Director of either Professional or Managed Services, CRM and Technical Lead.	CRM minimum of half year FToF/quarterly depending on potentiality, Director's minimum of half yearly FToF Technical Lead as appropriate to Client need
Bronze	<£25K	121	28%	To be validated	Desk based Account manager, Director Technical Leads, etc. called on depending on Client needs identified	Minimum half yearly/quarterly depending on potentiality

demanding of your time are those in the Bronze band, the least profitable. Without an effective Customer Contact Strategy, the risk is that you respond to your Bronze customer in exactly the same way as your Platinum customer, giving them a disproportionate amount of your time compared to their value.

Let me be clear, this doesn't mean Bronze customers aren't important, or that you shouldn't strive to provide them with an excellent service. It's about assessing whether it's commercially viable and sustainable to give them the same level of service as a Platinum customer.

Another important point is to understand how your customers want to be engaged. You might think they need quarterly face-to-face meetings when actually their preference is for one annual face-to-face meeting, backed up by quarterly calls. Many businesses over-complicate and over-engineer their contact model, introducing unnecessary cost and impeding the viability of their cost to serve.

A Customer Contact Strategy enables you to be systematic, structured, and logical in your approach with the goal of increased performance across the 'M' and 'R' parts of your AMR strategy.

Applying this knowledge to new customers

The majority of the chapter so far has focused on Maximization and Retention, but let's not overlook our 'A': Acquisition, as it is an equally critical strategic component.

Acquisition is a two-way street: customers have more choices and feel educated to make those choices, while organizations should be more strategic and targeted in the way they acquire new customers.

You'll recall the quote: 'the primary purpose of a business is to attract, maximize and retain the *right* customers.' The word 'right' isn't used loosely. To get great customer service, you have to be a great customer. Using the tools and techniques provided throughout *Built to Grow* and applying them to your business you should now have clarity on what a great customer looks like for your business.

It should be a two-way process; customers choose you as their partner of choice and you choose them based on their profile. Think of it as your 'customer headhunting programme'.

A key tool to help you understand where you should be focusing your customer headhunting activity is the Sales Map.

5. Your Sales Map

In sales, predictability is everything. Your ability to predict your sales results with a high degree of confidence is critical to keeping your entire business growth strategy on track. Culturally the one thing people dislike in sales is surprises. You see what happens to share prices when profit warnings are announced – they become extremely volatile.

The purpose of the Sales Map is to ensure there are no surprises coming from your sales strategy. Instead you deliver predictable, repeatable, sustainable results every time.

Think of the Sales Map as your satellite navigation

When you set your satellite navigation device, what is the first piece of information you type in? The destination, of course. The end point. The goal. And in understanding your current position, it is able to set a route for you to follow. You are immediately given all the information you need, including the time to the destination and the distance. It might even give you different route options in terms of the route you can take: major roads only or direct as the crow flies, taking in every minor road on the journey.

When you start the journey at any given point you have real time data in terms of your position. If there are road works, traffic jams, or obstacles ahead it proactively informs you, giving you options on alternative routes. It is an intelligent, dynamic system, putting you the driver 100% in control.

The Sales Map (Figure 10.3) is your satellite navigation device for your business. You set the destination, type in the critical data, and the intelligent dynamic tool does the rest. Its job is to get you where

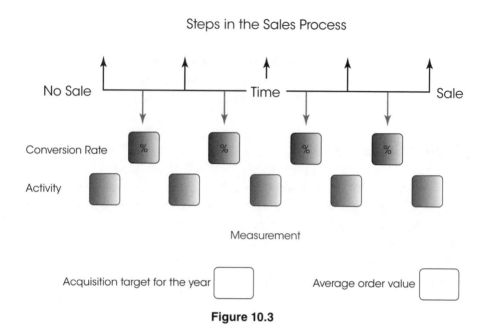

Figure 10.3

you want to go in the best possible way and in the optimum time. Let's look at how it works.

The horizontal line represents time

The horizontal line represents time from No Sale to Sale. This is important, since knowing your average timeline from 'initial enquiry' to 'business won' is critical. For some businesses, it can be instant; for others it can be months or even years.

Why is the timeline critical? If your goal is to deliver £1 million, £10 million, or £100 million of 'realized' revenue then the definition of 'Sale' and the timeline become really important.

For example, the key sales period for a gym is January, what with the New Year's blues and all the well-intentioned goals people have at that time of the year! Let's imagine the gym wants to acquire 500 new members in the month, but only achieves a target of 300. For every month that ticks by during which it doesn't make up the 200 member shortfall, it loses incremental realized sales of 1/12th, which creates pressure to make up the 'gap' by having to increase the number of members month on month.

A second example might be a plant hire business that acquires a new customer with an annualized spend of £50K on equipment. If you win the customer at the start of the year, you will realize the full value within the year. However, if you only win the customer at the half-year mark, their contribution to the overall sales target for the year might only be £25K. In your planning and forecasting, therefore, the timeline impacts the personalization of your Sales Map.

Above the 'time' line: Identifying the key steps of your sales process

I use the word 'key' steps. This is not about every call, every ring back, or relentless follow up. What you need to capture here are the critical steps in your sales process.

Below the 'time' line

There are two key elements below the line: the conversion rates for each step in the process and the activity required at each step.

I have worked with very few businesses who track their overall sales conversion from No Sale to Sale, let alone conversion rates at each step in the process. Yet measuring this accurately is essential if you want to be truly world class at pipeline management and have certainty in your planning and forecasting.

By measuring the conversion rate of each step, you can deep dive into what is working and where blockers might exist. For example, skills and capability gaps of individuals who may be struggling with one particular step.

The second element is activity, the important part from a pipeline management perspective. The science behind the Sales Map will give you the activity required in order to deliver your overall sales plan for the year.

The numbers and a Sales Map in action

As a worked example, let's use a Sales Map for the £1 million revenue company we used earlier in this chapter – see Figure 10.4.

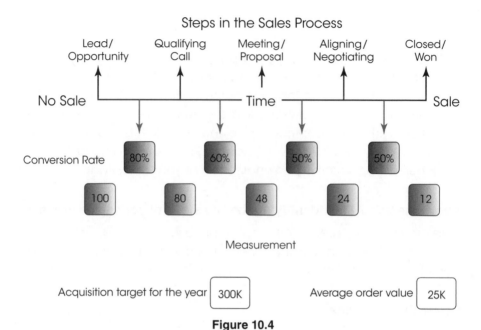

Figure 10.4

From the earlier example we calculated that to deliver a 10% growth to £1.1 million, the acquisition/new business target for the year needed to be £300,000. You'll see 300K inserted in the left hand box, at the base of Figure 10.4.

The next critical question: what is your average order value? Note the term 'average'. This is your mean average if you take out any one-off big deals or small deals, which might distort the figure. For this example, I've used a hypothetical figure of £25,000.

So based on an acquisition goal of £300,000 and an average order value of £25,000 you would need to acquire 12 deals this year, represented by the 12 inserted in the box on the right hand side of the Sales Map beneath the closed/won stage.

Now you might have already picked up that we're approaching this from an unexpected direction. When I do live coaching sessions with the Sales Map and ask the audience where they think the starting point is for personalizing the Sales Map tool: No Sale or Sale, 90% will default to No Sale. Wrong! If we are proactive in our planning and forecasting and we know where we want to be by the end of the year, we should work backwards to identify the activity required at each step to get us to our end goal.

So, having calculated the number of closed/won deals, the next step is to decide what you think the conversion rates are going to be at each step in the process. You may not be 100% certain about this and may have to present your best guess, gut feel, or intuition, but that's fine . . . we can work with that. The key is to use some baseline assumptions and then, over the course of time, validate whether they are reality or whether adjustments need to be made. The great thing about Sales Mapping is that it is a dynamic, fluid tool, which you can adjust as your insight and empirical evidence develop.

Finally, once you have inserted the conversion rates, you can calculate the activity required at each step in the sales process. To deliver £300,000 of new business, with an average order value of £25,000, equating to 12 new deals based on the conversion rates at each of the five steps, you will need 100 new leads/opportunities.

I have developed a Sales Map template for you to personalize for your business. Once you've downloaded the document just input your acquisition target, average order value, personalize the steps in your sales process, enter the conversion rates, and the tool will self populate. Download details are available at the end of the chapter.

Now, our final challenge is identifying how to source those 100 leads/opportunities, which brings us to our final idea and tool.

6. Your Sales Funnel

Your Sales Funnel (see Figure 10.5) is the tool that plugs into your Sales Map, acting as the feeder of quality opportunities.

The science behind the Sales Map will drive the total number of quality opportunities required (100 in our example). The question is where are they going to come from?

Your Sales Funnel enables you to track where potential sales are initiated from, and how they are progressing according to

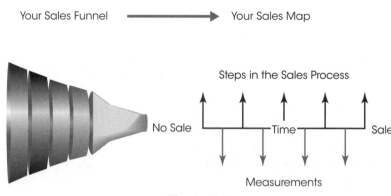

Figure 10.5

your sales activities. It is an invaluable tool because it delivers insight into:

1. Which of your sales and marketing activities are effective, both from an overall perspective and from a tactical perspective
2. Which of your sales activities related to those marketing activities are working and the effectiveness of the results of each
3. The number of prospects that enter the funnel and which result in closed sales
4. The strength and weakness of the sales strategy in driving prospects through the funnel and turning them into customers
5. The strength and weakness of individual salespeople.

How the Sales Funnel works

The funnel is divided into four categories (see Figure 10.6). The first tier nearest to the tip of the funnel corresponds to the most effective strategies: the low hanging fruit and optimum lead generation.

Working back through the three remaining tiers are strategies that you can use in your personalized lead generation model. There are hundreds of ideas that could be in here and some will depend on what works in your business and for your customer type. The purpose here is to seed the sense of possibilities, to give a structure to what and how you subsequently develop your lead generation activity.

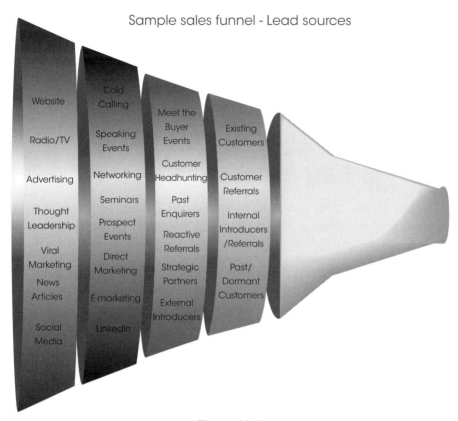

Figure 10.6

There is an obvious overlap between your Sales Funnel and your marketing strategy. The interdependency between marketing and sales becomes apparent when your sales teams have identified the lead generation activities they need to undertake, and marketing take these ideas and turn them into targeted and meaningful campaigns. Clearly, the return on investment from a particular campaign must be quantifiable and this is usually where positive tensions between sales and marketing arise. Working together will ensure both sides understand each other's perspective, but ultimately understand that everyone is working towards the same goal.

Summary: Selling Success

Your Business Development and Sales Strategy is one of the most vibrant and exciting parts of your business. Certainty, predictability, and 'no surprises' are key measures of success. Sales is the lifeblood of any business. The direct correlation between sales and revenue means there are no places to hide. Numbers don't lie; they paint a real time picture of reality. Do you really know your business reality? How effective is your planning and forecasting across AMR?

To move one step closer to understanding your business reality, download now your Sales Map template: **http://pti.world/ BTG-Toolkit**.

Chapter 11

People Strategy

'One of the greatest assets of your business walks out the door every night. What are you doing to get them to return next day inspired, motivated, and enthused to be the best they can be?'

John doesn't feel the same about work anymore. Something's changed. He used to approach it with commitment and drive, happily doing extra hours because he believed in where they were going and what they were doing as an organization. They were in this together. But now things are different. A new management structure has made him voiceless and depressed. Decisions he was once part of are now made behind his back. And the result? Discretionary effort; going the extra mile; working beyond contractual obligation have been withdrawn. Emotionally, John has checked out. The goodwill has gone. He takes more sick days now.

This hypothetical example describes a common and real scenario in businesses all around the world today, and worryingly, for many it may be considered the norm. You may not even realize, but the chances are high that within your own business you may have at least one John, perhaps even more.

One of the greatest assets of your business walks out the door every night. What are you doing to get them to return next day inspired, motivated, and enthused to be the best they can be?

Are People a Cost or an Investment in Your Business?

When I ask business owners, business leaders, and entrepreneurs what their biggest asset is, I routinely get the response 'It's their people'.

Yet most businesses don't act that way. There is a disconnect between words and actions, reflected in one significant phrase: Human Resources. The very term demotes people from being intuitive, instinctive, clever, and innovative individuals, to merely being a collective resource at the company's command. This attitude plays out elsewhere too: on a company's profit and loss statement, people typically fall into the category of 'overhead' not 'investment'.

Your people are one of the most powerful forces available to you in realizing your goals and ambitions, and the way you culturally think about your People Strategy is critical to your commercial and business success.

The BIG Idea: Creating Your Employee Value Proposition

In Chapter 7, I talked extensively about how a Compelling Value Proposition (CVP) is a key differentiator for your business in achieving competitive advantage. Similarly, in your People Strategy, your key differentiator is your Employee Value Proposition (EVP).

Your EVP is critical in helping you achieve one of the three key strategic Measures that Matter: employer of choice (see Figure 11.1).

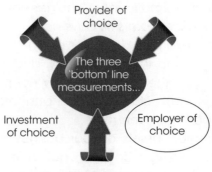

Figure 11.1

So what is a compelling EVP?

It's the balance of the rewards and benefits that are received by your employees in return for the skills, capabilities, experiences, and performance they bring to your organization. The EVP is employee-centered and designed through a deep understanding of what is important to existing and potential employees.

It must be unique, relevant, and compelling if it is to act as a key driver of talent attraction, engagement, and retention. Your EVP is the centre point of all your employee communication and experience management and, therefore, is one of your most compelling and exciting tools to inspire and motivate your people.

Is it really that important?

Gallup released numbers in 2015 indicating that only 13% of employees worldwide are truly engaged in their work. The other 87% vary from partially to fully disengaged. They come to work, go through the motions without any sense of enthusiasm that would encourage them to take ownership, and push to improve their own performance. That's terrifying!

Those numbers are echoed in other research too. According to the British Government's Office of National Statistics, in 2013 British workers took more than 15 million days off work, attributed to stress, anxiety, and depression, and in that same year a record level of absenteeism was reported. Similarly, the international healthcare group BUPA said that failure to unlock employees' *discretionary efforts* cut a potential £6 billion from the UK economy in 2012.

Unfortunately, there's no simple answer to the loss of motivation because there's no one simple cause. But perhaps a little happiness would help. A recent study by economists at the University of Warwick, England, found that happiness in the workplace led to a 12% spike in productivity, while unhappy workers proved 10% less productive. As the research team summarized: '. . . human happiness has large and positive causal effects on productivity.'

I often encounter stressed managers in the hospitality trade; despairing bankers who don't see their children; pressured recruitment consultants trying to seal the deal. Their emotional well-being is not a luxury; it's the energy source powering their performance. When it's low, their performance is low, which has both a short- and long-term impact on the business for which they work. Their well-being is measurable beyond business performance too; their lack of happiness has an impact on their health.

Jutta Tobias from the Cranfield University School of Management says: 'If you were to practise mindfulness for a couple of minutes right now, and a medical doctor had taken your blood pressure pre and post this short practice, your blood pressure would probably be measurably reduced after.'

A good exercise for any decision-maker, surely?

Maintaining a work–life balance is a topical subject and close to the hearts of many prospective and existing employees. You ignore this at your peril. Staff retention and absenteeism are real issues for business. In 2016, people management specialist, Investors in People, reported that 57% of the workforce plan to leave their jobs within 12 months.

So in answer to the question 'Is it really that important?' a compelling People Strategy is not just a 'nice to have' in your business growth strategy; it is a 'must have'. The success of your organization is hardwired to the productivity of your people, and since that calls for them to contribute their whole self, there is an absolute need for a strong, compelling EVP.

Building your EVP

Developing an EVP for an organization with a conventional HR department plays to its often untapped strengths. HR has been under pressure over the past decade to become more commercially minded and strategic. Bearing in mind the people-rich data HR departments have at their disposal, they are ideally positioned to undertake strategic people planning, delivered through a compelling EVP.

However, you don't have to have a dedicated HR function to develop an EVP, which is essential for a business of any size. To support you in building your EVP, I have developed an EVP template ready for you to personalize. You can download details at the end of the chapter.

In building your EVP, it's important to consider the entire end-to-end lifecycle of your People Strategy; from identifying people gaps, to building a robust people pipeline, growing and developing your people, and ultimately retaining them (see Figure 11.2).

1. Identifying your people gap

Are your organization's business growth strategy, vision, aspirational goals. and values aligned with a clear people and talent strategy for sustained business success? Where are the potential gaps in leadership, front line capability, support functions, and specialist/ technical expertise?

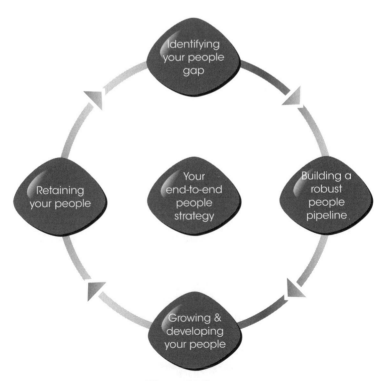

Figure 11.2

2. Building a robust people pipeline

How do you define talent? Are you unlocking potential and harnessing talent internally, and selectively recruiting externally?

3. Growing and developing your people

Have you got the right people in the right jobs doing the right things, with the mindset, skillset, and toolset to drive sustained peak performance?

4. Retaining your people

Are you keeping the back door firmly shut? Is your business perceived as the employer of choice through your compelling EVP?

Let's look at each one in detail:

1. Identifying Your People Gap

Identifying your people gaps is imperative if you want to grow your business in a sustained, controllable way. Undertaking a gap analysis will help build a clear picture of whether you have the right people on board today and where there is a need for new hires aligned to your vision and business growth strategy.

So where do you begin?

Translating your Strategic Plan into your organizational design

There are nine interlocking strategies, which together form the Strategic Plan for your business. One of the challenges is to consider how this translates into your organizational design.

For example, today you might not have a dedicated person whose sole responsibility is customer strategy. Are you going to create a new role within your organizational design or merge the ownership for this strategy into an existing role?

So the starting point is to overlay all nine interlocking strategies onto your existing organizational design, identify where possible gaps exist, and decide how you are going to close those gaps.

A leader-leader culture

In Chapter 3 we discussed at length the leader-leader model: how you can achieve great improvements in effectiveness and morale and also make the organization stronger. We also explored the cultural benefits of inverting your organizational charts or structures, with the CEO at the base, the senior executives above him or her, and the customer-facing people at the top. Then enable all decision-making to rise to the top.

In evaluating your current and future organizational design it's worth revisiting that chapter and reacquainting yourself with the merits of adopting both the overarching leadership framework and the inverted visual representation of your structure.

Is your current organizational design function or personality driven?

There is a fundamental challenge, which happens in all businesses over time. They stop viewing their organizational design from a functional perspective where roles are defined by the skills and attributes they need employees to have, and allow themselves to become personality driven. The challenge with personality driven design is it can be emotionally driven; not always in the best interests of the business and certainly not based on the 'best person for the role'.

Scenarios play out similar to these: Frank is the Managing Director's best friend, so we need to give that role to him, or Sarah has been loyal to the business, we know she is not right, but we need to keep her on. Organizational designs get increasingly complex over time because companies tend to adapt the ideal design to fit their people rather than finding people who fit an ideal design. It's counterproductive and often leads to compromises which make it harder to achieve your aspirational goals.

So here's what you can do. Once you've reviewed your current organizational design in alignment with your Strategic Plan and the leader-leader model, the next key step is to remove all personalities from the boxes on your organizational charts and focus only on the functional requirements of each role.

Ignore for now that you have a salesman named Steve, who is currently working in face-to-face sales and instead, define the skills, experience, and qualifications an ideal salesperson would have if that role was fulfilled to its greatest potential. I'll make a prediction right now: completing this exercise will have a profound impact on your thinking.

Once you have an aspirational picture of your organizational design, from a purely functional perspective, overlay your current roles and people to examine whether your real requirements match your current design. In most organizations it won't be the case at all. Redesigning from scratch gives you clarity to identify the need for additional skills training, to reassign people into new roles, or hire new people altogether.

Any early stage business owner, business leader, or entrepreneur, by completing this exercise, will see their name in many of the functional boxes. That's normal, but it's also a warning for the future. You cannot grow your business if you are sucked into performing too many operational roles so it's important to consider succession planning.

With the framework of your organizational design reviewed and future proofed against your business growth strategy you can then move into . . .

2. Building a Robust People Pipeline

In building a robust people pipeline, a leading HR Director shared with me a key principle: 'always be recruiting and developing people and talent'.

In order to deliver accelerated, sustained, and profitable business growth, your People Strategy has to be fluid and agile. You must be able to move internal talent around, to switch roles between people, and identify gaps where you need to recruit additional talent. In order for your People Strategy to work to its greatest potential, this process must be happening all the time.

In the process of 'always be recruiting and developing people and talent', it's essential you first define what talent looks like, feels like, and acts like in your business.

Defining talent in your business

It always creates a fascinating discussion when I ask business leaders, business owners, and entrepreneurs the pointed question: 'How would you define talent in your business?'

Most people challenges come about because the wrong people are in the wrong roles. This can occur for a number of reasons: a skills gap, poor behaviours, a bad attitude, lack of desire or will to develop further and grow with the business, misalignment in personal and business values, or a disconnect between an individual and their line manager. In fact, the last two reasons are actually two of the top three reasons why people leave organizations.

Ownership of some of those challenges lies with the individual, but the majority lie with the organization itself. The business leaders have not clearly articulated what excellence looks like for a particular role and end up recruiting the wrong people into the business, and we all know the impact that can have.

The right people in the right role can accelerate your journey exponentially. The wrong people can set you back 12 months in a heartbeat and be an expensive lesson both in terms of real cash and missed opportunities.

The solution is not complicated. Simply define the type of person who will thrive in your business. Here's a simple model for you to personalize.

The 2Ps . . . Performance and Potential

Talent is about an individual's performance combined with their longer-term potential (see Figure 11.3). If you're on a growth journey

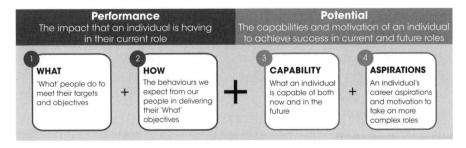

Figure 11.3

with your business, the potential part will be important for you moving forward.

In terms of performance, the WHAT is about whether an individual functionally gets the job done and how well they do it. The HOW is whether they are living the Values, demonstrating the right behaviours, and being role models for their colleagues. In a performance review and culturally as a business the WHAT and the HOW should be given equal weighting.

In terms of potential, CAPABILITY is about whether an employee is able to grow at the required pace. Some employees reach a ceiling in terms of their capability, where others continue to stretch and grow. ASPIRATIONS refer to whether employees have the desire and will to want to grow, to better themselves and fast track their career.

It's probably obvious that employees with neither performance nor potential will not last very long and they're the wrong people to have in any business. People with performance and potential on the other hand, may be the future stars of the organization. But what about employees that have one in abundance, but not the other?

Performance without Potential:

- Indicates a high performing individual who may not have the aspiration and/or the capability to go further.

Potential without Performance:

- Indicates an individual new to their role who may not have had the opportunity to demonstrate sustained high performance. Or . . .
- Indicates an individual who isn't able to utilize their capability to the fullest and may be in the wrong role

This definition of talent will be important for you to assess in conjunction with your broader strategic review of your organizational design. How can you do this?

Take stock of your people

Building a robust people pipeline requires you to take stock of where your people opportunities and challenges are so that you have a clear line of sight as to where you direct your energies. The strategic review of both your current and future organizational design will have kick started this process and given you high level insight. To do this deeper level of analysis, I recommend an audit of your people utilizing the performance and potential criteria for assessing current and future talent. There are a couple of ways to do this.

Applying Pareto's 80/20 rule provides some interesting insights

We used Pareto's rule in the business development and sales strategy as a tool for analysing which customers contribute the majority of sales and profits. A second application is for identifying and unlocking talent. Here's how it works:

- 20% are top performers
- 70% are the heart and soul of your business and . . .
- 10% are disruptors.

The toughest part for leaders is adjusting their leadership style according to the three categories. How you lead and manage a top performer will be completely different from how you lead and manage a disruptor.

Experience tells me most leaders get drawn into spending a dis-proportionate amount of time in the 10% category. Just like the bottom 10% of customers in the Pareto sales example who contribute the least profit and are the most problematic, so are the disruptors within your People Strategy.

There's no sugar coating this – most of the time the people who fall into this category are just not right for your business. If you have a business with clear performance expectations and a systematic review process – then the people in the bottom 10% know who they are.

When you share this with them, they usually leave before they're asked. A business has no spare seats and there are no free rides; seats or roles are all filled with the right people, doing the right things, at the right time, and in the right way. HR procedures and governance to manage the disruptor group requires significant amounts of time.

The challenge as a leader is this: from a people perspective which group or groups of people are going to enable you to fast track your growth agenda at break neck speed?

First, it's the top 20%: top performers

The challenge with top performers is that they coast in fifth gear. The exciting opportunity is that they always have reserves in the tank and can easily find sixth gear.

The top 20% are probably team members who deliver consistently year on year. They need little management – you set the goals, point them in the right direction, and they're off. They have a great atti-tude, are self-motivated, and know precisely what they need to do in order to exceed their targets and goals. If you need quick wins or to squeeze more results from the team, the top 20% are the people who'll rise to the challenge.

Contact with your top 20% is key – not focusing on the specifics of what they are doing – just communicating with them, keeping them updated and informed and, most importantly, giving them the praise and recognition they desire. There is no mistaking the stars of a company. They are the best and are treated that way.

Second, the 70%: your heart and soul

The 70% represent a significant percentage and applying Pareto's principle specifically to this category gives you a further level of worthy insight:

- 20% are future top performers
- 40% are the heart and soul and . . .
- 10% are potential disruptors

The heart and soul of your team are enormously valuable to your business – 20% of these have the potential to be your future top per-formers. What are you doing to identify, nurture, and develop this talent pool?

A word of caution: keep your eye on the future top performers to prevent them from becoming sliders. During the course of the year you might see differential performance as their motivation levels fluctuate or external distractions dilute their focus and drive. Spotting this is key as leader and coach. Knowing when you need to invest quality time to refocus and get them back on track is essential. Forty percent are the heart and soul – they will deliver results. They need managing more closely, training, regular contact, focus, and tactful goal setting – but they'll either hit or get close to their objective and goals. Ten percent are potential future disruptors. The people who do just enough. You question their attitude, commitment, and values. Do they really want to be here? Do they really want to be part of a team?

Managing the 70% is about identifying people with potential to move up, and cultivating them. Everyone in the middle 70% needs to be inspired and made to feel they belong. The 70% is where the majority of your time and effort should be spent and where you'll see the greatest returns.

The traffic light audit

With your new organizational design, a clear definition of talent and Pareto's 80/20 principle, the final piece of building a robust people pipeline is a traffic light audit helping you identify people in terms of where they fit:

- **Green** reflects your top performers based on both performance and potential
- **Amber** reflects the right person in the right place that might need developmental help, or the right person in the wrong place, who might have an excellent attitude, but whose skills could be better utilized in another role within the business
- **Red** reflects the wrong person for the organization.

Categorizing your people according to this method gives you a clear picture of where your developmental efforts should be applied and where your people potentiality lies, aligned to your aspirational goals.

Aligning your People Strategy with the business growth objectives ensures each employee's developmental growth plan ties into future business plans. If you know that in five years' time, the business intends to expand into new areas requiring new technical skills that aren't available in-house, you're able to develop a training strategy to create the skills or a plan to recruit new hires.

Assessing where to invest first

Working through the previous exercises you may have identified people in your organization who should be reallocated in terms of your organizational design or identified several new roles that will need to be filled in the next 18 months. The question is, which do you action first? Your People Strategy is one of nine interlocking strategies making up your broader Strategic Plan. Your recruitment and development must be aligned to the optimum return which delivers the bigger picture organizational goals.

A robust People Strategy will save you from having to do what many businesses do, which is to hire reactively, rather than proactively as part of a structured plan.

3. Growing and Developing Your People

Repeated studies have shown that a key aspect of employee engagement and retention is employees feeling they are growing and developing. If employees are able to link their personal and professional growth to the organization, they are more likely to stay and participate at a higher level through increased commitment.

Growing and developing is a two-way partnership between the individual and the organization. I think of it as the 'soft contract', the rules of engagement for how both parties can achieve maximum value from the relationship.

There are three core principles, which underpin this thinking:

A. An individual's never-ending thirst for learning
B. The singular most important question for unlocking people potential
C. Empowerment without enablement is a train crash!

An individual's never-ending thirst for learning

I believe every person owns their own performance through the conscious choices they make and one of those is undoubtedly having an attitude of constant curiosity for learning.

A great scene in a movie called *The Blind Side*, starring Sandra Bullock, reinforces the importance of this point. In the scene, she is dropping her birth son and adopted son at the school gates, and her parting words to them both are: 'Have fun and learn something new today'. Now, while the 'have fun . . .' part is important, it's the second part that really struck me as central to success: '. . . learn something new today'.

Sometimes, particularly as adults, we slip into the trap of complacency, operating in a state of unconsciousness where it feels like we are just going through the motions. But the day you stop LEARNING is the day you stop EARNING! It's the day you slip into a place that I call 'the groove or the grave' – no man's land. It's the day you accept your place in the world of mediocrity where just enough is good enough. It's the day when you lose your edge and stop being your best self.

In an increasingly competitive world, there is no such thing as standing still. All around you, people are actively moving forward and standing still really means you're falling behind.

As part of a leader-leader culture, each individual in the organization must take ownership for his or her development and be their own performance coach. It fosters a learning culture where every individual has a relentless thirst for learning smarter, identifying better ways of doing things, and creating a never-ending pursuit of excellence.

What if you and every single one of your employees at the end of each working day asked a simple question: 'What have I learnt new today which is going to help me to be even better tomorrow than I was today?'

The singular most important question for unlocking people potential

One of my clients is a large publisher of UK regional newspapers. One day, an editor walked into the CEO's office and shared his frustration about a non-performing team member. The CEO asked how long they had been underperforming and the editor replied: 'Oh, at least ten years'.

She asked him what he had done to inform the individual that they weren't performing, what evidence he could show of performance conversations, and what training gaps had been identified to improve their performance. The answer: none. Whilst you could question whether the individual had taken ownership of their own performance, they had undoubtedly been let down by their leader and the organization.

This scenario happens all too often. I am often saddened when I read exit interviews of employees who have left a business with a high rate of people attrition. Comments often include: 'If only I had been told that I was underperforming 12 or 18 months ago, I could have done something about it.'

The newspaper publisher may sound like it's misfiring, but actually, the same conversation could have taken place at any organization. On the whole, organizations are poor at setting their people up for success. Changing that hinges on asking the singular most important question for unlocking people potential:

> 'Do your people know what world class looks like, feels like and acts like from a behavioural and numerical/ KPI perspective?'

Now pause for a moment. If you have 1, 10, 100, 1,000, or 10,000 people, and you asked that question right now, how do you think they would answer? I guarantee you would hear a broad range of ideas, rather than a clear and unified response. That's a serious issue. If you haven't created absolute clarity about what the expectations are for their role, explained to them what *great* looks like, and set them up for success, it's almost predictable that you and your people will be working to different models and interpretations of what great looks like.

Aligning perception and reality so there is only 'one version of the truth' is critical to unlocking and harnessing the power of your people asset. More importantly, asking this question should not be an annual tick box exercise. Roles evolve, and therefore regular check-in and clarity management is essential.

Empowerment without enablement is a train crash!

I wish I had a pound for every time I'd coached a leader or manager and heard them complain that despite their efforts to empower their people, they're just not seeing the results they were expecting.

Mindset   Skillset   Toolset
Figure 11.4

The challenge is that empowerment is an overused word that means little without enablement. The one without the other is simply a train crash. If we really want to set people up for success, they need to be enabled with the mindset (the attitude, determination, and will), skillset (the specific technical or soft skills to excel) and toolset (the tools to do their specific job) to truly unlock their potential and deliver excellence within their role (see Figure 11.4).

Delivering these key components of enablement begins with an individualized learning and development plan for each employee.

An individualized learning and development plan

Individualization of learning and development needs is not a new idea, but it is still a fairly uncommon one. Often training is created to serve the majority of the needs of those carrying out a general role, rather than catering for the individual needs of each unique employee. Although there is some efficiency in the traditional way of thinking, there is magic in making learning and development suit the individual.

These learning and development plans should sit right at the heart of a robust performance development review system.

Unlocking people potential through a robust performance development review system

There has been an undercurrent in recent years, with large organizations such as Deloitte, Accenture, and Adobe announcing that they will no longer perform annual performance reviews. The media frenzy followed with headlines: 'Accenture dumped performance reviews', which should be read with caution.

During an interview with *The Washington Post*, Accenture CEO Pierre Nanterme confirmed that, `. . . beginning September 2015, [Accenture] will be doing away with annual performance reviews and rankings throughout its 330,000 people organization. The Fortune 500 Company will instead implement a more flexible system with ongoing feedback provided to employees right after assignments.'

He went on to say, about their performance reviews: `We are not sure spending all that time on performance management has been yielding a great outcome. Performance is an ongoing activity, it is every day.'

I am 100% aligned with the thinking behind organizations like Accenture, Deloitte, and Adobe. Performance reviews are not just a yearly appraisal – they are about live, in-the-moment inspirational and developmental feedback and coaching, each and every day!

A common mistake in many organizations is the emphasis of performance conversations taking place solely in the formal yearly or half yearly one-to-one. If you embed the culture of live, in-the-moment feedback, the annual and half yearly performance reviews should be the fastest and easiest conversations you have all year. Why? Because through regular inspirational and developmental feedback, perception and reality on performance have constantly been calibrated throughout the year.

Think about it for a moment. If you're a parent how much time have you spent, and how much are you still spending, on conversations about what is acceptable and what isn't? Why do you put so much emphasis on this? Because you know consistency is everything and live, in-the-moment feedback is the only message your child understands. You can't just compile the feedback for an annual performance review or even a weekly performance conversation. Live in-the-moment real time inspirational and developmental feedback is the only way. Regular performance conversations in business should be no different.

Where I do differ from Accenture, Deloitte, and Adobe is that for most organizations I believe a robust performance review process is essential.

First, employment law today favours the employee over the employer and if you do not have an audit trail of documented regular performance conversations then you will leave your organization exposed.

Second, performance reviews should be a positive experience. People should look forward to them as a way of capturing the great performance they have delivered and the contribution they have made to the broader organizational goals.

Third, and finally, you must keep score. From an employee perspective, it allows the individual to benchmark their performance against their peer group. From the perspective of the company, which expects to pay individual bonuses or company profit share, without a robust performance review system, it becomes hard to decide which payments should and should not be made.

4. Retaining Your People

One of the highest costs associated with people is recruitment, induction, and retraining following the loss of an employee. This is just the hard cost. It excludes the 'opportunity cost'; the lack of continuity with customer relationships, the change in team dynamics, and the lead-time an individual requires to become fully operational, all of which impact the capability of your business to deliver your accelerated growth plans.

Though some attrition is unavoidable, for your business to grow, it should be a priority to retain your good people. When good people leave, it's a certainty that one or more aspects of *Built to Grow* haven't been correctly applied. Inspirational leadership, personal and professional growth, clarity of purpose, alignment with values, a deep connection with the WHY, a belief in the organization, its reputation, its name and its social behaviours, and an expected level of reward and remuneration are all triggers for employees to choose to stay or go. They are all key ingredients, which are an integral part of your compelling EVP.

In a world that has become impersonal, where the big things make little difference, it's the little things which make a big difference. Personal job satisfaction is driven by far more than financial factors such as salary and benefits. Your EVP therefore must have the right blend of non-monetary rewards.

Non-monetary rewards

Increasingly, non-monetary rewards are becoming key differentiators, highly valued by employees. These include relocation services, career development, choice of location, and flexibility to spend time with children and attend school functions and sports days.

Organizations that consider people as merely a resource tend to have difficulty retaining good people. They generally end up over populated with amber and red employees and under populated with green employees. Organizations that value people as their greatest assets and demonstrate it through their actions are positioned to retain their good people and top performers who are the strongest catalysts for business growth.

A well-formed EVP will result in increased attraction and retention of key talent, help prioritize the HR agenda, create a strong people brand, help re-engage a disenchanted workforce, and reduce hire premiums.

If an organization's EVP matches their people's personal values then a win/win/win scenario exists. An employer can count on a motivated, committed worker who will go the extra mile. The worker will experience his/her job as meaningful and fulfilling and both will benefit from a mutually beneficial long-term relationship.

Summary

Earlier in this chapter, I asked a challenging question: do you view people as an overhead or as the lifeblood of your organization? How you view your people will determine how you create your People Strategy. Organizations that have highly energized and engaged teams deliver superior and sustained results, with people who are prepared to go the extra mile through tapping into their optional and discretionary commitment. They truly have skin in the game!

How compelling are your EVP and People Strategy for your business?

To accelerate your journey and develop your personalized EVP download now your EVP template: **http://pti.world/BTG-Toolkit**.

Chapter 12

Operational Excellence Strategy

'Every job is a self-portrait of the person who did it. Autograph your work with excellence.'

—Jessica Guidobono

If I were to ask what you thought the seven most expensive words in business are, what do you think you'd answer? Personally, I've got seven that pop into my mind: 'Because we've always done it that way.' Or perhaps, its sister statement, the equally costly: 'We've never done it that way before.'

How often do you hear words like these in your organization? If you're a mature business, the chances are they're common; if you're a newer business, you might be lucky enough not to come across such untested assumptions, and my advice would be to ban them right now, before they even raise their expensive heads.

Both statements hide a cultural issue that you need to ferret out. They don't just apply to operations, but it is here perhaps that they are most common. They are joined by any number of other red flag statements that are harbingers of a looming operational challenge, such as: 'The system says I can't do that' or 'That's not our process or procedure' or 'There's a problem with x y and z so I did a short term workaround.'

The first of those statements makes me want to break into a rant. If there is one thing guaranteed to kill your customer experience and turn off your customer, it's any statement that begins with the words 'The system says . . .'.

Businesses fall into a common trap: they make do with what they have, however much this may demand a compromise, or they do a quick fix workaround to get away from the constraints of the internal systems. This is admirable in a way, because it suggests an innovative mindset, but actually all it does is put a brave face on a very dark reality: most businesses design their operational processes and systems around a mindset of constraint. They start with what they believe they can't do, and then build the design from there. The net result is strange designs and workflows that don't seem to make sense. It's crazy, and it gets worse when you look at the downstream effect.

The workforce memorizes, learns, and applies the absurd process. They follow it tirelessly and in detailed fashion, critique each other about how well they know it, and write manuals that institutionalize it. Years pass. The world turns. The original designers move on, get promoted and retire, and your organization becomes one where people know what they need to do, but have no idea why.

'We've always done it that way' is a code phrase for 'I don't know why we came up with this design, or any of the details behind it, but I sure can tell you how to get all the steps in.'

'We've always done it that way' represents an unwillingness or inability to really understand what is needed and work out the *best* way to get it done. It's a way of avoiding what could be a lot of work, and could raise some sticky or embarrassing questions.

'We've always done it that way' also means 'I'm not in a position to evaluate anything else because I can't effectively tell if something new is better or worse.'

There are numerous funny stories about this, and many will leave you scratching your head in disbelief and questioning whether they could possibly be real. One that comes immediately to mind involves a report which a British engineering firm had been using for years to capture data about productivity, very happily following a process that it had always done. When it invited a quality management con-sultant in to help improve efficiency, the report was one of the doc-uments they gave him to evaluate. At the top-right corner on page one, there was a small box, which seemed to serve no purpose, but the consultant noticed that it had been routine for staff members to fill the number '0' into it; something they had been doing literally for decades. He asked several of them why they did it, and their response was they had been told to by their supervisor. When he asked the supervisor, he said he didn't know what it was about either, but that he had been taught to fill a '0' in when he first arrived at the business 25 years previously, and had simply done so ever since.

With curiosity getting the better of him, the consultant went to the original designers of the form, a company that had been in busi-ness for generations and which, as luck would have it, kept meticu-lous records of their designs going way back in time. He searched those records and discovered that the first time that small box had appeared on the form, which had been specifically created for this engineering firm, was in 1941, at the height of the London Blitz.

In its original format the box had had a heading, which had, over time, been removed, but which revealed a very telling story not just about the history of the time, but also about the effects of unques-tioned assumptions. The box into which the staff of that engineering firm had been entering the number '0' for more than 30 years origi-nally bore the heading: *Number of Air Raids Today.*

The next time you hear the phrase 'We've always done it this way' don't admire the person for sticking to it, but rather think about whether they are positioned to drive improvement, or continuously repeat the inefficiency of the past.

Practice Makes Perfect . . . or Does It?

I learned a really important lesson, albeit frustratingly, some years ago. I go through fads in terms of the sports I play and about three years ago, during the summer, my chosen sport was golf. As soon as the weather changed from winter to spring, I got my clubs out and I was at the driving range three nights a week, hitting buckets of 200 balls at a time. Two hundred balls, three times a week over ten weeks, meant I must have hit 6,000 balls on the driving range that summer, and most of them, I have to say, weren't very good.

You see, as I was driving, the balls had a tendency, repeated again and again, to hook left and off into the trees. I couldn't get around it, but I was determined to at least try, so I got my head down and practised harder, thinking that if I only persevered, I would get better. It didn't happen.

Then, towards the end of the summer, my wife Jane bought me a golf lesson with a pro, and I decided to take it on the driving range. 'Okay, Royston,' said the pro. 'Hit three balls for me.' I did, and sure enough, they went off to the left and into the trees. Frustrated, I turned to the pro, but he nodded calmly and said: 'Okay, here's what I want you to do. I want you to shift your left hand on the golf club a few degrees and bring it round to the front semi-clockwise.'

I did. It felt odd and uncomfortable because it wasn't what I was used to, but when he instructed me to try again, I hit six balls, one after the other, straight down the fairway.

It was an Aha! moment for me. Practice makes perfect? No. Practice makes permanent, and if you're practising the wrong things, those wrong things stay with you forever in the form of bad habits. Practice doesn't make perfect; the right practice makes perfect.

In business . . . in *your* business . . . unless you have world-class processes from day one, all you are making permanent are bad habits.

The Need for a Robust Operational Strategy

Operations is a little like sales: when everything is going well, the credit is shared around the organization; in fact even if the credit actually belongs with operations another department seem to grab the limelight. But when things go wrong . . . well, operations is in the spotlight. Almost every aspect of operations is high profile: right at the front end of the business, the customer interface every minute of every day.

Without a robust operational strategy, it doesn't matter how much work you've done on the other aspects of your business growth model. You can invest considerable time thinking about what business you're really in, and understanding your purpose and reason for being; you can analyse your market potential and design a truly compelling product and service proposition and have completed all the key components of Zone One of your Business Growth Transformation Framework®.

You can design your end-to-end customer experience; align with marketing to create a compelling online and offline strategy and enable business development and sales to bring the business in. You can make a significant investment in people and financial capital and watch with excitement as momentum builds, and then . . . bang! Disaster strikes because your operations strategy is weak and your business falls over.

Most business improvement opportunities lie hidden in undefined, broken, or poorly executed processes. Operational excellence is about defining, innovating, aligning, and sustaining business processes to enhance customer experience, mitigate risk, alleviate silo mentality, and create the foundation for accelerated, sustained and profitable business growth.

Applying the 7 Guiding Principles in Your Quest for Operational Excellence

To deliver and live up to the promises made to your customers and the marketplace, I want you to complete an audit of your systems, processes, and procedures and have a spring clean. Interrogate them. Ask why they exist; what purpose they serve, and whether there is a clear reason to be doing the things you are doing, in the way that you are doing them.

To help you achieve this I want you to assess your operations in the context of the 7 Guiding Principles of the Business Growth Transformation Framework®. These were detailed in their broadest definition in Chapter 1, but let's look at how they support your Operational Excellence Audit.

Principle 1: Simplicity

We overcomplicate things in operations, and it can be really dangerous to our business when we do. I recall a real life example that illustrates this point well. We were called in to work with the customer support and sales teams of a major UK bank, because the senior leaders believed the teams were ineffective. As part of our investigation, we completed a time and motion study and discovered something alarming. For customer-facing teams implementing best practice, you'd expect to see 70% of time spent on client activity, 20% spent on planning and preparation and 10% spent on admin work. At this bank, however, those ratios were almost completely reversed; the support and sales teams were spending 70% of their time on admin and just 10% on client activity! It's astonishing. No wonder they were ineffective.

When we delved deeper, we discovered that this bank had bought businesses on a focused acquisition drive over several years, resulting in nine distinct tools for tracking customers. In addition, the business was suffering from compliance fatigue with additional processes, systems, and checks being introduced which again diluted the teams' focus from value-adding customer-facing time.

We knew the customer tracking process could be simplified and by consolidating the nine tools into two, we achieved a significant reduction in admin time. Along with a number of other innovations, efficiencies, and simplifications we were able to turn the percentages on their head with 70% of the support and sales teams focused on where they could do their best work: serving customers.

The bank, without intending to, had simply been over-engineering processes for years, making them more complicated than they needed to be. It's common for businesses to do that, probably more than you realize. They introduce one-off workarounds, systems, processes, and tools without looking at the big picture and without fully appreciating the time impact for the people and the customer experience.

Could you be doing this too? In your quest for operational excellence, simplification must be one of your most aggressive goals.

Principle 2: Primary Purpose

Strategically, the primary purpose of a business is to Acquire, Maximize, and Retain the right customers. Everything which contributes to this is an investment. Anything which doesn't is a cost! We covered this principle in depth in Chapter 1, but it's worth a revisit.

What's a cost and what's an investment in your business?

Imagine if you went through your entire operational excellence strategy step by step using this statement. That means questioning every single part of your operations strategy, every process, every decision, from the point of view of whether it adds value in Acquiring, Maximizing, and Retaining customers. This is a simple but incredibly powerful exercise to do.

Principle 3: 'Outside In' Thinking

Principle 3 is fundamental to operational excellence. One of the things that irritates me the most is how system software implementations, which are intended to help deliver your customer experience strategy and drive slicker operations, are allowed to limit your capabilities, rather than enhance them. When big implementations are underway, it's common to hear things like: 'I know you want to achieve x and y, but the system isn't designed to do that.' It's madness. Your strategy shouldn't be limited by the capability of your systems. All strategic thinking in this area should focus on making you easier to do business with, so the systems should be designed around the customer experience, not the customer experience around the systems. Make sure you don't fall into this trap or, if you already have, it might be an angle you need to revisit in your quest for operational excellence.

Principle 4: Empirical Validation

Thinking beyond, and testing small before going BIG

Elite performance in business, sport, personal, and professional life is not necessarily about doing major things differently. It's about the disciplined execution, repetition, and relentless focus on doing the small things consistently and flawlessly. The aggregation and multiplying effect of these small things has an exponential, compounding effect on the end result.

It's called marginal gains, the buzz phrase which means the aggregation or the drive to perfect every controllable detail in search of optimal performance. Marginal gains were made famous in recent times through the work of Clive Woodward with his England rugby team and Dave Brailsford with British Cycling and Team Sky.

In his book *Winning*, former England rugby coach Clive Woodward describes how, when he took over the team in 1997, he set out to effect a wholesale culture change, restructuring the players' experience *from driveway to driveway*; that is, from the moment the English players left home to play for their country to the moment they returned, everything would be considered, analysed, and aligned with the team's values, purpose, and strategy. He says that success can be attributed to how a team works together under pressure, how they understand the importance of team work and loyalty, and how they are willing to do a hundred things just 1% better.

The final aspect Woodward called *the critical non-essentials*: a fresh jersey at halftime, the same bus for every home game, a more inspiring locker room at the Twickenham rugby ground; every little thing, every marginal gain helped Woodward's England team win the 2003 Rugby World Cup.

Britain's Olympic cyclists call it *marginal gains*. In their preparation for a home Olympics in 2012, in which they won an incredible seven out of 10 gold medals, the details included: customized aerodynamic helmets; hot pants (worn to keep muscles warm between races); sweat resistant clothing; alcohol sprayed on the wheels to enhance traction at the start; and hypoallergenic pillows to help stop riders catching colds.

Performance Coach, Dave Brailsford, explained that the whole principle came from the idea that if you broke down everything you could think of that goes into riding a bike and improved it by 1%, you will get a significant increase when you put it all together.

Just think what impact this could have if you did the same exercise across your business and the entire Business Growth Transformation Framework®! Most businesses are not realizing their full potential, but when you truly develop laser beam focus on marginal gains across all areas of your business, you can achieve profound increased results. Growth to the top line, reduction in cost base, increased productivity and efficiencies in the middle, all when multiplied together have a significant impact on your overall business growth.

It just works! Starbucks applied the principle when focused on its exponential growth. The focus: 'one cup of coffee at a time!'

At McLaren Formula One, they call it 'Tenths'. The entire team is galvanized by the idea of shaving tenths of a second off the lap time. All F1 teams do it, of course, but at McLaren they make it their central operating principle.

Marginal gain can be technical, physical, practical, operational, and even psychological. In the film *Any Given Sunday*, the Al Pacino character calls it 'Inches':

> 'You find out that life is just a game of inches. So is football. Because in either game, life or football, the margin for error is so small . . . On this team, we fight for that inch. On this team we tear ourselves, and everyone around us to pieces for that inch . . . because we know when we add up all of those inches that's going to make the difference between WINNING and LOSING.'

Where are your inches this year? Where are you going to find your marginal gains in your operational excellence and across your wider business strategy?

Principle 5: Disciplined Execution

Day-to-day business processes serve as arteries carrying the lifeblood of an organization. Whether these business processes are efficient or inefficient, effective or ineffective, boring or exciting (rarely are they ever exciting), they are the foundation required for all companies to function. When things go wrong, the intelligent approach in the pursuit of disciplined execution is to look at what I call the two Ps: process and personality, to see which is at fault.

If the process works on examination, the thing that led it to fail must be personality; specifically, a person. On the other hand, if the person has followed the process perfectly, then the personality isn't in question and there is a fundamental problem with the process. The two Ps is a simple but effective way to be able to diagnose quickly within your business where problems and opportunities exist.

A well-designed process may be an incredibly useful tool, but only if it is followed by people that understand it fully, and that's a common challenge for many organizations. It's been my experience that most companies think they know their business processes and how they should work, but they very rarely have those processes documented. This is the frequent and common response: 'We believe our people know what they should be doing from a process point of view, and therefore fail to see the potential for things like misunderstanding, modification or shortcutting, over time.'

We've identified 11 key process challenges over the past 20 years of working with businesses worldwide, which you can use in parallel with the 7 Guiding Principles for your Operational Excellence Audit.

1. **Process not defined:** because processes spring up out of a need to solve a business challenge, and then evolve toward a state of acceptance, most organizations do not have processes that are well designed and defined.

2. **Process not owned:** organizations are commonly managed vertically, where the organization chart lays out a hierarchical structure of cascading leadership and management responsibilities and accountabilities. Yet work processes flow horizontally, across vertical boundaries. Why? Because the customer end-to-end journey cuts horizontally through your business. If you want to create a seamless customer experience, you have to break down the traditional silo mentality of functions and departments working in isolation. Of course you will have realized by now that the methodology and approach through the Business Growth Transformation Framework® is designed to do exactly this. The effective leadership and management of work must include the individual ownership of processes that cross boundaries and functions aligned to the overall customer experience.

3. **Purpose not understood:** a process needs a worthy purpose to justify its existence. Without a worthy purpose, the entire process is non-value adding and should be eliminated. Even for the simplest process with a single output, the process must provide something that a customer (internal or external) values and align to the overall goals and vision of the business.

4. **Process not followed:** perhaps the most obvious one but also the most common. Processes are designed to be followed. When they are, they can deliver a predictable, repeatable, sustainable result; when they are not, you lose control of the outcome. This is usually a personality problem, rather than a process one.

5. **Customer not understood:** every process serves a customer and should create something of value, but process owners (assuming they exist) rarely know who their actual customers are, what they want from the process, and what they think of the value of the process in terms of how it meets their needs.

6. **Supplier not understood:** a supplier also serves every process. Just like the customer, most process owners do not know the supplier of their process, what the process needs from their supplier, and to what extent the process needs are being served effectively by their supplier.

7. **Cumbersome to execute:** because processes frequently grow into existence without intentional purpose or design, they tend to meander across organizations through the development of *good ideas* that add extra steps, poorly designed tasks, and additional workaround activities intended to accomplish what may have started out as a clean and simple process requirement.

8. **Loaded with non-value added work:** value added tasks are defined as those tasks the customer would be willing to pay for. Limited value tasks are those that are of questionable value for the customer. All others are non-value added. For every process developed what are the value added, limited-value added, and non-value added tasks?

9. **Performance not measured:** when organizations have front line measurements in place, they tend to be oriented vertically toward the organization chart's definition of responsibility and

accountability. They also tend to be reactive (and too late to adjust) versus proactive. Good process measurement captures both process effectiveness (the extent to which the process satisfies the customer's need or want) and process efficiency (the extent to which the process uses the minimum possible resources to do so).

10. **Not linked to strategy:** we frequently hear senior leadership say things like: 'We are committed to our strategy, but we can't get the organization to execute.' Strategy without strong process is like a head without a body. Without having operational control of processes, it is nearly impossible to move the organization toward a vision of the future.

11. **Don't understand what business they are really in:** we covered this concept in detail in Chapter 5, but because it is so important I think it's worth reiterating wherever I can, and worth you constantly asking, to get to the purest version of your answer. Remember that nothing is as galvanizing for your employees than a clear answer to your WHY. It also gives you enormous power of purpose when questioning, refining, and developing your processes to ensure they effectively lead you toward your WHY.

Principle 6: Productive Paranoia

What if the infrastructure goes down? What if your platform fails? What if there is a fire or a flood at your premises? What is your Plan B or Plan C, or even your Plan D? Most companies don't have a back-up plan in case things go wrong. They've literally never considered an alternative scenario to business as usual, and when they are challenged, even a small obstacle can be enormously damaging. Productive paranoia can mean anything from having a regular data back-up plan, with data copies stored off site so that your business information is safe, to running worst-case scenarios that may stretch the imagination.

Some years ago, I learned about the back-up systems for the computer centre that powers the NASDAQ stock exchange in the United States. The NASDAQ, like stock markets around the world, has a huge impact on the economy and the data centre is therefore considered to be a Class A priority site. To ensure it keeps running 24/7/365, there is a dedicated power station, just for the computer facility. That dedicated power station is backed up by another identical facility to kick in instantly, should the first one fail. Talk about leaving nothing to chance!

But that doesn't even scratch the surface. Rooms full of batteries back up those dedicated power stations, which will power the entire facility should the power stations fail. Those rooms full of batteries are backed up by a second lot of rooms full of batteries, which are in turn backed up by a third.

But those batteries aren't expected to run for very long. They're only there to take up the slack while the diesel powered generators in the basement kick in, and get up to speed. One of those generators will run the entire facility indefinitely, as long as it is refuelled, but nevertheless, the NASDAQ data centre has three. A failsafe against the failure of generator one, and a further failsafe in case both one and two don't start.

Finally, the diesel fuel is stored in a contamination proof tank, and completely refreshed every two weeks. Oh, and there is an identical facility in another state, ready to step in immediately, should a meteorite obliterate the first. Each of these fail safes is automatically triggered by the failure of the preceding one, in a matter of seconds. That's productive paranoia in action.

It also requires a significant investment in infrastructure of course, which isn't for everyone, so let me suggest an alternative, much more low cost solution to productive paranoia, that requires nothing but the power of human brains.

Productive Paranoia – your tenth man strategy

In the movie *World War Z*, starring Brad Pitt, the world is overrun by zombies and Israel is the sole survivor for a real-life reason that has prevented it from being caught napping for more than 40 years. In 1973, while its Arab neighbours mobilized their military forces in plain sight of Israeli intelligence, the Israelis nevertheless concluded that an imminent attack was unlikely. The Jewish festival of Yom Kippur was coming up, and rather than step up their defences, the Israelis opted instead to stand down.

It was a near fatal mistake. The attack came, the war was quick but brutal, and the Israeli leaders were left with a lot of very difficult questions to answer. In response to that event, they adopted what is known as a tenth man strategy, which is very simple: if ten people are in a room and nine agree on how to interpret a piece of information, the tenth man is required to disagree and run the alternative scenario. His duty is to find the best possible argument against the general thinking of the group. Their view is that playing devil's advocate increases the quality of their overall decisions. Whilst it's called the tenth man strategy, it doesn't matter if it is six people, four people, or less. The key is to have one person whose only reason for being there is to challenge, disagree, and run the alternative scenario.

Back to the movie: the Israeli military intercepted a message from India speaking about a zombie attack. Because of their tenth man strategy, the tenth man was literally compelled to take the message seriously and build defences against zombies. As it turned out, he was exactly right to do so. Productive paranoia in each instance was about preparing for the unforeseen, and running scenarios however improbable.

Principle 7: Proud Factor

A business with operational excellence is able to underpin the reliable, predictable, admired service promises it makes to its customers, whilst allowing for stretch to chase the adventurous and market-leading ideas and innovations. Laying the foundations for real pride in your work, for all employees, contributes to achieving operational excellence.

Applying the 7 Guiding Principles helps us to make sense of the complexity in the pursuit of operational excellence, but you may be asking whether you need to do this at all. Well, if you're in doubt, let's examine it from another angle.

Ask yourself . . .

. . . how can your organization automate, evaluate, measure, or improve your business performance without a common company-wide understanding of current business processes?

Business processes evolve over time, with constantly changing business needs such as employee turnover, acquisitions, change to strategy and so on. It would be foolish for a doctor to operate on a patient without understanding the patient's current condition and medical history, I am sure you would agree. Yet, many companies operate businesses without continuously assessing current applicability of internal processes and without understanding why and how these processes evolved.

Successful organizations invest the time and money necessary to continually update business processes. Benefits are seen immediately. Comments like 'I didn't know we could do that' or 'We agreed to stop doing that a long time ago' in response to questions such as 'Why are we handling that invoice three times instead of once?' or 'If we changed this process just a little could we save time and money?' will be heard. All business functions and projects stand a better chance of success when business processes are documented and understood up-front. Similarly, evaluating, measuring, reorganizing, and improving your business performance will also be easier, more accurate, and much more efficient.

So back to that focused question . . . how can an organization automate, evaluate, measure, or improve its business performance without a common company-wide understanding of current business processes?

The answer: it can't!

Embracing Technology as a Competitive Advantage

I have a view, expressed earlier, that one of the biggest challenges when it comes to operations is the fact that systems are developed almost in isolation, based on the constraints of the system software architecture, with little or no thought given to the customer engagement strategy. That doesn't imply that I am down on technology – in fact quite the opposite. It offers a real competitive advantage to those organizations that embrace it with the customer experience in mind: those that think 'outside in', not inside out.

I have mentioned previously in *Built to Grow* that venture capital, private equity, and accountants have a specific checklist of defined criteria for valuing businesses. Technology businesses or those businesses that leverage the power of technology as a key component of their business growth strategy tend to attract a premium multiplier on their business valuation.

Technology is what enabled Facebook to provide services to so many users that, if it were a country, it would have the third largest population in the world. Technology is the reason GroupOn managed to become a global brand, serving local businesses in 250 cities, and attain a valuation of $1 billion in just 18 months, the fastest company in history to hit that valuation.

An example of an organization that has got technology absolutely right, not just on the internet, but by combining it with a traditional bricks and mortar infrastructure, is a British bank named Metro Bank, which opened its doors in 2010. It was the first new high street bank to open in the United Kingdom for more than 150 years and its customers immediately noticed a difference such as lollipop jars and water bowls for dogs, which were fun and unusual. But what really sets Metro Bank apart is its state-of-the-art IT system. New customer accounts are opened and, their debit and credit cards enabled within 15 minutes, and all customer data is stored in one place.

Banks, historically, have been hindered by the legacy of their long-standing need for data. Back in the 1960s, when computing power began to offer meaningful benefits, banks built systems, which were adapted and modified over the years until there was a messy legacy of systems that often created a poor or at least an average customer experience. Because your bank account and credit card data are stored on different systems, the experience of calling a contact centre could be a really trying one, taking far longer than necessary, with the constant repetition of information.

That's the problem Metro Bank decided to try and solve. All information in one place, the bank says, enables it to be faster, more efficient, and much more customer friendly. There is no doubt that at its inception, Metro Bank and its clever customer-focused use of technology is causing its competitors to sit up and take notice. It is disruptive and challenging and has acquired significant market share in the UK retail banking market.

Operational Improvement Never Stops

Small marginal gains, constant questioning, and alignment around your WHY, are all part of the relentless drive for operational excellence. Great companies around the world know this and over the years detailed process and operational strategies have evolved to become established working practices. To go into the complexities of such models as Six Sigma, Kaizen, and others would require another book entirely, but just so you understand how seriously the greatest companies in the world take the task of operational excellence, let's look at some of the biggest ideas in brief.

Six Sigma

Six Sigma simply means a measure of quality that strives for near perfection. Six Sigma is a disciplined, data-driven approach and methodology for eliminating defects. To achieve Six Sigma, a process must not produce more than 3.4 defects per million opportunities (a Six Sigma defect is defined as anything outside customer specifications). Six Sigma is generally implemented in organizations when incremental improvement isn't enough and a much deeper set of improvements are required.

It was significantly popularized by Jack Welch as the CEO of General Electric, gained worldwide popularity during the 1980s and 1990s, and is still widely used today. One of the quirks of Six Sigma is the training of its coordinators, whose certification is held in very high regard, and who achieve Judo-style titles to specify their level of training: Six Sigma Green Belts, Six Sigma Black Belts, and Six Sigma Master Black Belts.

Kaizen

Kaizen is a Japanese philosophy that focuses on continual improvement throughout all aspects of life. When applied to the workplace,

Kaizen activities can improve every function of a business, from manufacturing to marketing and from the CEO to the assembly-line workers. Kaizen aims to eliminate waste in all systems of an organization through improving standardized activities and processes. By understanding the basics of Kaizen, practitioners can integrate this method into their overall efforts.

The purpose of Kaizen goes beyond simple productivity improvement. When done correctly, the process humanizes the workplace, eliminates overly hard work, and teaches people how to spot and eliminate waste in business processes.

Among the key points underpinning Kaizen are the following:

- Replace conventional fixed ideas with fresh ones
- Start by questioning current practices and standards
- Seek the advice of many associates before starting a Kaizen activity
- Think of how to do something, not why it cannot be done
- Don't make excuses – make execution happen
- Do not seek perfection – implement a solution right away, even if it covers only 50% of the target
- Correct something right away if a mistake is made.

The Toyota Way

The Toyota Way is the name of a book by Dr Jeffrey Liker, a University of Michigan professor of industrial engineering, in which he referred to the Japanese car maker's philosophy as 'a system designed to provide the tools for people to continually improve their work'. The focal points of the Toyota Way are the principles of continuous improvement and respect for people. Those principles empower employees, despite the bureaucratic processes, to have the authority to stop production to signal a quality issue, emphasizing that quality takes precedence.

According to Liker, the Toyota Way has been driven so deeply into the psyche of employees at all levels of the organization that it has morphed from a strategy into an important element of the company's culture.

Summary

As you started to read this chapter, perhaps you had a sense that operational excellence would be heavily focused on the technical aspects of process and you may be surprised to discover how tightly the topic is woven into business culture. Well, that's not an accident; it's important that every department or business function adopts the 7 Guiding Principles and challenges the status quo in order to deliver a seamless and consistent customer experience that supports and contributes to your growth ambitions.

Chapter 13

Finance and Governance

'Your net worth to the world is usually determined by what remains after your bad habits are subtracted from your good ones.'

—Benjamin Franklin

Throughout my career, I've come to appreciate and really value the attributes that define a company's success: having a compelling vision; a great product and service proposition; a powerful brand; great leadership and people; ethical business practices; evolving business strategies and values-based decision-making.

However – and *there is a however* – there is one fundamental attribute that is missing, without which you cannot have any realistic control over your business: Finance and Governance.

A documented and robust Finance and Governance strategy understood by all and implemented across the business will create the headspace for you to channel your time and energy into the creative, innovative aspects of building and running your business. This does not mean you abdicate responsibility for this important function, but instead delegate responsibility as you have now set the solid foundations for your corporate governance.

So, be honest with me now: if you browsed the table of contents of this book, what came into your mind when you saw there was a chapter called Finance and Governance? Was it the sort of feeling you had at school when it was time for your least favourite subject or perhaps one that really challenged you; something that you had to do, but knew before you even got to it that you'd never be able to make a connection? Or was your instant response: 'It will be interesting to see what is included in there and how that chapter is bought to life. That's an area I definitely need to sharpen up on.'

In my experience, the challenge many business leaders face in this area is that it is perceived as too specialist to warrant them putting in the time to learn it. But let me draw you an analogy to explain why I believe that thinking is absolutely flawed.

For close to 30 years, starting in 1978, motorsport fans used to watch with awe as a field of adventure seekers thrashed it out for dominance in the Paris to Dakar rally; a race that, for the most part, played out over the sand dunes and rocky terrain of the Sahara Desert in North Africa. The adrenaline had audiences mesmerized as the drivers threw their cars headlong down an often brand new path, at high speeds. It wasn't for the faint-hearted.

It wasn't for those who were unfamiliar with the technical aspects of their vehicles either, because out in the desert, there are no service stations, so when anything broke, as it frequently did on that brutal landscape, it fell to the drivers to put it right. I remember watching one year as two drivers had to stop in the middle of nowhere; hundreds of miles of sand in every direction, and they had to change the clutch on their car. To ordinary people, that's a very complex repair that can only be done by experts. The two drivers did it in less than an hour, on their own.

There's a point to this story: if the drivers of that car had been like many business leaders, only interested in driving fast, then they'd have been out of the race almost before it started. That specialist knowledge was incredibly valuable to them. For your business, Finance and Governance is that essential specialist knowledge. It is what enables all the other parts to happen. Without getting this right, you'll never create predictable, repeatable, and sustainable results in your business.

Change Your Mindset . . . Change the Game

I am going to have to make a very rare demand before we get cracking on this chapter. To get to grips with Finance and Governance, you'll need to bring the right mindset to the table from the start. Many business leaders, business owners, and entrepreneurs have come from a financial, accountancy background so if you're already in that headspace, then great. If not, there is a great quote that says: 'Change your mindset and you change the game.'

People that run high performance businesses unquestionably understand the numbers that underpin those businesses, understand what is going on in their finances, and have built a robust platform of sound governance. They find the best advisors and professionals they can to assist them, and make it a constant unwavering priority to get it right. So should you. The great news today is that these specialists and professionals do not necessarily need to be on the payroll. They can be outsourced, strategic partners who are working with a portfolio of businesses like yours. You don't need to do it all yourself.

This was a lesson I can say, upon reflection, was one of the best I ever learned early in my business career. Hire and surround yourself with the best advisors and professionals; the cost might be higher initially, but the payback will be huge. It is a golden rule I have never skimped on in any of the businesses I have been involved with, built, or run.

However, whether you bring expertise in-house or outsource it, the assistance of an expert shouldn't be used as an excuse for you to abdicate responsibility for the results; you should still be intimately aware of how to read, interpret, and gain valuable insight from the financials in order to then make informed, empirically validated decisions. At the end of the day the buck still stops with you.

Wise old Benjamin Franklin, who opened this chapter for us, is also credited with the often-repeated saying: 'In this world, nothing can be said to be certain, except death and taxes.' The way I think about this in terms of 'keeping score' and specifically when it comes to Finance and Governance is this: the size of your tax bill tells you one of two things: either how good you are, or how bad your accountant is.

My goal is for you to fall into the former of those two groups by applying the principles of *Built to Grow* and by building your business into a high performing, sustainable, legacy organization that fulfils all your personal and professional goals. So, let's explore what the critical ingredients are in your Finance and Governance strategy to make this happen.

Keeping Score . . .

In Chapter 10 we talked about keeping score, knowing your numbers and, perhaps most importantly, defining for your business the Measures that really Matter. There is a plethora of measures and ratios and other complex numbers that underpin your robust Finance and Governance strategy, some of which will vary and change depending on the nature of your business.

However, this is not a book to educate and teach you the principles of finance. There are books, resources, and specific courses out there which will do a much more in-depth job of this. What I am going to do instead is use this chapter to draw out and highlight the critical essentials every business leader should know, whatever the size or nature of your business.

IMPORTANT NOTE: If you are a seasoned business professional you might be thinking: 'Royston, this is basic stuff and common sense'. However, I urge you to stay the course and read with a fresh pair of eyes and think of this as a 'thermometer check'. You and I both know that, as time passes, it is so easy for bad habits to creep in; habits that if you're not careful can end up costing you a fortune.

The Challenge

Financial freedom and success are available to those who learn about them and work for them and are disciplined in achieving them. However, the challenge is that common sense is not that common and you only need to look at some of the seismic failings of recent times to evidence my point. Financial naïveté exists at all levels, even to seasoned and experienced business professionals.

Consider the catastrophic collapse of Enron in December 2001; a company that enjoyed a share price of more than $90 just 18 months before it came to an abrupt halt at a share price of less than a dollar. The Enron collapse wiped out billions of dollars in investment, destroyed the faith of many in business, and cast a stain on the truthfulness of business leaders for many years afterwards.

But it wasn't market pressures, competing products, or a lack of ideas that killed Enron; what destroyed it was awful financial management, reckless financial practices, and what appears to have been an almost complete lack of good corporate governance. The Board of Directors was unaware of the activities endorsed by CEO Jeffrey Skilling and by the time they were made fully aware, it was too late to do anything about it. Skilling is still serving a 14-year jail sentence for a number of financial crimes at the time of writing.

Enron created a ripple effect, which resulted in the *de facto* dissolution of Arthur Anderson, one of the five largest audit and accountancy partnerships in the world. In addition to being the largest bankruptcy reorganization in American history at that time, Enron was cited as the biggest audit failure.

But it gets worse . . .

The collapse of Lehman Brothers, a sprawling global bank, in September 2008 almost brought down the world's financial system. It took huge taxpayer-financed bailouts to shore up the industry across the globe.

Between 1850 and the early 2000s, a period spanning more than 150 years, Lehman Brothers was a significant force in American finance. Indeed, even on the day it dramatically shut its doors in September 2008, it was still the fourth-largest investment bank in the United States behind Goldman Sachs, Morgan Stanley, and Merrill Lynch. What killed it on a macro scale was the collapse of the United States housing market, which created a record number of defaulting loans; what killed it more specifically however was the fact that Lehman Brothers, more than any other bank, made very poor financial

choices. Despite 150 years of success, when Lehman Brothers executives began to realize the nature of the miscalculation that meant
they owned billions of dollars in worthless paper, it was too late. It
collapsed in a single weekend.

Think about that for a moment. Who would have thought that in
the 21st century we'd be having conversations about banks going
bankrupt and find ourselves asking whether the safest place for our
money is under the mattress at home? This was the reality for many
people; especially those who didn't really have a handle on what
caused the crisis in the first place.

Who would have thought there would be questions being asked
about our major financial institutions; not only raising fears about
their strength, but their reliability? It wasn't that long ago that an
investment made in a major bank was a safe and unadventurous
one, that could expect to yield slow, but consistent returns over
the long term – that was precisely why some investors liked them.
Across the Atlantic from Lehman Brothers, around about the same
time, a similar scenario played out at Royal Bank of Scotland (RBS),
which flew too high, became embroiled in a very poorly chosen and
poorly executed merger with Dutch bank ABN/AMRO, and ultimately
got bailed out by the British Government. I personally know many
people who had their bonuses, pensions, and retirement savings all
wrapped up in RBS shares, only to see the whole lot wiped out when
RBS went into rescue.

And it wasn't just banks. When the economy began to crater, car
companies such as General Motors and Chrysler, both of which had
been battling poor financial fundamentals for decades, found themselves in real existential peril. Insurance giant AIG became almost
wholly owned by the United States Government to prevent it from
folding. Fannie Mae and Freddie Mac, the two biggest mortgage
insurers in the United States, were rescued only by massive government injection of funds. In Dubai, the tallest skyscraper in the world
was rapidly renamed from the Burj Dubai to the Burj Khalifa before it
opened, in recognition of the financial bailout given to the Emirate
of Dubai by the UAE Government and the Emirate of Abu Dhabi;
the Khalifa designation recognized the involvement of the financial

lifeline extended by the ruler of Abu Dhabi and president of the United Arab Emirates, Khalifa bin Zayed Al Nahyan.

The list went on and on throughout 2008 and 2009, proving again and again that strong Finance and Governance principles are the most critical shield any organization can have against uncertainty. Get this wrong, and it doesn't matter how glamorous your brand, how large your customer base, or how audacious your vision; the next challenge you face could be your last.

And even worse . . .

What I am talking about is not isolated and doesn't just apply to businesses and major institutions like banks. It actually applies to entire nations. Whole countries can get their Finances & Governance woefully wrong with sickening consequences. Never mind about taking your money out of your bank and tucking it under your mattress, many people have to ask whether their money is safe even in the country in which they live or the currency they spend.

In Europe in the mid-2010s, the PIIGS countries (Portugal, Italy, Ireland, Greece, and Spain) have bounced from crisis to crisis, all built on terrible economic management. Greece in particular has endured more of the spotlight than it would have wished for, which has exposed such things as the appalling state of its revenue collection capabilities. In Greece, tax evasion is the norm for the country's rich elite; residents of the wealthy suburbs of Athens have for years failed to declare taxable items such as swimming pools, and the Greek tax authorities have done little about it. As the nation of Greece teeters on the edge of bankruptcy, its tax authorities are only now taking aim at tax-evaders. The problem isn't a small one either: using satellite photos, the tax authority examined the claims of the residents of Athens' wealthy suburbs and discovered that, rather than the 324 swimming pools claimed by the locals, there were in fact *16,974* of them.

In summary, it is not just small businesses, big businesses, or major institutions; it is countries too that need to sharpen their focus and capabilities in the areas of Finance and Governance. Just as businesses are competing on the global landscape for customers, so too are countries. So now we've explored the importance of your robust Finance and Governance strategy from a number of angles, let's drill into the Measures that Matter in keeping score and make this relevant for you and your business.

Measures That Matter

Throughout *Built to Grow* we have spoken about the three high level Measures that Matter to any business (see Figure 13.1).

Our specific focus for this chapter is on the last of these three: are we the investment of choice? To keep this really focused we are going to hone in on three areas: revenue growth, profit generation, and cash management.

You may have heard the expression: 'Revenue is vanity, profit is sanity and cash is reality'. If ever there was a philosophy which I passionately believe in, it is this. However, there are some important nuances, which we need to unpack in this expression. Let's look at each of them in turn, starting with . . .

Revenue growth

Revenue is often referred to as the top line in a Profit and Loss state-ment (P&L). However, it can be something of a vanity number and many businesses can place too much emphasis on it. It's pointless having high revenue if at the end of the year it equates to zero profit.

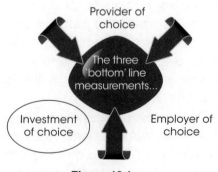

Figure 13.1

This is not a formula for success in building a high performing, sustainable, legacy organization.

However, profit point aside, revenue growth is critical because, once your fixed costs and overheads are covered with a carefully managed and controlled direct cost of sale, scale and growth in your top line will massively fast track your growth and success. That's why you see many organizations constantly price testing in the market or acquiring business at different margin/profitability aligned to their growth ambitions.

It comes down to some of the questions we covered in Chapter 1: The Fundamentals of Business Growth and Chapter 6: Market Potential Strategy – whether your goal is to be at one end of the scale: a niche low volume, high margin business, the other end of the scale: a high volume, low margin player, or a hybrid, somewhere in-between. In creating a clearly defined revenue strategy, these are the levers you have to play with and when they are aligned to a clear understanding of your direct costs, fixed costs, and overheads, you can make conscious, informed, educated decisions about how and when to drive the top line revenue in your business model.

There are a couple of other key points which we must cover in revenue growth: the first is being crystal clear about what revenue is and what it isn't; the second involves two really important finance principles; revenue recognition and accrual accounting. These two principles are where a number of organizations have been caught out in recent times with some even being fined heavily by the governing authorities for false accounting.

What revenue is and what it isn't

Revenue is the total amount of money that you have *earned*, coming into your business over a defined period of time. For most businesses this is a monthly accounting cycle rolling up into a yearly financial period. It is *not* the total amount of cash coming into your business. Cash can come into your business for a variety of reasons: financing, advance payments for services to be rendered in the future, payments of invoices sent months ago.

Understanding the difference between 'revenue' and cash' leads us to two important finance principles which I referenced earlier. Let's start with . . .

Revenue recognition

Revenue recognition determines how much revenue you will put on your accounting statements in a specific time period. For a start-up company, revenue recognition is not normally difficult. If you sell something, your revenue is the price at which you sold the item and it is recognized in the period in which the item was sold. If you sell advertising, revenue is the price at which you sold the advertising and it is recognized in the period in which the advertising actually ran on your media property. If you provide a subscription service, your revenue in any period will be the amount of the subscription that was provided in that period.

However, this leads to another important concept called *accrual accounting*. When many people start keeping books, they simply record cash received for services rendered as revenue. They record the bills they pay as expenses. This is called *cash accounting* and is the way most of us keep our personal books and records. But a business is not supposed to keep books this way. It is supposed to use the concept of accrual accounting.

Accrual accounting

Let's say you hire a contract developer to build your smartphone app and agree to pay him $30,000 to deliver it to you. Then, let's say it takes him three months to build it. At the end of the three months you pay him the $30,000.

In cash accounting, in month three you would record an expense of $30,000. But in accrual accounting, each month you'd record an expense of $10,000 and because you aren't actually paying the developer the cash yet, you charge the $10,000 each month to a balance sheet account called Accrued Expenses. Then when you pay the bill, you don't touch the P&L; it's simply a balance sheet entry that reduces cash and reduces Accrued Expenses by $30,000.

The point of accrual accounting is to perfectly match the revenues and expenses to the time period in which they actually happen, not when the payments are made or received. This is so fundamental in your Measures that Matter. One of my golden principles in business is always that there are 'no surprises'. From a financial perspective that means I want to know on a monthly basis my 'real time' business position and performance from a financial perspective. Effective revenue recognition and accrual accounting enable you to determine that 'real time' position with confidence and certainty.

So that's revenue growth and some essential principles. Let's now move in to the second of the three areas I promised to cover . . .

Profit generation

When we speak about profit, it's common for there to be some confusion about exactly what it means. To be as simplistic as possible, profit is the amount that is left over after each sale, once you've deducted all your costs, which I have no doubt you already understand.

However, I think it's worth looking at the different types of profit (yes, there are different types, or perhaps different stages of profit) so that we can clear up any confusion that might exist.

Gross profit

The first key profit indicator in your Finance and Governance Measures that Matter is gross profit, which is a company's total revenue (equivalent to total sales) minus the cost of goods sold (COGS). Gross profit is the profit a company makes after deducting the costs associated with making and selling its products, or the costs associated with providing its services.

As a simple example, if a company sells goods for $100, and the cost to the company to produce the goods is $70, the company's gross profit is $30, equating to a gross profit margin of 30%.

Gross profit margin provides an indication of a company's profitability. It is not a precise indication because you still have to deduct overhead, payroll, and taxation, but as a measure it is important. It's also worth noting that gross profit is different from what some people term operating profit (earnings before interest and taxes).

Gross margin is often shown as a percentage of revenues. I prefer to invest in high gross margin businesses because they have a lot of money left after making a sale to pay for the other costs of the business, thereby providing capital resources to grow the business without needing more financing. It is also much easier to make a high gross margin business profitable. The greater your gross profit margin, the stronger and more independent you can remain, and the closer you get to that key overriding measure that matters: being an investment of choice.

Other costs not directly associated with the generation of revenue are often referred to as overhead (sometimes fixed costs), and these are the costs that will exist even if you have no revenue. So now we've defined what gross profit is, and why it is a measure that matters in profit generation, what is net profit margin?

Net profit

The second key profit indicator, net profit, is a more accurate measure of a company's profitability because it takes into account not just the direct costs of sale and production but all the fixed and variable costs of running the business. Net profitability is an important distinction, since increases in revenue do not necessarily translate into actual increased profitability. Net profit is the gross profit (revenue minus cost of goods) minus operating expenses and all other expenses, such as taxes and interest paid on debt. The formula for net profit margin is as follows:

Net profit margin = (revenue - cost of goods - operating expenses - other expenses - interest - taxes)/revenue

Examining its net profit margin can help a company gain a much clearer picture of its overall expenses. Now let's look at the final measure within profit generation.

EBITDA

Earnings before Interest, Taxes, Depreciation, and Amortization (normally written in the acronym format EBITDA) is an indicator of a company's financial performance which is calculated in the following manner:

EBITDA = Revenue - Expenses (excluding taxes, interest, depreciation, and amortization)

Why does it matter? EBITDA is one of the operating measures most used by analysts in understanding the underlying performance of a business. EBIDTA allows analysts to focus on the outcome of operating decisions while excluding the impacts of non-operating decisions like interest expenses (a financing decision), tax rates (a governmental decision), or large non-cash items like depreciation and amortization (an accounting decision).

By minimizing the non-operating effects that are unique to each company, EBITDA allows investors to focus on operating profitability as a singular measure of performance. Such analysis is particularly important when comparing similar companies across a single industry, or companies operating in different tax brackets. This measure is also of interest to a company's creditors, since EBITDA is essentially the income that a company has free for interest payments.

In general, EBITDA is a useful measure for large companies with significant fixed assets, which are subject to heavy depreciation charges (such as manufacturing companies), and/or for companies with a significant amount of debt financing. EBITDA is also a key measurement when a company has a large amount of acquired intangible assets on its books and is thus subject to substantial amortization charges (such as a company that has purchased a brand or a company that has recently made a large acquisition).

It is rarely a useful measure for evaluating a small company with no significant loans. However, I share it with you because as a business leader, business owner, or entrepreneur it is sensible to have a sound understanding of what it is and why it is used.

Managing the double lines

Managing the double lines (driving top line revenue growth and, in parallel, focusing on the overhead and cost base), will allow you to deliver accelerated, sustainable, and profitable business growth. However, managing the double lines in your growth model can easily be derailed if you don't have one eye on your cash management strategy.

Remember the expression: 'Revenue is vanity, profit is sanity and cash is reality.' Cash is king, but if not carefully managed it can be the Achilles heel of your growth ambitions.

Your cash management strategy

More businesses go bust coming out of a recession than they do going into one. Why? Because they overtrade and stretch themselves beyond their financial reserves, which have already been substantially diminished during the recession itself.

Managing cash is critical and this is the third of our Measures that Matter in your robust Finance and Governance strategy. Your cash management strategy in terms of your daily/weekly/monthly/yearly trading is fundamentally about one measure that really matters: your debtor to creditor ratio. It still amazes me today how many senior business leaders, business owners, and entrepreneurs don't instantly know what their debtor and creditor numbers are running at, whether for the year to date or as a trend.

The simple fact is that nearly every business is both a creditor and a debtor, since businesses extend credit to their customers, and pay their suppliers on 'delayed' payment terms. Cash can be what stifles the growth potential in businesses and proactively managing the ratio between these two levers is key to being able to fund your growth ambitions for your business.

Your debtor management . . . you're not a bank

When I work with clients and we start drilling into their financials, cash management and, even more specifically, debtor to creditor management come up as a key discussion area, without fail.

I'm normally drawn into a focused conversation where I end up making the following statement: 'I didn't realize that a secondary part of your business proposition was providing financing for your customers.' I'm sure you know where I'm headed with this point. You are not there to provide a free credit facility for your customers, yet too many businesses indirectly fall into this trap. Don't let your debtors treat you like one. It will cripple your growth potential and will lead to sleepless nights for many business leaders, business owners, and entrepreneurs, because they can't pay their employees and bills.

It doesn't have to be this way if you are proactive in your debtor management, and the great news is that this is not complicated to fix. On the customer side it is about two things: firstly, how creative you are in positioning your compelling value proposition and the associated payment terms; and secondly, your ability to negotiate effective terms, especially if you're a small business and cash is tight.

Consider the builder who builds a wall around your house and then comes to you with a bill; if he hasn't already got part payment from you to cover the materials – the bricks, cement, plaster, and paint – then he is using his own capital to secure those items. In the worst-case scenario, where a delinquent customer decides not to pay, or drags his feet in making payment, the supplier is not only waiting on an invoice, he is out of pocket. When I recently replaced my decking at home the supplier asked me to pay for the materials before he installed anything. At the very least, he wasn't funding the job on my behalf.

Stage payments are a sound financial strategy in business today and most customers will understand that, as they are probably doing it themselves. Your customers simply need to pay you. There is nothing wrong with creating that expectation, nor any sense in being too polite about it. Not that your cash collection should be reminiscent of a hungry shark, but it must be consistent and it must focus on ensuring that your own cash management needs are taken care of.

One final thing that can make the world of difference for you in your debtor strategy is this: do credit checks. Where feasible make it an integral part of your up-front processes to check a customer's credit rating at the point of agreeing to work with them. This used to be a cumbersome and expensive process. However, today it is simple – there are a number of credit check websites. It's not just debtors paying late that can stifle the growth of your business, but the potential of having to write off bad debt. If a potential customer comes up with a poor or indifferent credit rating you need to make a conscious and deliberate choice about whether you should be doing business with them in the first place, or, even more importantly, whether you can *afford to.*

Once you've got your debtor strategy on track you can then turn your attention to your creditors.

Creditors

The second lever, creditors, is all about your effectiveness in nego- tiating payment terms with suppliers and partners to ensure you're maximizing your debtor to creditor ratio.

Of course there are other creative ways in which you can unlock the cash in your business, such as invoice factoring (see below), but this goes back to the gross profit margin you're making, as there is always a cost involved in such solutions. While creative ideas such as these can work, you're far better off managing your cash effectively so you can avoid the costs associated with using them.

A word of caution about your cash management

Though it sounds mad, it often happens that companies get mud- dled up about the amount of money they have on hand at any one time, because often they're simply holding it for someone else. Consider, for example, the revenue you collect on behalf of the Gov- ernment in the form of corporation tax and VAT (or whatever the taxes are called in your country or jurisdiction). Those amounts come into your account on payment of every invoice, but it's critical that you ring fence them, perhaps by putting them into an entirely separate account, because they aren't yours to spend.

I frequently see companies get a corporation tax or VAT bill – which is predictable and happens at regular intervals – and then have to scramble to find the cash to pay it because they've made the mistake of thinking that 100% of the cash in their accounts was their free cash flow to fund their daily business activity. Corporation tax, VAT – or your equivalent – is not operating capital and if you find yourself using it as such, your business model simply isn't working and you need to revisit the fundamentals of your business growth model.

Your Three Most Important Financial Tools

In order to have a strong Finance and Governance strategy, at a minimum there are three financial tools you must have, and must get used to reading. Not just get used to reading but also develop the skill and ability to interpret the insights from the numerical data they provide, in order to make informed, well educated, empirically validated decisions, to drive your business forward.

1. The Profit and Loss (P&L) statement, which is a report of the changes in the income and expense accounts over a certain period of time (monthly and yearly being the most common).
2. My preference is for a trended P&L, which shows the trends in revenues and expenses over a period of time, for example three to five years. This will allow you to see the high level year-on-year trends with revenues increasing (hopefully) and tight management of the cost base (hopefully less than revenues). The trended monthly P&L is also a 'must have' financial tool; a great way to look at a business and manage your short-term position aligned to your medium and longer-term growth strategy. Remember the key in business is always 'no surprises'.
3. The balance sheet which records the balances of all asset and liability accounts at any given point in time.
4. The cash flow statement; a report of the changes in all of the accounts (income/expense and asset/liability) in order to determine how much cash the business is producing or consuming over a certain period of time (monthly and yearly being the most common)

Don't try to navigate your business blind. Use these tools constantly as part of your daily routine, and stay on top of your numbers.

Reality Check

While this is a chapter on Finance and Governance, there is an important caveat here, which is that numbers don't tell you everything about a business. No P&L can tell you if the product is good and getting better. It can't tell you how the morale of the company is. It can't tell you if the management team is executing well. And it can't tell you if the company has the right long-term strategy. Or at least, it *can* do those things, but only after it's too late to do anything about them. So, as important as the P&L and sound financial principles we've covered in this chapter are, they only represent one set of data points you can use in analysing your business performance. You have to get beyond the numbers if you want to know what is going on.

By far the most important means of predicting how your organization is behaving, and of being confident that you're collectively creating the environment wherein your financial goals can be achieved, is a robust Governance strategy.

Your robust Governance strategy

On one of my clients' websites, there is the following statement: 'We are very proud of our approach to governance and believe it is vital to ongoing value creation for our customers, employees, shareholders and all our stakeholders.' This actually sits within their customer promises.

There are a number of reasons why I believe this is powerful. The first is how they are viewing governance: change the mindset, change the game. They are positioning it 100% 'outside in' as a benefit to the customer, giving them total peace of mind that they are dealing with a credible, professional organization. Just think about all the examples we discussed earlier of business failings and their lasting impact.

Second, they are actually positioning their governance as an enabler for value creation, therefore saying it is fundamental to their business growth strategy and to building a high performing, sustainable, legacy organization. This is a really clever strategy.

How is 'governance' perceived in your business: as an integral part of your daily business or, at the other end of the scale, where you have centralized and dedicated governance, risk, or compliance departments or teams? However simple or complex your governance, the one universal safeguard that it provides is the checks and balances to ensure that your business is behaving appropriately. Far from being limiting, it can be the most liberating part of any business, if culturally it is set up in this way. Unfortunately, in my personal experience many organizations perceive it as a 'prevention department' as opposed to an enabler of value creation.

The Exciting News

Your Business Growth Transformation Framework® is in essence a governance framework in itself. Think about it for a moment; a robust health & safety policy within operational excellence is part of your overarching organizational governance. A HR policy on diversity or how to deal with underperformance is a key part of governance in your people strategy. Brand guidelines in marketing define what can and can't be done with the brand . . . the list could go on. However I'm sure you've understood the point I'm making.

So depending on the maturity of your business, in each area of the Business Growth Transformation Framework® you might already be well defined and have all the i's dotted and the t's crossed. If there are any gaps you've identified through reading *Built to Grow*, you certainly now have the blueprint to plug those gaps.

There is one final, critical point about governance. The expectation of regulators, investors, and other stakeholders regarding governance has massively shifted over the past few years. The spotlight is shining on this area more than ever before. Stakeholders now see business leaders, business owners, and entrepreneurs as more accountable for the effectiveness of their overall governance process. This shift is real, and it is significant, and is likely to amount to an expectation of greater involvement in the means by which governance is effected, and for more active oversight by business leaders and their teams.

It's no longer just a business responsibility; it's an individual responsibility. Make sure you have the expertise, people, and resources available and have sound best practices in place in your business.

Funding Routes: The Upsides and Downsides

It would be remiss of me to have a finance chapter without any reference to funding routes to fuel the growth ambitions for your business.

With each passing year there is another new trending idea for how to achieve this, which is added to the already very strong list of potential business finance ideas outside traditional bank lending: private equity, venture capital, crowd funding, angel investment, product pre-sales to name just a few.

Reviewing all the different funding options available could be a complete chapter in *Built to Grow*, so I have created a report detailing all the options, their benefits and their downsides. You can find download details at the end of the chapter.

Summary

If your net worth to the world really is determined by what remains after your bad habits are subtracted from your good ones, a strong Finance and Governance strategy is a critical means of adding tremendous weight to your good ones. It's a major advantage that every business leader, business owner, and entrepreneur should place high on his or her list of priorities. Where are you on the journey?

Remember to download the Funding Route report at **http://pti.world/BTG-Toolkit**.

Chapter 14

Control the Controllable

'God grant me the serenity to accept the things I cannot change, the courage to change the things I can, and the wisdom to know the difference.'
—Reinhold Niebuhr

The business landscape in which we compete today is volatile, increasingly competitive and, certainly over the long term, unpredictable. It may seem on the surface to be a hostile landscape for anyone who wishes to start or build a business by purposeful design as there are so many shifting variables. However, there is ample evidence to justify precisely the opposite argument.

Throughout history, challenge and adversity have forged many great successes. More millionaires and billionaires are created during stormy economic times than during times of calm. Success has always required focus, commitment, and a journey of personal mastery. For business owners, business leaders, and entrepreneurs who embrace these principles, the world today is bursting with opportunities.

Through globalization, the world has become one big business arena, and the emergence of the internet and technologies that surround it means that tools to compete are readily available to you. The pace of change is driving a never-ending surge of innovation with new ideas every day. The best ones have yet to be even thought up.

Whether you are a great inventor of new ideas, an innovator of existing ideas that reinvent the category they're in, or a disruptor of markets through finding better ways to serve customers, the competitive edge is yours to steal. Opportunities abound.

The important thing is not to get overwhelmed. Change will always be a constant and you cannot control everything. If you master the art of controlling the things which are controllable, you'll have a stunning platform for sustained growth in any economy. That is *Built to Grow*.

So what is controllable?

- Creating a compelling business purpose – a WHY and setting the bar high in terms of audacious goals
- Understanding your market potential and where you can make a profound difference
- Creating a compelling value proposition which speaks directly to the needs of the customer now and in the future
- Placing the customer at the epicentre of your thinking and becoming obsessed in delivering memorable experiences every time
- Capitalizing on disruptive, innovative marketing which maximizes online and offline channels and positions you and your business as the thought leader in your chosen market
- Creating predictable, repeatable results in your business development and sales, resulting in accelerated, sustained, and profitable business growth
- A people strategy delivered through a compelling employee value proposition for attracting, maximizing, and retaining the best talent
- Operational excellence as a norm throughout all the arteries of your business
- Robust finances that keep the growth agenda on track and governance as an effective conscience making sure it's not just what we do, but how we do it
- And finally, inspirational leadership as the enabler pulling it all together.

Built to Grow is a multi-part jigsaw puzzle. A simple metaphor to illustrate a business with interlocking strategies and deep interdependencies, which when executed together, create an unbreakable strategic plan. The pieces of the puzzle are all controllable parts, over which it is possible to exercise mastery. Focus on that, and you become a business capable of embracing change . . . relishing change . . . even driving change . . . and no longer a business that fears or ignores it.

Set yourself on a path to achieve the highest echelons of greatness. A business that is truly *Built to Grow.*

Chapter 15

Your Journey to Mastery

'There are no crowds lining the extra mile!'

There is a saying: there are no crowds lining the extra mile. Masters of their craft, whatever their specialist field of endeavour, are part of a select group of people who really live this saying.

Why? Because the extra mile is where they spend most of their time. They don't subscribe to the tribe of life; the herd mentality. For them, a life of mediocrity is not an option.

Instead they invest their time every day in being the best of the best, raising their personal standards and chasing perfection. Even though perfection isn't truly attainable, they know by going the extra mile they may just catch excellence on the journey.

If you have read *Built to Grow*, you can call yourself a part of this group, committed to achieving greatness, already living your life on the extra mile. If this is your first experience of *Built to Grow*; if you're one of those who opens at the end, this chapter will give you several excellent reasons to explore the rest of the book.

Being Committed and in the Arena

Famed Scottish mountaineer W. H. Murray put it rather beautifully, thus:

> 'Until one is committed, there is hesitancy, the chance to draw back, always ineffectiveness. Concerning all acts of initiative (and creation), there is one elementary truth that ignorance of which kills countless ideas and splendid plans: that the moment one definitely commits oneself, then Providence moves too. All sorts of things occur to help one that would never otherwise have occurred. A whole stream of events issues from the decision, raising in one's favour all manner of unforeseen incidents and meetings and material assistance, which no man could have dreamed would have come his way. Whatever you can do, or dream you can do, begin it. Boldness has genius, power, and magic in it. Begin it now.'

In Chapter 3: Inspirational Leadership, I outlined the seven traits of inspirational leaders and I promised we would discuss the seventh: Achieving Mastery, after we had explored all of the components of *Built to Grow*. Let's do that now.

Whether you manage people, develop products, run IT systems, take care of the organization's finances, or carry out a role in any of the other disciplines within your business, the difference between being good, or even great, and being masterful is immense. Why? Because there is no short cut to mastery, and anyone who has committed themselves to the time and effort required to achieve it, simply exists in a different category; an easy occupant of the extra mile.

So how can *you* get there?

A Never-Ending Pursuit of Personal Mastery

Perhaps you're familiar with the theories of author Malcolm Gladwell, particularly as detailed in his *Outliers: the story of success*, in which he suggests that becoming a master of anything is a matter of practising it for ten thousand hours. If this is new to you, let me break it down a little bit, because this is a really compelling idea, and one that has had a dramatic impact on leadership training and ideology since it first made its appearance around 2008.

One example he uses is The Beatles. We spoke earlier in the book about how The Beatles were rejected early in their career, but it seems all the more remarkable when you consider just how firmly on track to superstardom they already were thanks to a random twist of fate. The Beatles were clearly an unusually talented act and the song writing capabilities of John Lennon and Paul McCartney are surely not open to any credible challenge. But the world is littered with talented men and women who haven't had the success the Fab Four had, leaving Gladwell to speculate that there must be something entirely different going on.

Enter, the ten thousand hours rule.

You see, The Beatles burst onto the scene in 1962, gaining prominence in 1963 and really hitting the big time from 1964 onwards . . . but they had been playing together since 1957. That's significant for reasons that I will share in a moment.

It adds some context to an interesting fact about The Beatles however: their greatest achievement according to many Beatles fans is the album *Sgt Pepper's Lonely Hearts Club Band*, which was recorded just three short years after their breakthrough . . . but actually, it was fully ten years after they formed. Far from being an unusual artistic achievement, could their talent have been an act of purposeful design? Let's look at their back-story.

In 1960, after they received credit as a club band, they were invited to play in Hamburg, Germany. It wasn't a traditional concert tour they were contracted into however: the terms of their agreement were that they would play for eight hours per day, seven days per week, as a permanent musical act at a club. Customers would come and customers would go, so the boys made every song they played last 20 minutes with 20 solos in it.

I said earlier in *Built to Grow* that practice doesn't make perfect but permanent . . . but the right practice makes perfect. In this case, it couldn't have been better practice for The Beatles. That daily repetition meant they learned to read each other, to work together predictably, and to play their instruments and the music they made, with increasing skill.

John Lennon had this to say about it, according to *The Beatles: The Authorised Biography* by Hunter Davies:

> 'We got better and got more confidence. We couldn't help it with all the experience playing all night long. It was handy them being foreign. We had to try even harder, put our heart and soul into, to get ourselves over. In Liverpool, we'd only ever done one-hour sessions, and we just used to do our best numbers, the same ones, at every one. In Hamburg, we had to play for eight hours, so we really had to find a new way of playing'.

In Hamburg, between 1960 and 1962 alone, The Beatles played nearly 2,700 hours together on stage. By the time they had their first success in 1964, they had played more than 1,200 times. It's an almost unheard of number; most bands never play that many times in their entire careers. The Beatles did it before they even made it big.

Philip Norman, who wrote another biography of The Beatles, titled *Shout!* said that Hamburg was the making of them. 'They were no good on stage when they went there and they were very good when they came back . . . they weren't disciplined on stage at all before that. But when they came back, they sounded like no one else . . .'

Mastery takes time, and dedicated pursuit. Choosing mastery is about choosing to dedicate your focus to constant improvement, and finding that extra fuel in your tank, even when you think you've arrived, to kick on to the next level and squeeze that extra potential from within. The masters in their chosen fields are never okay to be just okay; excellence is the game they play and the extra mile is their arena and where they spend their time.

Are you committed to the journey of mastery and truly becoming the inspirational business leader, business owner, or entrepreneur known for thinking BIG? I hope this book has given you the inspiration, desire, and will to accelerate your journey in your pursuit of personal excellence and ultimate mastery.

So what now? You have two choices:

First, you can put this book on the shelf and allow the ideas to fade into memory. As the author, I hope you don't, but not from a perspective of personal gratification. I passionately believe the ideas in this book can help you build an organization destined for greatness and I want to see you realize your personal and professional goals and ambitions.

Which brings us to choice number two: you can actively implement the lessons that you've learned. You can mark the pages, underline and highlight ideas, and use it as the blueprint in the laboratory of your own company. If you do that, I look forward to being a part of your journey through the words on these pages and I look forward to writing about your Built to Grow organization in a future book!

You now have the ideas, you now have the tools: over to you to personalize and apply them to your business. It's been an enormous privilege to share them with you.

Good luck. I know you've got it in you to build a legacy business of enduring greatness, which will deliver accelerated, sustained, and profitable business growth.

Your Business Growth Coach
Royston

Bibliography

Adidas. Available at www.adidas.co.uk. (Accessed March 2016).

Airbnb. Available at www.airbnb.co.uk. (Accessed March 2016).

Aldi. Available at https://en.wikipedia.org/wiki/Aldi. (Accessed February 2016).

Amazon. Available at https://en.wikipedia.org/wiki/Amazon.com. (Accessed January 2016).

Any Given Sunday (1999) Directed by Oliver Stone. Warner Bros.

Apple. Available at http://apple.com. (Accessed March 2016).

Arthur Andersen. Available at https://en.wikipedia.org/wiki/Arthur_Andersen. (Accessed January 2016).

Asda. Available at https://en.wikipedia.org/wiki/Asda. (Accessed February 2016).

Audi. Available at https://en.wikipedia.org/wiki/Audi. (Accessed February 2016).

BBC News Magazine (2015) 'Should we all be looking for marginal gains?'. Available at http://www.bbc.co.uk/news/magazine-34247629. (Accessed March 2016).

Billmoria, Karan (2007) *Bottled For Business.* UK: Capstone.

British Airways. Available at https://en.wikipedia.org/wiki/British_Airways. (Accessed January 2016).

Buffett, Warren. Available at https://en.wikipedia.org/wiki/Warren_Buffett. (Accessed February 2016).

Burj Khalifa. Available at https://en.wikipedia.org/wiki/Burj_Khalifa. (Accessed January 2016).

Carroll, Lewis (1865) *Alice's Adventures in Wonderland.* New York: Macmillan Company.

Centre for Economics & Business Research (2013) 'The State of Workforce Wellbeing'. Available at http://www.cebr.com/

reports/the-state-of-workforce-wellbeing. (Accessed February 2016).

Churchill, Winston. Available at www.winstonchurchill.org. (Accessed January 2016).

Coca Cola. Available at www.coca-cola.co.uk. (Accessed January 2016).

Conwell, Russell (1901) *Acres of Diamonds*. Philadelphia: John D. Morris and Company, reprinted from *Modern Eloquence* edited by Thomas B. Reed.

Countrywide statistics. Available at www.countrywide.co.uk. (Accessed March 2016).

Cunningham, L. (2015) 'In Big Move, Accenture will get rid of performance reviews & rankings', *The Washington Post*, 21 July 2015.

Davis, H. (1968) *The Beatles: The Authorised Biography*. New York: McGraw-Hill.

DFS. Available at www.dfs.co.uk. (Accessed March 2016).

DHL. Available at www.dhl.com. (Accessed January 2016).

Disney. Available at www.disneyinternational.com. (Accessed March 2016).

Dragons' Den. Available at https://en.wikipedia.org/wiki/Dragons. (Accessed March 2016).

easyJet. Available at https://en.wikipedia.org/wiki/EasyJet. (Accessed March 2016).

Enron. Available at https://en.wikipedia.org/wiki/Enron. (Accessed January 2016).

Facebook. Available at https://en.wikipedia.org/wiki/History_of_ Facebook. (Accessed January 2016).

Gallup. Employee engagement statistics. Available at http://www .gallup.com/services/190118/engaged-workplace. (Accessed February 2016).

Gartner. Importance of the customer experience. Available at https://www.gartner.com/marketing/customer-experience. (Accessed February 2016).

Gates, Bill. Available at www.gatesnotes.com. (Accessed March 2016).

Gerber, Michael. Available at http://michaelegerbercompanies
.com/web. (Accessed January 2016).

Gillette. Available at http://gillette.com (Accessed March 2016).

Gladwell, M. (2008) *Outliers: The story of success.* New York: Little,
Brown & Company.

Google. Available at http://google.com. (Accessed February 2016).

Groupon. Available at https://en.wikipedia.org/wiki/Groupon.
(Accessed March 2016).

Hamilton, Lewis. Available at www.lewishamilton.com. (Accessed
February 2016).

HSBC. Available at www.hsbc.com. (Accessed February 2016).

Hunt-Davis, Ben and Beveridge Harriet (2011) *Will It Make The Boat
Go Faster.* UK: Matador.

IDC. Technology statistics. Available at: http://www.forbes.com/sites/
louiscolumbus/2013/09/12/idc-87-of-connected-devices-by-2017-
will-be-tablets-and-smartphones/#. (Accessed April 2016).

Innocent Smoothies. Available at https://en.wikipedia.org/wiki/
Innocent_Drinks. (Accessed January 2016).

Investor in People. Employee statistics. Available at www
.investorsinpeople.com. (Accessed March 2016).

Jenkins, Jamie (2014) 'Sickness Absence in the Labour Market:
2014.' Available at https://www.ons.gov.uk/employment
andlabourmarket/peopleinwork/labourproductivity/articles/
sicknessabsenceinthelabourmarket/2014-02-25. (Accessed
February 2016).

Jobs, Steve. Available at https://en.wikipedia.org/wiki/Steve_Jobs.
(Accessed January 2016).

John Lewis. Available at https://en.wikipedia.org/wiki/John_Lewis_
Christmas_advert. (Accessed March 2016).

Jones, Peter. Available at www.peterjones.com. (Accessed
February 2016).

Jordan, Michael. Available at https://en.wikipedia.org/wiki/
Michael_Jordan. (Accessed March 2016).

KPMG. Customer growth statistics. Available at Wreden, N. (2005) *Profit Brand*. London; Kogan Page, P77, (e-book: https://books .google.com).

LEGO®. Available at www.lego.com. (Accessed March 2016).

Lehman Brothers. Available at https://en.wikipedia.org/wiki/ Lehman_Brothers. (Accessed January 2016).

Leicester City Football Club. Available at www.lcfc.com. (Accessed May 2016).

Lencioni, Patrick M. (2002) 'Make Your Values Mean Something', *Harvard Business Review* (July) 113–117.

Lidl. Available at https://en.wikipedia.org/wiki/Lidl. (Accessed January 2016).

Liker, J. (2004) *The Toyota Way*. New York: McGraw-Hill.

Lincoln, Abraham. Available at https://en.wikipedia.org/wiki/ Abraham_Lincoln. (Accessed March 2016).

L'Oréal. Available at www.loreal.com. (Accessed January 2016).

Macquet, David L. (2012) *Turn the Ship Around!* New York: Penguin.

McCarthy, Edmund Jerome (1960) *Basic Marketing: A Managerial Approach*. Homewood, Ill: Irwin.

McDonalds. Available at www.mcdonalds.com. (Accessed March 2016).

Metro Bank. Available at www.metrobankonline.co.uk. (Accessed March 2016).

Morrisons. Available at https://en.wikipedia.org/wiki/Morrisons. (Accessed February 2016).

Mother Teresa. Available at www.motherteresa.org. (Accessed January 2016).

Murray, W.H. (1947) *Mountaineering in Scotland. Undiscovered Scotland*. London: Dent.

NASA. Available at www.nasa.gov. (Accessed March 2016).

NASDAQ. Available at https://en.wikipedia.org/wiki/NASDAQ. (Accessed March 2016).

New Zealand All Blacks. Available at www.allblacks.com. (Accessed April 2016).

Nicklaus, Jack (2005) *Golf My Way*. New York: Simon & Schuster.

Nike. Available at www.nike.com. (Accessed February 2016).

Norman, P. (1981) *Shout.* New York: Simon & Schuster.

Oswald A J., Proto E. and Sgroi D. (2014) 'Happiness and Productivity'. University of Warwick. Available at https://www2 .warwick.ac.uk/fac/soc/economics/staff/eproto/workingpapers /happinessproductivity.pdf. (Accessed February 2016).

Pet Grooming statistics. Available at http://www.euromonitor.com /pet-products. (Accessed March 2016).

PFMA. Pet ownership statistics. Available at www.pfma.org.uk. (Accessed April 2016).

Pizza Express. Available at www.pizzaexpress.com. (Accessed January 2016).

RBS. Available at https://en.wikipedia.org/wiki/The_Royal_Bank_of_ Scotland. (Accessed January 2016).

Red Arrows. Available at http://www.raf.mod.uk/reds. (Accessed March 2016).

Retton, Mary Lou. Available at http://marylouretton.com. (Accessed February 2016).

Robbins, Tony. Available at www.tonyrobbins.com. (Accessed February 2016).

Ryanair. Available at https://en.wikipedia.org/wiki/Ryanair. (Accessed February 2016).

Sainsbury. Available at https://en.wikipedia.org/wiki/Sainsbury. (Accessed February 2016).

Santander. Available at http://www.santander.co.uk/uk. (Accessed January 2016).

Sapient. Marketing trends. Available at http://www.sapient.com/ content/dam/sapient/sapientnitro/pdfs/insights/5_Trends. (Accessed March 2016).

Shell. Available at www.shell.com. (Accessed January 2016).

Sinek, Simon. Leadership in action. Available at https://www.ted .com/talks/simon_sinek_how_great_leaders_inspire_action. (Accessed February 2016).

Singapore Airlines. Available at https://en.wikipedia.org/wiki/ Singapore_Airlines. (Accessed February 2016).

Stallone, Sylvester. Available at http://sylvesterstallone.com. (Accessed March 2016).

Stella Artois. Available at https://en.wikipedia.org/wiki/Stella_Artois. (Accessed March 2016).

Tesco. Available at https://en.wikipedia.org/wiki/Tesco. (Accessed March 2016).

The Blind Slide (2009) Directed by John Lee Hancock. Warner Bros. Based on the 2006 book *The Blind Slide: Evolution of a Game* by Michael Lewis.

The South Pole Expedition. Available at https://en.wikipedia.org/wiki/Comparison_of_the_Amundsen_and_Scott_Expeditions. (Accessed February 2016).

Tobias, J. (2014) 'Mindfulness and Performance'. Cranfield University School of Management, UK. Available at https://aperoand.files.wordpress.com/2014/05/jutta-tobias_mindfulness-and-performance-for-aperoand_may2014.pdf. (Accessed February 2016).

Uber. Available at https://www.uber.com (Accessed March 2016).

UK Government people at work statistics. Available at https://www.gov.uk/government/organisations/department-for-business-innovation-skills. Accessed February 2016).

United Nations. Available at www.un.org. (Accessed January 2016).

Virgin Atlantic. Available at https://en.wikipedia.org/wiki/Virgin_Atlantic. (Accessed January 2016).

Welch, Jack. Available at https://en.wikipedia.org/wiki/Jack_Welch. (Accessed February 2016).

Wimbrow, Peter Dale Sr. (1934) 'The Guy in the Glass.' *The American Magazine.*

Woodward, C. (2004) *Winning!* UK: Hodder & Stoughton.

World War Z (2013) Directed by Marc Forster. Paramount Pictures. Based on the 2006 novel *World War Z* by Max Brooks.

Index

Continue your Journey to Mastery

In Chapter 15: Your Journey to Mastery I outlined two choices you have upon reading *Built to Grow*. First, put the book on the shelf and allow the ideas to fade into memory, or second, actively implement the lessons you've learnt.

My preference for you is clearly the latter, and to help you with the next stage of your journey here are some further ideas:

 Built to Grow

Mindset

Having bought and read *Built to Grow* you now have the thinking and growth mindset to deliver accelerated, sustained and profitable business growth

 Your Built to Grow Toolkit

Toolset

To support you in the personalization of Built to Grow for your business or organization, I referenced throughout the book a number of resources and tools available. Don't miss out on your FREE Built to Grow toolkit. Simply download at **http://pti.world/BTG-Toolkit**.

Skillset

Built to Grow Boot camps, Online Programme, and Coaching

Built to Grow Boot camps – Work 'ON' your business through 2 or 3 day live boot camps run by Royston and the Pti team. A deeper dive into the Built to Grow strategies, tools, and ideas; the opportunity to network and learn from other like-minded business leaders, owners, and entrepreneurs and walk away from a high impact event with your own personalized Built to Grow blueprint for your business.

Built to Grow Online programme – A unique modular multi media experience giving you a greater breadth and depth of understanding, personalization, and application of Built to Grow strategies, tools, and ideas to your business. At your own pace, whenever you want, wherever you want.

Built to Grow Coaching programme – A tailored and personalized experience with Royston and the Pti team helping you every step of the way with the implementation and personalization of Built to Grow.

Please go to **www.pti-worldwide.com/store** for further details.

Feel Inspired?

Any questions, feedback or comments on the book I'd love to hear from your directly. Email: **royston@roystonguest.com** or connect with me at:

www.roystonguest.com
Twitter: @Royston_Guest
Facebook.com/Royston Guest
LinkedIn.com/roystonguest

Pti Blog and Resources

Visit the Pti blog and resources to access exclusive resources, tools, case studies, interviews, videos, webinars, and our latest Facebook live bitesize sessions: **www.pti-worldwide.com/blog-and-resources**